I0062573

Praise for *Already Smarter*

"This enjoyable book presents a rich tool kit of techniques to help any reader become an effective, lifelong learner. Concrete examples, research findings, and the author's experiences coalesce into a seamless road map for forging productive mindsets, increasing motivation, establishing fruitful habits, adopting effective learning strategies, and creating supportive learning environments. All learners will find something of value here."

—MARK MCDANIEL, PHD, coauthor, *Make It Stick: The Science of Successful Learning*; professor emeritus and research scientist, Department of Psychological and Brain Sciences; director, Center for Integrative Research on Cognition, Learning, and Education (CIRCLE), Washington University

"Based on cognitive science, neuroscience, and the learning sciences, this book is a valuable manual of practical, personal strategies for increasing your learning abilities."

—CHRIS DEDE, PHD, coeditor, *The 60-Year Curriculum: New Models for Lifelong Learning in the Digital Economy*; senior research fellow, Harvard Graduate School of Education

"*Already Smarter* offers sage guidance for anyone who wants to learn anything at any stage of life. Jeff Bergin draws on a wide range of research, theory, practice, and his own experience as a teacher and learner to offer concrete, focused strategies for effective learning. He helps readers understand that learning is not just a cognitive activity; it also involves affect—emotions and feelings that can foster or hinder learning. The key to success is a growth mindset— believing that we are capable of learning new skills and knowledge."

—DUANE ROEN, PHD, coauthor, *The McGraw-Hill Guide: Writing for College, Writing for Life*; professor emeritus, Arizona State University

"I wish I had this book earlier—it's the kind of guide every lifelong learner needs. Practical, encouraging, and built for real life, *Already Smarter* is an invaluable resource for learners, educators, and anyone seeking to grow. I took away strategies I'll use myself and share with others. Each chapter blends research, relatable stories, reflection questions, and clear action steps. Jeff Bergin approaches learning in a truly holistic, human way—and makes it feel not just possible but truly energizing."

—SARAH DEMARK, PHD, vice provost, Western Governors University; interim executive director, Open Skills Network; coauthor, "Charting a Future With Skills: The Need for a Skills-Based Education and Hiring Ecosystem"

"I wish I had this book when I first stepped into educational leadership. *Already Smarter* offers readers more than approaches rooted in the science of learning—it charts a path for transformational change. With a focus on codesign between educators, leaders, and learners, Bergin shows how understanding students' needs can foster a growth culture and strong collaboration. Drawing on his deep experience as a leadership coach and his forward-thinking insights into the role of technology—especially generative AI—Bergin offers invaluable guidance for building smarter, more responsive learning environments."

—DR. SHERRY RANKINS-ROBERTSON, department chair and professor of writing and rhetoric, University of Central Florida; faculty fellow, Institute on AI, Pedagogy, and the Curriculum, AAC&U

"*Already Smarter* is a standout blueprint for learners, educators, and coaches seeking to build the habits, mindset, and confidence essential for active, lifelong learning. Dr. Jeff Bergin skillfully bridges cutting-edge learning theory with real-world application, making research both accessible and actionable. This is exemplified in the book's 'Simple Strategy' sections— concise, practical steps that translate complex concepts into clear, usable actions. Particularly compelling is the book's emphasis on setting meaningful, motivating goals that help learners align their efforts with personal values and long-term aspirations.

Equally powerful is Bergin's integration of the mind–body connection, including guidance on rest, movement, breathing, and mindfulness. He makes a compelling, evidence-based case that how we feel physically and emotionally profoundly influences how well we learn. This holistic approach reinforces that effective learning depends not only on intellect and willpower but also on structure, self-awareness, and intentional strategy.

In an era of rapid technological change—defined in part by the meteoric rise of AI-powered learning tools—*Already Smarter* arrives as a timely and essential resource. It offers practical, research-driven techniques to help learners across higher education and workforce development avoid becoming passive consumers of technology and instead become empowered, intentional users of both emerging tools and their own cognition.

More than a book, *Already Smarter* is a comprehensive tool kit for navigating a lifetime of learning with clarity and confidence. It will serve as a trusted resource for students, educators, mentors, and workforce professionals at every stage of the learning journey."

—HOWARD LURIE, senior vice president for research and evaluation, Academic Programs International / The API Foundation

"In *Already Smarter,* readers have the opportunity to benefit from an approachable translation of complex research from an expert in learning that can immediately be put into action in a variety of practical contexts. Dr. Bergin guides readers to think about how to effectively cultivate learning engagement, embrace ownership, and seize opportunities to maximize learning. A must-read (and do) for anyone guiding or navigating a learning journey of any kind throughout life."

—SHAWN MAHONEY, PHD, leadership and learning executive advisor; board chair, *Education Week*; former global lead, Sales University, Amazon Web Services (AWS)

"This powerful book challenges a common misconception—that when someone struggles to progress, it's simply due to a lack of motivation or skill. With clarity and compassion, *Already Smarter* reveals how success often requires more than just grit. The book makes a compelling case for the essential role of mentorship, mental health support, and holistic care. It offers a timely and necessary perspective for anyone committed to helping all learners and workers thrive—no matter where they start or where they're headed."

—**DESIRÉE JEWELL,** senior vice president of marketing and communications, SkillUp Coalition

"Finally, a learning book that meets people exactly where they are! This isn't just for 'struggling learners'—it's for anyone ready to unlock extraordinary capabilities within themselves and others. Packed with holistic, evidence-based practices delivered in short, digestible sections, it lets you read quickly and apply techniques immediately in various contexts. The author's compassionate yet practical approach rewrites what's possible when we combine the right research, tools, and support with a radical belief in people. From identifying misbeliefs to building new habits, *Already Smarter* shifts how we understand human potential entirely. With strategies that work for real people facing life's daunting challenges, this book doesn't just change how we learn—it transforms how we see ourselves as learners."

—**HOLLY ANN CUSTARD, PHD,** senior director of data ecosystem partnerships, Strada Education Foundation

"You don't need a degree in education or psychology to understand how to self-improve. In *Already Smarter*, Dr. Jeffrey Bergin synthesizes cutting-edge research across a wide range of learning sciences to offer a wonderfully readable, informed, hands-on guide to becoming a better student and learner—at any stage of life. Grounded in rich scientific literature, this book is valuable not only for those eager to take charge of their own learning but also for researchers seeking a gateway into foundational work across multiple disciplines. Let Dr. Bergin be your guide, as he has been for me through this book."

—**PJ HENRY, PHD,** global network associate professor of psychology, NYU Abu Dhabi

"*Already Smarter* is more than a book—it's a generous, deeply human invitation to rediscover the learner within. Jeff Bergin writes with the clarity of a researcher, the soul of a coach, and the wisdom of someone who has walked this path himself. His voice is both compassionate and compelling, reminding us that learning isn't just a skill—it's a lifeline to our potential, asking us to elevate our own human experience.

I've seen firsthand Jeff's unwavering belief in people's capacity to grow. That belief is a clear theme in every chapter, from dismantling limiting beliefs to designing smart habits and championing others. If you have ever felt stuck, underestimated, or unsure where to begin, this is a great place to start. It's also for those of us who know the power of learning but need a nudge to reengage with it fully.

Jeff doesn't just teach us how to learn—he shows us why it matters now more than ever. If you're ready to stop saying 'maybe later' and start becoming who you're meant to be, this book is your moment. *Already Smarter* is also a great book for parents helping to guide young adults. As the mother of five adult-ish children, this is an incredible tool to remind parents that everyone has their own potential and path."

—**STACIE BAIRD,** chief people officer, Community Medical Services; host, *The HX Podcast with Stacie Baird*

"Dr. Bergin has created a useful and accessible road map for learners who are stranded by education system barriers and barriers of their own making. This guidebook is empathetic but also crafted with solid counsel that is useful and easy to consume. All learners who want to get out of their own way will find support and help here."

—**JAN JONES-SCHENK,** DHSc, president, JJS Associates; executive dean emeritus, Western Governors University

"This book is what every reader needs to thrive in a world where change is constant and learning is no longer optional. *Already Smarter* offers the mindset, tools, and momentum to move forward—at any stage, in any direction. In a world flooded with advice, *Already Smarter* stands apart: practical without being preachy, empowering without oversimplifying. Jeff brings learning to life not as a one-time event, but as a lifelong habit that fuels purpose, momentum, and progress. This book doesn't just teach you how to learn; it helps you believe in your capacity to grow and gives you the tools to actually do it. Every chapter opens a door to what's possible."

—KARA SMITH MCWILLIAMS, PHD, chief product
officer, National Conference of Bar Examiners

"*Already Smarter* is a refreshing, practical, and deeply thoughtful guide to learning. Jeff Bergin makes complex ideas accessible and actionable, inviting readers to rethink how they learn—and why. This book is an empowering resource for adult learners, educators, and anyone committed to personal growth."

—JAMES GRIGSBY, SPHR, MSW

"As both a student and an educator, I found *Already Smarter* to be refreshingly practical, compassionate, and deeply empowering. It breaks down learning in a way that is doable—even for those who have been told they're not 'good' learners. This book doesn't just offer strategies for learning; it builds confidence and reclaims agency. I wish I had read it earlier—for both my own learning and for my students."

—ALLISON CHRIST, teacher

"Anyone looking to enhance their ability to learn more effectively is going to want to have this book in their tool kit. Each chapter breaks down the science of learning into simple, digestible strategies that anyone can apply and offers practical tips with real-world examples. The content in Jeff Bergin's book is easily absorbed and allows readers to learn about themselves while making their learning dreams and goals a reality."

—ELIAS ANTELMAN, student

ALREADY SMARTER

SIMPLE STRATEGIES
FOR EFFECTIVE LEARNING

JEFFREY BERGIN, PhD

FC

**FAST
COMPANY**
Press

This publication is designed to provide accurate and authoritative information in regard to the subject matter covered. It is sold with the understanding that the publisher and author are not engaged in rendering legal, accounting, or other professional services. Nothing herein shall create an attorney-client relationship, and nothing herein shall constitute legal advice or a solicitation to offer legal advice. If legal advice or other expert assistance is required, the services of a competent professional should be sought.

Fast Company Press
New York, New York
www.fastcompanypress.com

Copyright © 2025 THINKALOUD LLC

All rights reserved.

Thank you for purchasing an authorized edition of this book and for complying with copyright law. No part of this book may be reproduced, stored in a retrieval system, or transmitted by any means, electronic, mechanical, photocopying, recording, or otherwise, without written permission from the copyright holder.

This work is being published under the Fast Company Press imprint by an exclusive arrangement with *Fast Company*. *Fast Company* and the *Fast Company* logo are registered trademarks of Mansueto Ventures, LLC. The Fast Company Press logo is a wholly owned trademark of Mansueto Ventures, LLC.

Distributed by River Grove Books

Design and composition by Greenleaf Book Group
Cover design by Greenleaf Book Group
Cover images used under licence from © Adobestock.com

Publisher's Cataloging-in-Publication data is available.

Print ISBN: 978-1-63908-126-4

eBook ISBN: 978-1-63908-127-1

First Edition

For all the teachers, coaches, friends, and colleagues who encouraged me to learn—especially the hardest lessons and the ones learned during the hardest times.

Disclaimers

*A*lready Smarter was written to empower learners—in particular adult learners—with insights, strategies, and encouragement for building greater self-awareness, confidence, and learning effectiveness. The ideas and tools offered throughout this book are designed to support reflection and personal growth, but they are not intended as a substitute for individualized professional advice, medical treatment, or mental health support.

The stories, examples, and scenarios are illustrative and intentionally relatable. Any names, characters, organizations, or events are fictional or composites based on real-world patterns the author has observed across years of work with diverse learners. They are not representations of specific individuals. Any resemblance to actual people or events is purely coincidental.

Everyone's learning journey is different. Results will vary, and success depends on many personal factors—including your unique context, goals, and support systems. While the author believes in everyone's potential to learn—and to learn more effectively—this book does not endeavor to guarantee any particular learning outcome.

Importantly, this book does not specifically address attention deficit disorder (ADD) or attention deficit hyperactivity disorder

(ADHD), both of which can significantly impact learning. If you believe you may have ADD or ADHD—or face other learning challenges—please seek formal evaluation, guidance, and care from a qualified health-care professional.

All endorsements featured in this book reflect the personal opinions of the individuals providing them. They do not represent the views of the organizations with which the endorsers are affiliated nor do they imply any specific learning outcomes for readers.

While every effort has been made to ensure the accuracy and usefulness of this content at the time of publication, the author and publisher disclaim any liability for outcomes related to the use or misuse of information in this book, including but not limited to any liability arising from errors, omissions, negligence, or any other causes. Readers are encouraged to adapt strategies thoughtfully and consult trusted professionals as they navigate learning, wellness, and career decisions.

Contents

Part IV: Optimize the Mind-Body Connection

Part V: Resolve to Evolve

Preface

I set out to write this book because of a nagging thought that began to preoccupy me. I kept thinking about how many people were, inadvertently, failing themselves—almost the way my middle school gym and math teachers had both literally and figuratively failed me at different points. *Is this something we internalize*, I wondered? I've seen people fail themselves by not investing in their learning—or worse, not believing in the power of their learning. In fact, learning is not something that is confined to places called schools, colleges, or training centers; learning is the lifeblood of all our ambitions and aspirations. Learning is the bridge that takes us from where we are today to where we want to go tomorrow. Without learning, we stagnate, and our skills, minds, and lives begin to decay.

A fellow coach summed it up nicely: We should never create glass ceilings for our clients by indicating that what they are doing at any moment is "just fine." Yet this is exactly what we do to ourselves when we don't indulge our innate desire to learn, grow, and change. By accepting that things are "just fine," we minimize our potential rather than maximizing it. By postponing our learning, we risk our careers, stall our talents, and delay our goals. We tell ourselves *maybe later*, which all too often means maybe never.

This moment is the kairotic moment—the exact opportune time—to advance our learning. We are at the convergence of three things: increasing evidence around how we learn (what is called learning science), increasing need for lifelong learning (for employment, cognitive health, and mental health), and increasing adaptation to changes in our modern world (climate change, sociopolitical change, and technological change). Now is not the time for glass ceilings; now is the time for us to embrace our inner learners and activate our lives. This book is intended to do just that. It is for everyone who wants to learn more, think big, go further, start over, or just do better. None can be done without learning. In particular, it is for people who no longer want to accept the premise that being unfocused or unmotivated is a fault of their own, rather than a symptom of not having the proper tools and support.

I have held plenty of misconceptions about my own learning, and perhaps it was my struggles that have made me addicted to improving it. Becoming a learning researcher and instructor made me realize why people weren't learning. Becoming a coach made me realize how to help them. By setting goals, devising strategies, and working together, month after month, learning happens. And where learning happens, growth and change follow. So, I dedicate this book to the learners who have allowed me to coach them. Their resilience, strength, and persistence have inspired and enlivened me. I dedicate this book to each of them—they know who they are—and to those of you who are ready to take the next step on your learning journey. I hope I can help you along the way.

Introduction

If you picked this book up, chances are you are contemplating learning something new, changing your life in some way, or simply wondering how you can be more productive. Maybe you're following your curiosity in a new direction, pursuing a lifelong dream, beginning a learning program, starting (or advancing) a career, launching a business, contemplating a side hustle, or simply trying to figure out a DIY project. The reasons for learning are endless, but they all boil down to one critical skill: being able to learn *effectively*. Despite all of the learning we do in our lives, learning itself is rarely something we learn about; rather, it's just assumed that we will figure it out along the way.

Learning is not as intuitive as one might think. Sure, we all know a bit about learning from our own experiences and from what we have read or been told. The problem is: Many of the things we believe about learning are inaccurate, outdated, or nuanced. In some cases, we may actually know what works but stop short of applying it to our own learning process. In fact, I conducted an informal survey with one hundred adults who explored their perspectives and behaviors around learning strategies and found that people often report *knowing* about a learning strategy, but do not actually put that strategy into practice in their daily learning lives.[1] It's sort of like knowing what's healthy but choosing the unhealthy option anyway.

Some of you might be thinking, *Well, I've done alright so far, why change now?* In fact, the time couldn't be better to change our approaches to learning, because learning is, increasingly, an imperative. It's not just something that helps us in the context of a class; it's required to get and maintain any kind of job, career, or business. Learning is the lifeblood of work—as well as passion projects and big dreams.

Learning Is Imperative

If you have noticed the proliferation of educational opportunities, it may seem like everyone should be learning. That's not too far from the truth. According to the American Psychological Association, 74 percent of Americans report having undertaken some kind of learning activity to improve a hobby or an interest, and 63 percent report learning something new to help them professionally.[2] Today, learning is more important than ever. The world and the workplace are changing rapidly and require us to update our knowledge, skills, and abilities at a faster pace than ever before. Consider the skills that were needed ten, fifteen, or twenty years ago. Many of these have been made obsolete by advances in technology, professional practices, and workplaces themselves. At the same time, people are living and working longer than ever before, requiring them to refresh their skills at an alarming pace. Indeed, lifelong learning is quickly becoming the norm.

Michelle R. Weise, author of *Long Life Learning: Preparing for Jobs That Don't Even Exist Yet*, writes, "We are all going to have to prepare for jobs that don't even exist yet. Enter the concept of long-life learning. Through the lens of longevity, the future of work becomes inextricably tied to the future of learning."[3] Weise continues: "No matter our current station, we will all become working learners, flexing between working and learning, or juggling both at the same time—looping continuously in and out of learning and navigating more job transitions than we ever dreamed possible."[4]

According to a Pew Research Center survey, 87 percent of workers believe that they will need retraining and new job skills throughout their lives.[5] Similarly, research conducted by the Bureau of Labor Statistics reveals that most people hold about twelve jobs between the ages of eighteen and fifty-two. Not only do job changes require learning, but learning itself also pays dividends. In fact, income *increases* and the likelihood of unemployment *decreases* with educational attainment.[6]

Learning doesn't just help us land or keep jobs; it also helps us build the very tool that we use to learn: our brains. Learning activities—such as literacy, cognitive activity, and educational attainment—all build our cognitive reserve.[7] Cognitive reserve has the potential to reduce the risk of dementia or delay its onset.[8] For those with a genetic predisposition to Alzheimer's disease, higher education and cognitive activity deferred the onset of impairment by almost nine years.[9] Learning doesn't have to be formal or traditional to yield these benefits; learning actions such as engaging in computer activities, games, reading, and social interactions help maintain cognition later in life.[10] And it builds confidence, too. In fact, 87 percent of learners felt that the process of learning something helped them feel more capable in their lives.[11] So not only does learning help you acquire new knowledge and skills, but it also helps you feel better about yourself.

Learning Is the Secret Ingredient to Success

Learning is here to stay. It is now the key ingredient in any career—and one that employers are prioritizing. And if you don't sharpen your learning skills, you face the very real risk of being replaced by another human or a machine. But that's actually not the worst thing that could happen—after all, people reinvent themselves every day. The worst thing is that without knowing how to learn, you may be left with a sense of regret and failure over something left undone. You may feel that you didn't achieve your human potential, earning potential, or what I call *purpose potential*. Not meeting your purpose potential means that you fell short of following through on an important part of your purpose. It need not be a big lofty purpose, but it could still be something meaningful in your life that you might look back on someday and think, *If only I had followed my heart when I had the chance.*

So what happens that prevents us from achieving our potential? Many things can get in the way, but one of the big things that may go unnoticed is *learning*. Feeling unable to learn, disinterested in learning, or unsuccessful in prior learning experiences can inhibit our progress in many areas of life. However, we may not instantly recognize that *learning* (or lack of learning) is the culprit. What are the clues?

- **Getting mentally stuck:** We may get stuck if we hold counterproductive beliefs about ourselves or our learning abilities, such as *I can't do this* or *I won't succeed at this*.

- **Holding on to bad strategies:** We may hold on to strategies that just don't work, but we may not realize it's the strategy that's bad, thinking instead that we are bad at something.

- **Getting caught in the weeds:** We may adopt small strategies—little things we believe help us learn—but fail to address bigger things like learning disabilities, poor sleep, or counterproductive habits that ultimately undermine our learning.

- **Knowing, but not doing:** We may know a few things about learning but not actually apply those things consistently or correctly to a learning experience or learning goal.

- **Overcomplicating things:** We may make learning something new way too complicated, too time-consuming, or too tedious to actually complete.

- **Blaming ourselves:** We may assume we are "bad" at something when in fact we just don't know how to go about learning it.

The bad news is that each of these beliefs sabotages effective, productive, efficient learning—and, therefore, sabotages the things that learning enables: education, career advancement, entrepreneurship, and ultimately, dream-making. There is good news, though. Each of these beliefs are self-inflicted and, therefore, under our control to correct. But how?

Help Is Here

Let's review. We must learn new and difficult things to achieve just about anything. Yet we get stuck along the way but can't quite figure out why. This prevents us from achieving some or many things, both big and small, even though we know we should be able to. Over time, this can erode our confidence and leave us feeling stuck, powerless, or regretful. Take a minute to think about times this may have happened to you or to your friends, family members, or other connections.

If you have felt this way, you are not alone. I've been there—and not only have I overcome some of these issues, but I've also helped other people overcome them, too. I started my career as a tutor working with college students and underrepresented high school students, many of whom struggled with not only learning strategies but also their self-confidence. From there, I went into organizational development, higher education, and workforce development, in each case working with adult learners who had a variety of learning and life goals but who needed the help, resources, or guidance to pursue their dreams. In each case—and especially as a community college instructor—I met numerous smart, conscientious people who struggled to learn—only because they lacked an actionable understanding of how to do so. The most difficult part was seeing people blame themselves, saying that they lacked the ability to learn when, in fact, they simply lacked the tools. Somewhere along the line, I stopped considering myself a learning designer, a learning instructor, or a learning leader and began simply to consider myself a learning coach. Today, I'm a learning and leadership coach, helping both learners and leaders build action plans to reach their dreams through a combination of coaching, mentoring, teaching, and, of course, learning.

What Is Different About This Book?

As I've coached a variety of people, each learning for very different reasons, I've found surprisingly few resources that explain—in concise language—how to go about the work of learning. Either the courses and books available are too dense and academic, or they are lacking evidence entirely. Either they are too theoretical, or they are too tactical. And in most cases, they fail to provide a holistic view into learning, including things as wide-ranging as neuroscience, habit formation, social connections, and artificial intelligence (AI). This book brings you simple, evidence-based practices that can help you improve your learning in big ways if you put them to use.

This book takes a much more holistic view of learning, with the understanding that beliefs, connections, spaces, motivations, habits, and actions all come together to produce successful learning, growth, and change. In general, research supports three broad theories of how humans learn: cognitivism, behaviorism, and social constructivism. *Cognitivism* focuses on how people receive, store, and retrieve information in their minds, emphasizing internal processes. *Behaviorism* focuses on how environments shape people, such as the spaces in which they learn and how they interact with the world, emphasizing environmental factors. *Social constructivism* focuses on how people construct knowledge by actively building upon what they know, emphasizing interactions.[12] This book builds upon each of these theories, incorporating research-based findings that you can apply to your thinking, behavior, and knowledge construction in simple, practical ways.

This book is divided into five parts: Set Your Intention, Establish a Solid Foundation, Engage Actively, Optimize the Mind-Body Connection, and Resolve to Evolve. Sequentially, the book starts by helping you identify what kind of learner you are and ends by helping you help others to learn. Each part has four chapters, and each of those chapters is designed around a very simple learning model: Each chapter begins with questions to get you thinking about your own learning, which also primes your prior knowledge. Each chapter then offers short explanations of learning research followed by simple, actionable ways to put the research into practice—generally, in three simple steps that make it literally as easy as 1-2-3. And each chapter concludes with an example of what I call the *cumulative effect*; that is, how the various techniques can work together to really propel you forward. This is followed by *Take Action: Make Your Own Plan*, which summarizes each chapter, challenges you to reflect on how these strategies may support your learning, and invites you to develop your own simple learning plan. Frankly, using a few of these strategies may help you, but the more strategies you learn, the more you may begin to see an amplified effect on your learning and your life. Even by just adopting a few strategies, you'll be in better shape than most people, who normally use very few strategies (as you will see from the survey results I share throughout this book).

As you scan through the chapter titles, you might think, *Hmmm, I already know some of this stuff.* When I am coaching people, I've heard similar sentiments. "This stuff sounds familiar," they might say. Or "Oh, I already know that," they might interrupt. It's true: Somewhere along the way, you may have heard of some of these things. But when I begin to press people, they realize that they know *of* something but not how to *actually do* that thing. In fact, this tendency surfaced in my own informal survey research, with many respondents reporting familiarity with a learning strategy, yet reluctance to use it in everyday practice.[13] The best analogy might be playing a sport: We may know about hockey, gymnastics, or polo but may not know how to effectively play these sports. In fact, if you are familiar with some of the learning strategies in this book, that is actually a great benefit. It means that you are primed with prior knowledge (see Chapter 7) and that will not only help you learn these more quickly but also help you put them into practice.

Your Journey, My Commitment

How you use this book is entirely up to you. You can use this book at any time in your learning journey. You can use it in the earliest beginnings—when you are just starting to contemplate learning something new—or you can use it immediately before you begin a new learning experience, in the days ahead of a workshop, course, or event. You can also reference it during a learning experience—focusing on those chapters and strategies that pique your interest. And perhaps surprisingly, you can also use it after an experience ends, which may help you see which things you have done, even if accidentally, and how well they worked for you. In fact, this kind of reflection is an important part of learning, as you will read in Chapter 8.

Each chapter in *Already Smarter* is short and simple by design. It's broken into straightforward chunks that you can read quickly and apply even faster. Select the strategies that really speak to you. You don't have to do everything in this book to become a better, faster learner—just do the things that resonate with you. For one person, this may be addressing anxiety, instituting a practice strategy, and building a robust learning network. For another, it might be using sleep-, exercise-, and sensory-based learning strategies to build healthy new learning habits. No two learning processes will (or should) look alike. Yours will be every bit as unique as you are. Please let me know what worked best for you; this will help me improve the book and the associated materials.

There are three main ways to use this book: as a manual, map, or menu.

- **Use this book as a manual.** You can use this book as a how-to manual to learn how to become a more confident, more efficient, and more productive learner. You can read this book cover to cover, modifying your learning techniques and processes in real time as you read. This is useful if you want to improve your learning ability for school, work, family, or personal reasons.

- **Use this book as a map.** You can use this book to map out a whole new learning journey by starting at the beginning and working clear through to the end. The sequence of the chapters functions as a step-by-step how-to book that can be applied in order. This is useful if you are contemplating making a change in your life, such as going to school, taking a course, or learning a new hobby. Reading this book will allow you to develop a map that will take you from where you are today into a whole new world of learning.

- **Use this book as a menu.** You can use this book as a menu, whereby you pick and choose strategies that appeal to you à la carte. Adopting just a few techniques will help, and the more you use, the more you may learn.

While learning has always been a fundamental aspect of being human, *learning how to learn* is becoming *imperative*. Understanding how to direct one's learning to meet our economic needs, navigate modern life, and flourish as we age is, now more than ever, a necessity. This book offers over one hundred research-based ways to improve your ability to learn almost anything. You can adopt five, twenty-five, or more of these. Whatever mix you adopt may ultimately help you become a better learner. While it's impossible to guarantee a specific outcome, especially since outcomes are based on effort, there are several things that I can commit to.

- My *promise* is that this book will provide opportunities to inform your thinking about the things that affect learning, whether cognitive, emotional, or technological.

- My *hope* is that you will find several strategies that really resonate with you that you will carry forward to every aspect of your learning and life.

- My *dream* is that you will feel more empowered to learn and reap the benefits of that learning in your interests, career, and big dreams.

- My *purpose* is to prevent you from experiencing the regrets that come with failing to pursue something—or the defeat that comes with failing to complete something.

You'll be positioned to work on one goal and then move on to the next in a virtuous circle of ongoing learning—a lifelong learning journey that brings growth, rewards, and opportunities. That takes you from *I'm thinking of learning something* to *I've accomplished something—and you can too*. My big learning goal is that everyone who learns something from this book will pay that learning forward to another person, who will in turn pay their learning forward to yet another person, filling the world not only with learning but with actualized people who have achieved their greatest goals. My dream is that everyone, starting now, is already smarter about learning itself and about how to improve their own learning journey.

PART I

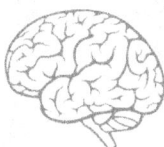

Set Your Intention

L earning begins the day you begin to yearn to do something different—or to simply do something *better*. The very first step in any learning journey is to set an intention. Setting an intention starts with believing that you have what it takes to do something new, daunting, or unknown. Possessing this belief is no small task. You may be consumed by self-doubt and convinced of your limitations. Stepping beyond these—into a more empowered perspective—takes effort and conviction.

The first part of this book is about that very conviction: It is about setting a new intention. The chapters within this part are focused on understanding that the first steps to learning are letting go of whatever limiting beliefs you have, beginning to change your mindset, igniting your motivation, and setting goals that stick. These chapters will help put you on a path from which all kinds of learning possibilities can emerge, and to leverage your mind, spark your motivation, and set your goals. If these are aligned, there's really no stopping you.

CHAPTER 1

Unlearn Limiting Beliefs

W hether you want to pursue a big dream—like getting scuba certified to contribute to marine preservation— or just tackle a home improvement project, getting it right may hinge on your ability to learn something—and to learn it with confidence. Yet many of us lack confidence because of the misconceptions we hold about ourselves.

In my experience as a learner, I have struggled with this too, often focusing on negative things I have been told about my learning or abilities. Such feelings can be hard to shake, or we may cope with them in ways that are counterproductive. In fact, most of the people I surveyed worry that how they handle their limiting beliefs may be based on outdated practices.[1] As a learning and leadership coach, I have worked with people to explore ways to overcome these challenges and improve their learning by addressing some of their most deeply held limiting beliefs. In doing so, I have seen how unlearning limiting beliefs can unblock so many of the things that typically hold people back.

This chapter can help you identify and address your limiting beliefs—one of the most important things that you can do early in your learning journey. It explores five very common limiting beliefs that many people experience and provides strategies to start to shift them toward more accurate and productive ones. By applying some of these strategies, you may find yourself feeling more confident with your learning and your ultimate goals.

Before you begin this chapter, think about how overcoming limiting beliefs could help you achieve your learning goals and life aspirations.

- What are the techniques that you currently use to identify and counter limiting beliefs?
- Why might managing limiting beliefs improve your learning success?
- How might managing limiting beliefs help you achieve your dreams?

Misbelief 1: I'm Doing Just Fine

Perhaps the most common misbelief is simply the acceptance that one is doing "fine" or "well enough." On the face of it, this doesn't seem like a particularly detrimental belief. After all, many people do pick up a few learning strategies along the way that work for them and put these to use, intuitively or automatically, when they are learning something new. The downside to this approach is that their performance may, inadvertently, remain suboptimal and cause low-grade feelings of malaise. Such feelings might be characterized by a sense of "not quite getting it" or "not being so good at it" that leads one to abandon a new pursuit because "I just wasn't feeling it." If these types of experiences build up, they can disempower us and cause us to languish, feeling a general lack of progress, purpose, and autonomy.

On the flip side, experts analyzed twenty-seven studies looking at the effect of study habits and learning achievement and found that study habits are strongly related to performance.[2] Simply put, by adopting a few learning strategies, you can get better at learning. By becoming a better learner, you can accomplish things both big and small. This, in turn, builds empowerment and agency—the sense that you can do whatever you want to or need to. In other words, learning becomes a superpower that enables not only academic learning but also career advancement, personal development, lifelong cognitive reserve, and the pursuit of big dreams. Effective learning, it turns out, underpins nearly every aspiration we possess.

Simple Strategy: Build a Learning Bucket List

This book should convince you of one thing: You can learn and, just as importantly, you can improve your ability to learn. By improving your ability to learn, you open your life up to new opportunities, build your income potential, and safeguard your brain against cognitive decline. To get started:

1. **Make a learning bucket list.** List all the things you want to learn to do, including things that pertain to your life purpose, job, interests, relationships, or way of being in the world.

continued

2. **Be choiceful.** Prioritize the list and select one or two things that you'd like to learn as you read this book. Consider selecting something that you have been hesitant to learn or that you have put off for a long time. This is your chance to give it a try!

3. **Use the strategies.** Begin applying the techniques in this book to your learning goals. Remember: The more techniques you use, the more you will be able to learn.

Misbelief 2: I Just Can't Learn *That*

Many people hold deep misbeliefs about things that they can and cannot do. "I'm just not good at that" is a common refrain for many of us, limiting what we try to achieve. Often these misbeliefs are based on biases—predispositions to feel strongly for or against something based on your experiences, environments, genetics, or some combination of these.

Biases are common among humans and something you need to be mindful of, both within yourself and others. Humans routinely focus more on negative events and information than positive ones. This is called the "negativity bias," and it may be part of evolution, as it helps us avoid harmful situations.[3] The negativity bias causes you to remember, consider, and believe negative information over positive information. So, if your ski instructor tells you that you have good balance and form but need to improve your endurance, you may just hear that you have poor endurance and disregard the rest.

Another common bias is the confirmation bias, whereby you only attend to information that confirms your initial beliefs and disregard information to the contrary.[4] Building on the skiing example, you may use the feedback about your endurance to confirm that you are not well suited for skiing—or any other endurance sport—and give it up altogether.

These two biases can deeply undermine your learning. If you do poorly on a test, project, or assignment, you may focus more heavily on that poor performance and, even worse, use it as a confirmation that you are not good at learning something—or at learning anything. Over time, these biases can undermine your confidence and cause you to avoid learning new things altogether. In actuality, everyone is capable of learning.

Simple Strategy: Stop Being Biased (Against Others and Yourself)

Anyone can keep their biases in check. To get started:

1. **Recognize biases.** Remind yourself that your biases undermine you and sabotage your learning.

2. **Spot and stop negativity.** If you find yourself focusing on negative information, remind yourself that this is your negativity bias kicking in. Balance this by recalling positive information, such as times you have been successful.

3. **Spot and stop confirmation.** If you perform poorly and are feeling discouraged, remind yourself that this may be your confirmation bias. Remind yourself that this was just one experience, and it does not represent the totality of your potential.

Misbelief 3: My Mind Won't Let Me Learn

While some beliefs may stand in your way unnecessarily, there are some very real differences that do make learning more challenging for some people. These learners face challenges when they try to learn, which are classified as diagnosable learning disabilities. Sadly, these are often misunderstood and misdiagnosed, which risks leaving many people feeling as if they are poor learners. How can you better understand what constitutes a learning disability and address any that might be affecting you?

"Learning disabilities" tends to be used as a general umbrella term describing specific conditions such as dyslexia (which affects reading), dyscalculia (which affects numbers), and dysgraphia (which affects writing).[5] According to the Learning Disabilities Association of America, learning disabilities are the result of factors that alter the brain in ways that affect learning.[6] They can interfere with reading, writing, math, organization, planning, reasoning, memory, and attention. However, while their outward symptoms may share some similarities, learning disabilities should not be confused with problems related to physical, emotional, environmental, or socioeconomic challenges.[7]

According to the National Center for Learning Disabilities, one out of every five children has a learning disability.[8] Many require ongoing management, for years or their lifetime, to prevent undue suffering and hardship in learning. Learning disabilities are unrelated to measures of intelligence. People who have been diagnosed with learning disabilities simply need support managing their specific disability.[9]

Interestingly, researchers proposed that at least one learning disability, developmental dyslexia, may not be a disorder, but may rather reflect a specialization for exploration, thereby serving an adaptive role in evolution by supporting discovery and creativity within groups.[10] Therefore, if you've been diagnosed with a learning disability, remind yourself that you may be uniquely adapted to process information in important, alternative ways.

Simple Strategy: Address Learning Disabilities

If you have a diagnosed learning disability or worry that you may have one, take heart. There are many resources and services available to help diagnose, manage, and support learning disabilities. To get started:

1. **Get informed.** The Learning Disabilities Association of America and the National Center for Learning Disabilities both have many useful resources on learning disabilities, including links to resources by state.

2. **Get diagnosed.** Work with a specialist in your area to diagnose your specific learning disability. Then save any documentation they provide so you can reference it later, if needed.

3. **Be your advocate.** Seek the services, support, and tools you need to manage your learning disability, including any accommodations you need to support your learning.

Misbelief 4: There Are Too Many Obstacles

Sometimes learning is made more difficult by legitimate obstacles that may stand in your way. Indeed, there are a wide variety of challenges that stop people from pursuing learning opportunities or trying to learn new things.[11] Many people face physical, emotional, socioeconomic, or environmental obstacles that make learning more difficult. Physical obstacles include disabilities that may affect when, where, and how you learn. Emotional obstacles include fear, anxiety, and depression about learning. Socioeconomic obstacles include impaired access to education, materials, resources, and support services. Environmental obstacles may include having small children, caring for an elderly parent, or needing to work multiple jobs. Some people face multiple obstacles simultaneously. For example, managing a physical disability alongside depression, financial insecurity, and family responsibilities can make learning seem entirely out of reach.

The good news is that many of these obstacles can be addressed. In fact, there are a few things those who overcome these obstacles tend to have in common: motivation to improve their lives, the belief that they can learn, and a clear sense of a learning path.[12] Importantly, they also have the support of friends, family, or other learners.[13] These factors can instill a sense of self-determination to act in a way that is aligned with their values, goals, and interests.

Researchers in the United States and Spain conducted a meta-analysis of the best ways to promote self-determination for learners with disabilities. They found that, in many cases, interventions promoting self-determination are effective ways to manage or overcome these challenges, regardless of grade level, disability, and setting (although effectiveness varied).[14] What are the best ways you can be more self-determined? Experts in self-determination believe the answer includes being intrinsically motivated, which includes three things: autonomy, competence, and relatedness.[15] When you feel you have freedom of choice, you are improving your competence and can better relate to or belong with others, and you will feel more motivated to tackle the obstacles you face.[16] Of course, some challenges are complicated by systemic barriers—such as socioeconomic status—that may require structural solutions in addition to personal effort.

Simple Strategy: Cultivate Determination

If you are being confronted by one or more obstacles, self-determination can help you overcome them. To get started:

1. **Identify obstacles.** The first step to addressing obstacles is clearly identifying them. List each of the obstacles that stand in your way and circle the obstacle that presents the biggest challenge.

2. **Consider solutions.** Consider at least five different ways you can address this obstacle. Some may be things you can do independently, while others may require outside help.

3. **Prioritize where to begin.** Begin to analyze each solution. Does the solution enable you to feel in control? Do you possess the ability to execute the solution? Will the solution make you feel more connected to other people? If you can find a solution that does all three of these things, you'll likely find it easier to use your self-determination to overcome the obstacle.

Misbelief 5: I Won't Succeed

Another common misbelief is that you may get started, but you probably won't succeed—or "stick with it"—so why try? Learning is like training a new muscle. Sometimes, that muscle gets strained or injured, or doesn't seem to be growing. But over time, that muscle does get stronger. The key is to have the right attitude that can survive the various setbacks and challenges that emerge. An attitude based on grit and resilience will ensure that you stick with whatever you are trying to learn—especially when it gets tough.

According to Angela Duckworth, author of *Grit: The Power of Passion and Perseverance*, "The highly accomplished were paragons of perseverance." She writes, "For most, there was no realistic expectation of ever catching up to their ambitions. In their own eyes, they were never good enough. They were the opposite of complacent. And yet, in a very real sense, they were satisfied being unsatisfied. Each was chasing something of unparalleled interest and importance, and it was the chase—as much as the capture—that was gratifying. Even if some of the things they had to do were boring, or frustrating, or even painful, they wouldn't dream of giving up. Their passion was enduring."[17]

Grit is the ability to persist at something, even in the face of obstacles.[18] It's similar to stick-to-itiveness: the ability to hang in there when the going gets tough. Grit has two secret ingredients: perseverance and passion.[19] If you feel passionate about what you are learning, developing your grit will be easier—and it will be more effective if you combine it with other learning strategies. However, if you don't feel so passionate about something, you might instead focus on your resilience.

Resilience is the ability to recover from difficulties, challenges, and setbacks. According to researchers, there are three resilient capacities: 1) having coping resources, 2) using a coping repertoire, and 3) having resilient beliefs.[20] In other words, you may have a friend who helps you when things aren't going well, a process for handling challenging circumstances, and the belief that you are resilient. If you systematically practice these three things, not only will your learning benefit, so, too, will your life.

Simple Strategy: Find the Hope to Cope

Anyone can cultivate an attitude of optimism and hope. Just tell yourself, *I can do this*—because you can. To get started:

1. **Rally.** Rally all your coping resources. These may include people, such as friends or colleagues, and practices, such as those described in this book.

2. **Remember you can cope.** Develop a coping repertoire. Establish practices that help you cope with learning obstacles. These may include strategies from this book that have resonated with you. Lean into these strategies when things get tough.

3. **Believe in yourself.** Foster resilient beliefs about your abilities, resources, and opportunities, including affirmations that you can use when you need them.

The Cumulative Effect

Have you ever put effort into learning something new but found yourself continuing to question your own abilities? Maybe you thought, *I'm not good at this*, or *I've always struggled with this*, or *I just don't think I've got what it takes right now*. That's where addressing limiting beliefs comes in. While each strategy presented in this chapter is a valuable way to overcome limiting beliefs, the right combination can be even more powerful.

Imagine that you want to learn something that is far outside of your comfort zone, like scuba diving. As you register for your first diving class, you begin to experience doubt. You begin to think of all the reasons why you can't learn this—or at least not right now. But you realize that this may be your negativity bias tricking you into thinking that something is too far outside of your abilities. Recognizing that these thoughts may be rooted in long-held biases is the first step in addressing them. Of course, you might also face some very real challenges. These could be learning disabilities that affect your ability to read the diving materials and gauges, requiring a diagnosis, support, or accommodation. Or there may be other obstacles in your way related to time, cost, or transportation, to name a few. You take time to identify each of these so you can begin to devise solutions and support. And when things get really bad, you lean into your own grit and resilience—grit to keep going and resilience to bounce back from failures. As you put these tools together, you begin to notice that you're improving—one dive at a time—until one day it dawns on you that you are becoming a confident, comfortable diver, free from some of the beliefs that held you back.

The strategies in this example aren't random choices—they're part of a deliberate plan intended to support learning. This plan includes things like countering biases, resolving real challenges—such as learning differences and obstacles—and building the grit and resilience to go forward. Remember the cumulative effect: combining strategies from this chapter with those in other chapters can result in a personalized learning strategy that may further empower you.

Take Action: Make Your Own Plan

In this chapter, you learned that one of the best things we can do for our own learning is to unlearn things that have limited us in the past. These may include things that have stopped us or inhibited our perceived ability to learn. To persevere in the face of difficulty, we need to believe we can do better, overcome our biases, address any learning disabilities, overcome challenges that have prevented successful learning, and ultimately find the grit and resilience to keep going.

Think about how your beliefs may be limiting your learning and stopping you from growing and changing. After contemplating the following questions, develop a simple plan to unlearn your limiting beliefs and consider sharing it with someone who is supporting your learning. If you need more support, be sure to read Chapter 18 on building a robust learning network. For additional resources, visit www.already-smarter.com.

- How does believing that the way you learn is "just fine" hinder you?
- How might you counter beliefs that there are certain things you "just can't learn"?
- How could you more effectively manage learning difficulties that have typically impeded your learning?
- How might the ability to overcome obstacles empower you?
- How can you harness your resilience and grit?

CHAPTER 2

Cultivate Your Mindset

Y ou may be interested in advancing your career—perhaps by enhancing your presentation skills—or simply looking to take a class with a friend. Regardless of your goal, your success may rest on your ability to learn—and to learn fearlessly. Yet, for many of us, learning something new comes with trepidation because of longstanding fears and anxieties around learning or doing certain things.

From my earliest days as a learner, I have wrestled with this too: fear of taking courses that may threaten or humiliate me somehow. Such feelings are quite common; in fact, almost a third of the people I surveyed want help improving how they manage their mindsets, anxiety, and fears.[1] In my work as a learning and leadership coach, I have helped people explore ways to overcome these types of counter-productive thoughts and improve their learning by managing their inner dialogue. Many of the folks I've worked with have reported that changing their mindset was one of the most important ways to truly begin learning something new.

This chapter can help you manage anxiety, reduce fear-based reactions, and adopt behaviors that enhance learning, such as meditation and deep breathing. It introduces five evidence-based strategies you may find useful to expand your learning—and your life. With ongoing practice, you might begin to feel more confident and optimistic as you cultivate a mindset that supports your growth.

Before you begin this chapter, think about how your overall mindset could help you achieve your learning goals and your life aspirations.

- What are the techniques that you currently use to elevate your mindset and manage things like anxiety?

- Why might managing your mindset improve your learning performance?

- How might managing your mindset help you reach your aspirations?

Go for Growth

When you think about learning, you can be your own worst enemy. It's easy to sabotage yourself before you even get started. Maybe you think you aren't smart enough, or believe you are only able to learn "so much," or wonder if you simply cannot learn certain things at all. But what if you could adjust this mindset to better serve you? How can you shift the very ways you think about learning?

According to psychologist Carol Dweck, author of *Mindset: The New Psychology of Success*, "The passion for stretching yourself and sticking to it, even (or especially) when it's not going well, is the hallmark of the growth mindset. This is the mindset that allows people to thrive during some of the most challenging times in their lives."[2]

Your mindset consists of the well-established attitudes and beliefs you hold. Dweck differentiates between a fixed mindset, in which people believe that they *can't* learn certain things or new things, and a growth mindset, in which people believe that they *are* able to learn new things. Possessing a growth mindset means believing that you are capable of learning, changing, and growing.[3]

Experts compiled nearly twenty years of research on the relationship between mindset and performance and came to the conclusion that mindset plays an important role in learning and achievement.[4] Learners with a growth mindset are more efficient at monitoring their errors and are more willing to receive feedback about their performance. As a result, possessing a growth mindset has the potential to spark motivation and promote lifelong learning.[5]

Simple Strategy: Aim for Growth

If you don't possess a growth mindset—yet—take heart: You can change your mind. With a little practice, anyone can develop a growth mindset. To get started:

1. **Focus on accomplishments.** Remind yourself you have already successfully learned many new things over the course of your life.

2. **Reframe challenges as opportunities.** Consider difficult or challenging things to be opportunities for personal or professional growth and focus on the learning process, not the outcome.

3. **Find growth-oriented connections.** Prioritize making connections with people—friends, colleagues, classmates—who also have a growth mindset. They can help you develop yours.

Believe in Yourself

Sometimes you undermine your efforts by believing yourself incapable of success. Sure, you may have a growth mindset, but ultimately, you may not believe you have the resources, capability, and circumstances to be effective. In other words, you may believe you have the ability to learn, just not a strong belief that you can effectively *achieve* your learning goal.

Belief in your ability to do what's needed to accomplish a specific achievement is known as self-efficacy.[6] Self-efficacy is associated with higher academic and workplace performance.[7] Indeed, self-efficacy and performance each contribute to the other in a virtuous cycle: Self-efficacy boosts performance, which, in turn, boosts self-efficacy.[8]

If you're worried you may be lacking in self-efficacy, the good news is you can build it. Students who received positive messages developed a stronger sense of self-efficacy and performed better.[9] In some cases, just having the *perception* that their instructors were encouraging them built self-efficacy and improved performance.[10]

If you don't receive positive messages or encouragement from external sources, you can give it to yourself by incorporating regular self-affirmations. Self-affirmations are statements you can make to yourself that assert your fundamental value. Experts believe affirmations activate key regions of the brain focused on future-oriented core values.[11] They also increase your self-efficacy, especially when you are feeling powerless.[12] Importantly, affirmations improve performance when you are feeling threatened or like you don't belong.[13]

Simple Strategy: Change Your Mindset

If you typically don't believe in yourself, now is the time to change that. Anyone can develop a stronger sense of self-efficacy, and that belief alone will help you to learn, grow, and change. To get started:

1. **Adopt affirmations.** Develop your own daily affirmation practice where you begin each day by stating a positive affirmation about your ability to learn.

2. **Find encouragement.** Surround yourself with people who provide encouragement and support. Avoid people who are critical and doubtful of your abilities.

3. **Celebrate success.** Celebrate small successes such as the completion of a learning task, event, or project.

Manage Anxiety

Mindset and beliefs aren't the only things that affect learning. Your mood can also affect how you learn. Anxiety, in particular, can erode performance. This has been well documented in the case of math anxiety. Many feel they are not good at math or some other difficult subject. For you, it could be writing, learning a language, or playing a sport.

Not surprisingly, anxiety impairs performance. Analyzing more than twenty-five years of research, researchers found that math anxiety, for example, negatively affects math achievement. This tends to start in childhood and remain consistent through adulthood.[14] That means feeling anxious about learning something may just feel "normal," even though it can be addressed.

Researchers in Taiwan set out to examine the role stress and social support play on learners' physical and mental health. They gathered data from 232 vocational learners and found that these learners were under "study stress" but that parental, teacher, and classmate support can relieve physical and mental study stress.[15] In other words, just having a support system helped reduce stress.

There are numerous ways to address anxiety and stress, many of which are covered in this book. Managing one's time and devoting time to leisure activities can help reduce stress.[16] So can stress-reduction activities such as incorporating mindfulness and breathing activities, feeling connected to others, and getting enough sleep.

Simple Strategy: Manage Your Anxiety

Anxiety is a condition that can, with practice and support, be overcome. You can conquer your anxiety. To get started:

1. **Manage time.** Manage your time carefully and plan for more than enough dedicated learning time.

2. **Find support.** Incorporate social support into your learning experiences.

3. **Relax more.** Incorporate regular leisure and relaxation activities, such as meditation, into your life and learning.

Breathe to Address Stress

Stress is an unavoidable part of life. Bodies change in response to stressful circumstances. The heart may seem to beat faster, breath may quicken, and palms might get sweaty. These are normal physiological responses. However, they may impair your performance. The good news, however, is that you can exert some control over this stress response through targeted breathing techniques. Such techniques can help you manage your nervous system.

Engaging in *focused breathing* enhances memory significantly more than normal or regular breathing. It may enhance cognition by improving relaxation and attention, which support learning in high-stress situations.[17] Focused breathing is simply exerting some control over your inhalations and exhalations, for example, to a count of four or six. The most intense form of focused breathing is diaphragmatic, or deep, controlled breathing, which lowers cortisol levels and improves attention and mood, which may also influence learning.[18] Such deep, slow breathing reduces the heart rate, diminishes perceived stress, and results in better focus and decision-making.[19] This state can enhance performance and learning.

Simple Strategy: Focus on Your Breath

By controlling your breathing, you can control your nervous system and your mind. Engage in focused breathing ahead of a test, exam, or any learning effort that requires you to make a decision. To get started:

1. **Slow down.** Take a slow, deep inhale and notice your belly rise.

2. **Hold it.** With your belly full, hold your breath for a few seconds.

3. **Release.** Slowly exhale, one second at a time, for a count of four or six.

Quiet Your Mind

There is a lot of buzz these days about meditation. It's considered a way of managing stress, improving well-being, and supporting health. You might meditate as part of your wellness routine, stress-management strategy, or spiritual practice. Mindfulness meditation involves focusing on the present moment and acknowledging one's feelings, thoughts, and sensations. This simple practice can reap major rewards. But you may not have considered meditation a way to improve learning.

Research has shown that meditation can improve attention, memory, and learning;[20] improve working memory, especially in high-stress contexts;[21] increase attention and decrease hyperactivity;[22] and support sleep (which affects learning).[23] Mindfulness meditation may even be generalizable to other cognitive tasks, such as attention.[24] Researchers studied the effects of mindfulness training on military personnel and found that mindfulness meditation boosted mood *and* memory capacity, seeming to serve a protective purpose against the functional impairments that can be associated with environments that are acutely stressful.[25]

Better yet, mindfulness meditation doesn't need to be practiced for very long to reap the benefits. Researchers tested a mindfulness meditation program on thirty-four learners, all of whom were diagnosed with a learning disability. They found meditation decreased their anxiety, improved their social skills, and boosted their learning in just five weeks.[26] Another study indicated that after only four sessions of meditation training, participants had reduced fatigue and improved anxiety, as well as improved cognition. They concluded that just four days of meditation training can help people improve their attention.[27] Just five to twelve minutes of mindfulness meditation each day is associated with decreased stress and anxiety.[28] While the results of any mediation program will vary based on the individual and his or her practice, this evidence nonetheless demonstrates an exciting connection between meditation and the mind.

Simple Strategy: Start Meditating

Anyone can meditate. The key is to find just a few minutes in your day and then stick with it. To get started:

1. **Find quiet.** Find a quiet space to sit, ideally with your feet on the floor and your hands on your lap.

2. **Make time.** Set a timer for the length of time you intend to meditate; between five and twenty minutes is good for beginners.

3. **Breathe.** Focus on your breath. If thoughts come into your mind, acknowledge them and release them, returning to your breath.

The Cumulative Effect

Have you ever embarked on learning something new but found yourself feeling inadequate, anxious, or overwhelmed? Maybe these feelings have manifested as racing thoughts, heightened awareness, sweaty palms, or rapid breathing. Or maybe they've caused a deep sense of dread. That's where addressing your mind comes in. Each strategy in this chapter helps you manage your mind, and together, they can have a stronger impact.

Imagine that you want to sharpen a valuable skill, like giving high-impact presentations, but that also strikes fear in you. You realize that the first step to learning isn't sitting down at your computer or registering for a course; it's preparing your mind. Getting started means adopting a growth mindset—a belief that you are fully able to learn and grow. But even with that core belief, you may still doubt your ability to succeed once you get started; you doubt your self-efficacy. So you boost it with encouragement, affirmations, and the decision to believe that, despite your circumstances, you've got this. And if anxiety and stress inevitably creep up on you, you don't cave into it; instead, you regulate your body. You lean into time management, deep breathing, and meditation—simple ways to lift your mood, focus, and performance. One day, just after giving a killer presentation, you realize how far you've come, not just with your presentation skills but with an even bigger skill: managing your mindset.

The choices in this example aren't haphazard—they're part of an intentional plan to support learning. This plan includes things like thinking about your beliefs and attitudes, managing your anxiety and stress, and using breath work and meditation to center yourself. Keep in mind the cumulative effect—blending strategies from this chapter with others can help you craft a learning approach that is effective for you.

Take Action: Make Your Own Plan

Have you ever heard the phrase "it's all in your mind"? When it comes to learning, there is no truer phrase. In this chapter, you explored how our mindsets, beliefs, attitudes, and moods have a huge effect on our learning—and, therefore, on our lives. By engaging in a few simple daily practices, we can prime our minds to learn and our bodies to better manage negative feelings that may accompany learning. These practices include adopting a growth mindset, cultivating a belief in our own ability to learn effectively, addressing anxiety, managing stress, and quieting our busy minds.

Take a moment to reflect on your mindset, beliefs, and moods and how these may influence your actions. After contemplating the following questions, develop a simple plan to cultivate a learning mindset and consider sharing it with someone who is supporting your learning. If you need more support, be sure to read Chapter 18 on building a robust learning network. For additional resources, visit www.already-smarter.com.

- Do you believe that there are some types of things you simply cannot learn? How might you let go of this belief?

- Do you find yourself giving up on your dreams because you worry that, in the end, things won't work out? How might you shift this perspective?

- What might you do to address any anxiety you experience while learning?

- How might a breathing or meditation practice help you learn?

CHAPTER 3

Ignite Your Motivation

S ometimes you may want to improve a skill that will also benefit other parts of your life. Take, for example, mastering the art
of negotiation. This certainly may come in handy if you have
a sales job, but negotiating may also serve you if you one day launch
your own business or simply want to bargain for a lower price at a
market. Regardless of your reason, your success rides on your ability
to learn how to negotiate—in a way that motivates you. Yet many of
us lose our momentum because we haven't aligned our learning to
our broader interests and motivations.

As a learner, I have grappled with this too: dropping courses that
didn't interest me or stopping activities shortly after they began. It
turns out that almost everyone struggles with motivation; nearly 95
percent of my informal survey respondents don't regularly leverage
their own motivation.[1] As a coach, I have worked with people to
explore ways to overcome their apathy and improve their learning
by igniting their motivation. In my experience, motivation is less

something we either have or lack; rather, it is something we can learn to tap into to propel ourselves forward.

This chapter can help you explore ways to leverage your intrinsic motivation—an important factor in seeing a task through to completion. It introduces five research-based strategies that may help you boost motivation and stay engaged in your goals, both big and small. With effort, you might find yourself shifting from disengaged to determined as you ignite your motivation.

Before you begin this chapter, think about how harnessing your motivation could help propel you through learning experiences and drive you to achieve your big dreams.

- What are some of the things you are most interested in or most motivated to do?

- Why might feeling motivated help improve your learning performance?

- How might leveraging your natural motivation help you achieve some of your biggest dreams?

Pursue Your Interests

Have you ever noticed that learning something that interests you often takes far less effort? The problem is you can't always limit learning to your main interests. In life, you need to learn things that interest you and sometimes things that disinterest you. The trick, then, is following your interests when you can and finding ways to make the disinteresting things slightly more appealing. How might your level of interest affect your learning?

There are differences among things that interest, engage, and motivate you. Generally, if something is of interest to you, it is also motivating and engaging.[2] However, you can be motivated to do things that are of relatively little personal interest. For example, you may have to take a class that's of very little interest in order to earn a degree or complete a required training or certification for a job. The key is to find things that are of interest, and, therefore, more motivating and more engaging, whenever you can. But when things are of disinterest to you, you can still find ways to make them *more* interesting. For example, you might not be interested in statistics unless you connect the data being studied with something you actually care about, such as sports, business, or world events. This connection can make something perceived as disinteresting far more relevant to your learning.

Simple Strategy: Follow Your Interests

You can follow your interests and make less interesting things more meaningful. To get started:

1. **Follow your heart.** Prioritize those experiences that play to your interests and strengths.

2. **Draw connections.** When something is not interesting, ask yourself: How might this relate to or benefit my interests? If you can't answer this question, then ask others for their perspectives.

3. **Be clear.** State this connection as clearly as you can and rephrase it as an interest. Say to yourself, *I am interested in X because it will help me to pursue my interest in Y.*

Harvest Your Intrinsic Motivation

Have you ever felt highly motivated to do one thing—play a sport, create artwork, or connect with friends—but completely unmotivated to do other things, such as cleaning or going to the gym? Sometimes the simple practice of staying motivated seems impossible.

Researchers analyzed more than 200 studies on motivation and found that while motivation has a positive effect on learning,[3] it can be a bit complicated. It's important to differentiate between *intrinsic motivation*, which is driven by internal rewards, such as enjoyment or the wish to improve, and *extrinsic motivation*, which is driven by the desire for external rewards or accolades.

Intrinsic motivation seems to be hardwired into the human brain. Exploration, learning new things, and interest in one's environment are related to dopamine levels in the brain, the release of which motivates us to seek out new experiences.[4] In fact, intrinsic motivation activates portions of the brain that help with memory formation.[5] And motivation greatly promotes and predicts academic achievement.[6]

In the workplace, intrinsic motivation is related to positive outcomes, while extrinsic motivation can have a negative impact on outcomes.[7] This means that being exclusively extrinsically motivated, such as doing a job only for the title or money, for example, results in poorer performance compared to that of people who are more interested in the job itself.

The key to success relies, in part, on one's intrinsic motivation to do things that are in themselves rewarding and growth-promoting, like being creative, reading, and engaging in hobbies.[8] However, if you are intrinsically motivated, getting negative feedback may demotivate you *unless it is extremely specific*. If you do receive negative feedback, seek out more details to learn exactly how you can improve.[9]

Simple Strategy: Tap Your Intrinsic Motivation

You can tap into your intrinsic motivation to propel yourself forward. To get started:

1. **Ask why.** Ask yourself why you are undertaking something. If it is for extrinsic reasons, such as influence, money, or status, consider whether it is something you are truly motivated to do.

2. **Connect to your intrinsic motivation.** Tap into your intrinsic motivation by connecting what you are learning to things that you are more motivated or interested in learning about. For example, if you are not motivated to learn statistics, find figures that do interest you—such as health, crime, or population data—and focus on these as you work through learning projects.

3. **Get specific.** If you get negative feedback, request specific feedback on your effort, progress, or work so that you can continue to improve.

Focus on Improvement, Not Success

When you try something new for the first time, do you focus more on doing it perfectly or just learning how to do it? Is it more important for you to perform highly or is the very process of learning a good enough goal?

The way in which you go about learning is directly related to how you view performance. How you approach tasks, including learning tasks, is called your "achievement orientation." According to experts, there are two dominant types of achievement orientation: mastery and performance.[10] Mastery goals are about continuing to improve your skills and abilities in a certain domain to be the best that you can be, whereas performance goals are directly related to achieving a specific outcome often tied to a reward or status.

Researchers studied engineers and technologists to understand how their approach to their goals affected their performance. The goal orientation that fostered the greatest well-being was a mastery orientation toward mastering a task rather than focusing on the perceived success that the task provides.[11] Indeed, this desire to achieve mastery has been shown to improve both academic performance and persistence.[12]

Simple Strategy: Adopt a Mastery Focus

When you're learning something new, you can adopt a mastery focus—and it will help you to master things even more. To get started:

1. **Ignore status.** Avoid thinking about short-term performance, grades, and recognition.

2. **Focus on each step.** Focus on each step in the learning process, with a vision of overall improvement and long-term success.

3. **Be an apprentice.** Consider yourself an apprentice, undergoing a constant evolution toward improvement.

Seek Rewards That Further Your Goals

Rewards are among the most powerful—and misunderstood—aspects of performance. You might think utilizing rewards means giving yourself a bit of a reward for completing something, such as a cold beer after a daily study session or your favorite meal at the end of a course. If that helps you to stay on task, then enjoy. But the effects of rewards are not always as straightforward as you may expect.

Experts analyzed 128 studies on the effects of intrinsic motivation and extrinsic rewards. They found that the use of rewards undermines intrinsic motivation. Rewards that were based on completing something reduced participants' interest, meaning that the more rewards they received the less they liked doing something. Rewards were even more detrimental and less effective for children.[13]

In general, there are two types of material rewards: transactional rewards, which are often like a gift, and relational rewards, which are things that support your ongoing growth. When people who were highly intrinsically motivated believed that they could receive a relational reward—the kind that helps them keep improving—the greater they performed (on creative or innovative work).[14] In addition to material rewards, there is a related kind of reward that *is* effective: praise. Positive feedback increased how likely people were to do things and to report being interested in doing things.[15] Rewards—including feedback—have the most benefit when they are specific and targeted to a specific behavior or experience.[16]

Simple Strategy: Be Careful of Rewards

When it comes to motivating yourself, reconsider what will help you achieve your goals. It may not be the big rewards when

continued

you've reached them; rather, it may be small encouragement from friends and family along the way. To get started:

1. **Avoid rewards.** Be cautious about striving for rewards, as they may undermine your intrinsic motivation. Counterintuitively, rewards are more likely to support things you already like doing.

2. **Request feedback.** Instead, solicit feedback from helpful and supportive individuals who are likely to provide positive feedback or specific constructive feedback that you can put into practice.

3. **Enable ongoing improvement.** If you do earn a reward or want to provide yourself with a reward, aim for one that is relational; that is, one that helps you keep improving. For example, after running a 5K, reward yourself with new running shoes.

Connect to a Greater Purpose

Contributing to a purpose is a powerful source of inspiration. Do you ever think about how you and your actions may contribute to a broader cause or sense of purpose? Maybe you work in a helping profession, where you are helping people heal, recover, or restart their lives. Or perhaps you are learning how to do something that will advance society or improve the environment. In both cases, you are likely motivated by a rewarding sense of purpose or service.

Researchers in Croatia wondered how contributing to a community through acts of service might also affect learners' academic performance and well-being. They studied 423 high school learners and found that helping one's family, friends, neighbors, peers, school, or community protected against depression, promoted self-regulation, and led to higher academic performance.[17]

Another set of researchers studied more than 2,000 adolescents and young adults. They found that having a purpose that transcended self-oriented motives, such as having an enjoyable career or improving academic performance, reduced the likelihood of dropping out, increased deeper learning, and sustained self-regulation.[18] In another study, researchers found that having a sense of purpose in midlife was associated with improved cognitive functioning, including improved memory, executive functioning, and overall cognition.[19]

Taken together, the studies indicate that being anchored by a larger purpose helps people of all ages improve and maintain their minds. Better yet, any given learning experience need only be *indirectly* related to your broader purpose. For example, while your bigger purpose may be helping stray animals, learning technical skills may help you secure a job working for a company that cares for such animals. Keeping your bigger, broader purpose in mind will help you through the difficulties of learning something that may be of less immediate interest but of longer-term benefit.

Simple Strategy: Draw Connections

Finding and connecting your goals to a larger purpose can help you stay motivated and learn more. To get started:

1. **Find a purpose.** Identify what gives you purpose in life— what you really value. You may have many purposes or your purpose may change from time to time, so don't get too hung up on finding one big purpose.

continued

2. **Align to your purpose.** Undertake learning activities that contribute to a broader purpose. These activities may help you achieve your purpose or simply draw upon your purpose as inspiration.

3. **Stay focused on the purpose.** Once you have drawn connections between what you are learning and your sense of purpose, keep these connections clear in your mind and strongly in focus.

The Cumulative Effect

Have you ever tried to learn something new but felt unmotivated and unable to connect what you were learning to your own interests, goals, and greater purpose? Maybe you kept asking yourself, *why do I need to learn this?* That's where igniting your motivation comes in. While each of the strategies in this chapter can harness your motivation, they can be even more powerful when combined.

Imagine you want to improve something that would benefit you in your job and your life, like becoming a persuasive negotiator to advocate for yourself and close sales at work. Yet every time you try to get started, you lose your motivation. You finally ask yourself, *how interested in this am I?* You admit that this isn't particularly interesting to you, but you know that you can still succeed if you link it to something that you *are* interested in—like getting deals and saving money. Focusing on what naturally matters to you—to something intrinsically motivating—boosts your likelihood of sticking with it. You also keep your focus on the satisfaction of making progress and learning something new, and you adopt a mastery orientation where you focus on small, steady improvements that will help you in the long run. Instead of rewarding yourself, you ask for feedback from someone you respect, connect your success to your purpose or values, and help others who are learning the same thing—all of which make for more meaningful rewards. One day, after successfully negotiating the lease terms on your apartment, you realize how far this skill has taken you and how your motivation can flex to fit the circumstances.

The techniques in this example aren't arbitrary choices—they're part of a deliberate plan intended to support learning. This plan includes things like pursuing your interests, harvesting your intrinsic motivation, focusing on improvement over success, seeking rewards that align with your goals, and connecting your learning to a greater purpose. With the cumulative effect of combining strategies from other chapters, the tools here can support a more personalized and powerful path forward.

Take Action: Make Your Own Plan

Throughout this chapter, you discovered that we learn more when we are interested in, and motivated by, what we are learning. Therefore, identifying what interests us and aligning what we are learning to our interests sets us on a path to success. By tapping our intrinsic motivation, rather than focusing on extrinsic rewards, we will get further, faster. Possessing a mastery mindset, rather than focusing on a status or performance goal, will help us take things one step at a time, especially when things get tough. The best rewards are often the simplest, in the form of acknowledgment, praise, or the ability to continue something you enjoy. And keeping a bigger purpose in your mind will help you feel energized and contribute to your memory and cognition.

Take a moment to reflect on your interests and motivations and the role they play when you undertake something new. After contemplating the following questions, develop a simple plan to ignite your motivation and consider sharing it with someone who is supporting your learning. If you need more support, be sure to read Chapter 18 on building a robust learning network. For additional resources, visit www.already-smarter.com.

- How might you lean into things that interest you—or connect what you are learning to those things?
- What types of things are you generally motivated to try, do, or learn? Why are these things more motivating for you?
- Are you more motivated by progressively mastering something or the final performance, outcome, or achievement?
- What kinds of rewards might help you further pursue your interests?
- In your life, what gives you meaning or purpose?

CHAPTER 4

Set Learning
Goals That Stick

There are times in life when you may find yourself pondering a big feat—like running a marathon or completing some other lifelong fitness challenge. These types of gargantuan efforts are tough to pull off without learning new things—in ways that lead to your ultimate goal. Yet many of us fail to achieve these types of big feats simply because we are bad at goal setting and goal achievement.

Like many people, I have long been aware of goal setting, but it took years to learn how to use goal-setting strategies as tools to actually achieve my goals. Indeed, most people are familiar with the concept of goal setting, but only one of every five people in my informal survey indicated that they actually use it regularly as a learning strategy.[1] I have worked with people to explore ways to overcome this inertia by establishing crystal-clear goals and even clearer paths to achieving those goals. Goal setting can be a powerful step toward beginning to learn—and creating meaningful change in our lives.

This chapter can help you explore how to set meaningful goals and work toward achieving them. It introduces five evidence-informed strategies that may help you make progress on your personal, career, and life goals. With the right techniques, you might find yourself shifting from goal-averse to goal-oriented as you develop learning goals that stick.

Before you begin this chapter, think about how setting learning goals could help you learn more and achieve more.

- How do you currently go about goal setting?

- Why might goal setting help improve your learning performance?

- How might goal setting help you achieve some of your biggest dreams?

Use Goals to Focus

Some of the best instructors ask learners questions that start with the word *why*. Why are you studying? Why are you hoping to learn something new? Why does this subject, topic, or course interest you? The answers to these questions often go beyond a desire to get a better job or meet an obligation. You may undertake learning experiences to achieve a variety of goals: curiosity, personal fulfillment, or the simple and very human desire to grow. Some of these goals are clearer and stronger than others. How do your goals set you on a path for learning?

Goal setting is one of the most important things that learners can do to foster their educational attainment.[2] Goal setting may be especially useful for those of you who have struggled with something previously or who don't have confidence in your abilities. Indeed, goal setting can improve performance by a full letter grade.[3] Goal setting has been found to be one of the most important ways by which learners can regulate their learning and complete specific courses.[4]

However, goals should be directly relevant to your life.[5] In other words, goals should be connected to your interests, personally meaningful, and relatively achievable. For example, setting a goal to complete a course that enables you to advance along your chosen career path is relevant and, therefore, more likely to be accomplished.

Simple Strategy: Set Goals That Support Learning

If setting goals seems difficult to you, think again. With a bit of practice, anyone can set and achieve goals. To get started:

1. **Take time.** Take time to think through your goals and ambitions. What do you most want to accomplish, and what do you need to learn to do so?

2. **Ask why.** When you set a goal, ask yourself why this is important to you. Draft a goal statement that includes your "why." For example, "I want to learn to throw pottery because ____." This goal statement will make your goal relevant and meaningful.

3. **Make it achievable.** Ensure that your goal is achievable. If not, revise it to make it reasonably achievable.

Keep Goals Bite-Sized

Do you tend to be someone with big, lofty goals, or do you prefer to take things one step at a time? Big goals, such as monumental career aspirations, may seem overwhelming, but smaller goals, such as completing a simple task, may not seem very inspirational. While neither may work well alone, big and small goals do work well *together*.

Studies have indicated that creating both *superordinate* and *subordinate* goals resulted in improved effort.[6] You can think of superordinate goals as being the bigger, longer-term goals and subordinate goals as being the smaller steps needed to achieve the larger ones. For example, a superordinate goal might be to become a doctor, while the subordinate goals might include getting a premed degree, then going to medical school, and then completing a residency. An even more subordinate goal may include taking your very first course. Nearly every big goal can be broken into smaller, more manageable subordinate goals that help us develop a clear path forward.

Simple Strategy: Set Smaller Goals

You can break your goals into smaller chunks that make them easier to pursue and accomplish. Get in the habit of breaking goals into smaller pieces. To get started:

1. **Think big.** What is your big goal? Maybe it's a dream career, a long-pursued interest, or a life goal. Try to articulate it as clearly as you can.

2. **Break it up.** Break the big goal into several more manageable goals. These may include seeking advice, reading books, and taking some courses.

3. **Decide where to start.** Decide on the easiest, most action-able first step. What is the very first thing you can do to get started?

Strategize to Achieve Goals

Have you ever set a goal but then failed to achieve it? New Year's goals, for example, are notoriously difficult to follow through. Sometimes our goals seem too difficult; other times, ordinary life gets in the way, or we simply lose interest. In any case, goals don't achieve themselves; they require thoughtful strategies.

Researchers found that learners who wrote down strategies for achieving goals experienced a 22 percent increase in their academic performance. This was true regardless of whether they wrote about academic goals, personal goals, or a combination of both. Just being "goal-directed" and reflecting on those goals improved their learning performance.[7]

A *strategy* is a way of getting something done. One strategy, for example, is involving others in your goal pursuit. In fact, people tend to stick with difficult goals that are set publicly and shared by others.[8] Another strategy is asking for feedback. Receiving feedback on a specific goal improves your motivation to achieve the goal, engagement in pursuing it, and performance toward ultimately succeeding (and keeps your mind from wandering to unrelated thoughts).[9] You can think of strategies as the glue that helps you stick to your goals.

Simple Strategy: Stick with Your Learning Goals

You can accomplish your goals if you generate strategies, share with others, and ask for feedback. To get started:

1. **List strategies.** Write down specific strategies to achieve your goal. List as many as you can think of and then prioritize them based on which strategies you are most likely to adopt.

2. **Share your goals.** Share your goal publicly and make it a topic of conversation. Then begin to involve others in the pursuit of it.

3. **Ask for feedback.** Request feedback on your goal. Ask others, especially those you respect, how you're progressing.

Start with the End in Mind

Are you a planner, or someone who tends to make decisions as you go? Planners tend to do a lot of research, think things through, and then come up with detailed, step-by-step plans. Some of these plans take people exactly where they had hoped to go, while other plans fizzle out or even backfire. After you set goals, the real work begins: determining how you can achieve those goals.

There are two primary ways to plan: forward planning and backward planning. *Forward planning* is planning the first, second, and third things you need to do. *Backward planning* means starting with the goal and working backward. While forward planning tends to be the go-to for most people, backward planning can yield even greater results. Backward planning doesn't just help you along your way; it also leads to greater motivation, higher expectations of reaching a goal, less time pressure, and better overall performance.[10] If you haven't tried backward planning, give it a try and find out where it takes you.

Simple Strategy: Plan Things Backward

You can achieve a goal if you imagine you have already succeeded and work backward, thinking through each step that got you there. To get started:

1. **Go in reverse.** Create a reverse timeline with your ultimate end goal being the first item you put on the timeline.

2. **Work backward.** Work backward, identifying what may happen immediately before achieving that goal, and before that, and before that.

3. **List everything.** Add learning experiences—including informal experiences—that may help you along this path.

Prime Yourself to Attain Goals

Once you have a lofty goal, broken into superordinate and subordinate goals, with strategies and a specific plan, there's only one more thing to do: Prime yourself to achieve the goal. Priming is when your goals are activated by external cues. It's like giving yourself a nudge in the right direction.

Priming can be conscious, subconscious, or both. In a learning context, conscious priming may include images of what learning something will enable you to do or become, whereas subconscious priming may be associating with other learners who share your goals or who have already attained them. Both types of priming work, and you can really improve your performance by complementing a consciously primed goal with additional subconscious priming.[11]

Priming can be tricky, though. Take the familiar goal of dieting. Some dieters *stop* dieting if they are primed to enjoy caloric foods (as soon as they spot these foods, they give in); others use caloric foods to further prime their self-control (as soon as these dieters spot these foods, they strengthen their resolve).[12] When you establish primes, you need to be thoughtful about whether they will trigger you to work toward your goals or inadvertently sidetrack your efforts.

And primes shouldn't always be easy. Experiencing more difficult primes may cause you to exert more effort, set additional difficult goals, and perform more highly.[13] So, when you prime yourself, aim high.

Simple Strategy: Prime Your Mind to Maximize Learning

You can prime your mind to achieve a goal. Priming can help on both a conscious and subconscious level. To get started:

1. **Prime everywhere.** Surround yourself with things that prime you to pursue your learning goals. This may include words or images related to what your goal will enable you to achieve, feel, or become.

2. **Place carefully.** Place primes not only where you learn but also in places that may inadvertently trigger you to undermine your goal achievement.

3. Find common connections. Begin to associate common objects with your goal pursuit. For example, you may begin to associate your morning coffee time with learning.

The Cumulative Effect

Have you ever wanted to learn something new but couldn't quite figure out what your goal was and were therefore unable to strategize, work toward completion, and prime yourself to achieve it? That's where setting learning goals that stick comes in. Each approach described in this chapter can help you establish and achieve goals, but their true strength emerges when used together.

Imagine that you've decided you're finally going to tackle your biggest fitness goal: running a marathon. But then again, this goal feels daunting. You know that setting a clear, meaningful goal serves as a guidepost on your learning journey, so you pick the specific marathon you're planning to compete in and then break it into several smaller goals: a 5K, a 10K, and a half-marathon. You work backward from the ultimate goal to make sure that there is adequate time to prepare for each of the smaller goals, ensuring that you also have enough recovery time between each of the milestones to avoid burnout or injury—two very real risks that threaten your big goal. You spend time brainstorming and researching strategies to achieve not only your ultimate goal but also the smaller races along the way, and you share your goal publicly, especially with people who support you. As each week takes you closer to your marathon date, you make your goal increasingly visible at home and at work, keeping race photos, gear, and healthy snacks nearby to remind you that you are making progress on your learning—and fitness—journey. One day, as you complete your final practice run, it occurs to you just how far you've come and how running is now a sign not only of fitness but also of knowing how to set and achieve goals.

These strategies aren't accidental choices—they're part of a purposeful plan intended to support your learning. This plan includes things like using goals to focus your efforts, keeping them bite-sized and achievable, strategizing effectively, starting with the end in mind, and priming yourself to attain your goals. Don't overlook the power of integration—bringing these approaches together with those from other chapters can meaningfully enhance your learning.

Take Action: Make Your Own Plan

This chapter focused on the importance of goal setting for learning. Effective goals must be relevant to our larger lives. Goals need to be the right size, with big or lofty goals broken into smaller, subordinate goals that are easier to manage. Regardless of what type of goal we are trying to achieve, writing down strategies will help us boost our performance. Planning backward from an ultimate end goal boosts motivation and performance. Priming ourselves to achieve goals involves establishing external cues that keep us on our path. These may be conscious, such as photos related to our goals, or subconscious, such as associating with environments or people who have already achieved a similar goal.

Take a moment to reflect on your experience setting goals and how you typically go about goal setting. After contemplating the following questions, develop a simple plan to set learning goals and consider sharing it with someone who is supporting your learning. If you need more support, be sure to read Chapter 18 on building a robust learning network. For additional resources, visit www.already-smarter.com.

- When you consider a goal, do you ask yourself why it matters to you or your life?

- Do you tend to set big, lofty goals or smaller, achievable goals? How can you use both kinds to support one another?

- How have you achieved a learning goal—and what strategies worked best for you?

- How might you develop a plan that supports one of your biggest goals?

PART II

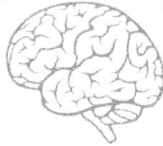

Establish a Solid Foundation

Once you've set your intention to learn, it's time to begin the action. How can you go about the process of learning—and which opportunities might you seize? By seeing your goals clearly, you can set out for them, and suddenly they become mere milestones on your journey. But taking these steps is easier said than done. It's hard to make time and not get overwhelmed before you even begin.

The second part of this book is about establishing a solid foundation. This part includes four chapters focused on going from idea to action: seizing opportunities, mastering your time and energy, starting strong to build familiarity, and driving your learning. These chapters will help you go from having a clear goal to taking steps on the path to that goal, with dedicated time and a strong start to succeed. Building a solid foundation is the first significant set of actions toward beginning to achieve your dreams.

CHAPTER 5

Seize Opportunities

Sometimes one small victory—say, learning how to bake a delicious dessert—can have a cascading effect on your life (like getting a booth at a farmers market or opening a bakery). Sometimes we even find that these types of surprise successes have resulted from learning or trying something new—provided we can find these experiences and afford them. Yet many of us miss the opportunities that are right in front of us.

Over the years, I have missed out on numerous growth opportunities, only discovering them when it was too late to get involved. I'm not the only one who has failed to find unexpected learning opportunities; when asked, more than 90 percent of those surveyed indicated that they don't routinely look for them either.[1] As both an instructor and a coach, I have worked with people to explore ways to find different types of resources that are readily available—often at little or no cost. I have seen learners becoming excited to spot new opportunities that they hadn't previously seen.

This chapter can help you learn about the kinds of resources that may be available all around you. It introduces five important strategies for uncovering learning opportunities that fit your budget, time, and values. By applying the right techniques, you might find yourself feeling more engaged and energized as you discover new ways to learn.

Before you begin this chapter, think about how hidden learning opportunities could help put you on the path to achieving your learning goals and life aspirations.

- What kinds of simple, affordable opportunities might interest you?

- Why might free or short-form learning opportunities improve your learning performance?

- How might free or short-form learning opportunities help you achieve some of your life goals?

Consider Costs—and the Return on Investment

Learning something new takes time, energy, and, often, money. In some cases, learning may take you away from your family, friends, and hobbies; in other cases, it may require a significant financial investment or postponing the use of that time to earn money more immediately—this is known as *deferred income*. These are the inherent costs of learning, and they need to be weighed against the return on that investment. The return, of course, can be earned income or things like enjoyment, personal growth, or career mobility. Devising a plan for how you will pay for a learning experience, and the subsequent return on that investment, can be critical for your success.

Imagine that you currently earn $50,000 per year and that you are considering a graduate program that costs $15,000 per year and takes two years of full-time study to complete, forcing you to quit your job and take out a student loan to cover tuition as well as about $25,000 in living expenses for each year. That total investment is around $180,000 and might not seem worth it. However, if it doubles your income, you'll pay for it in two years and then have much stronger earning power thereafter. In this case, it might well be worth it.

When considering the return on a learning investment, there are a couple of important catches. Financially, will you be able to achieve the salary that you expect, or will that take a few years or longer to get to? Emotionally, will you want to do whatever job you will be qualified to do? In other words, will the job be satisfying and meet your bigger needs, hopes, and dreams?

A big part of considering the return on investment (ROI) is looking into the likelihood that the expected result is both realistic and satisfying. Will a learning experience improve your life ambitions, personal satisfaction, or career goals? Will it make you feel better about yourself, how you spend your time, and how you contribute to society? Not all learning takes you closer to your goals. Sometimes people invest in learning experiences that they later find aren't in line with their values or interests.

Simple Strategy: Calculate the ROI of a Learning Experience

If you've never calculated the ROI, don't worry. With a bit of practice, this can become a habit of mind. To get started:

continued

1. **Consider the total costs.** This includes tuition and other expenses such as books, transportation, and childcare. Also be sure to include the cost of lost income if you need to take a pause from working to create time for learning.

2. **Consider the future return.** If it is a financial return, be realistic about how much income it will bring you and for how many years you will realistically earn that income. If it is some other kind of return—for example, providing more work-life balance—be clear about the value of this to your life.

3. **Do the calculation.** Subtract the costs from the future return and ask yourself if this is "enough" to warrant the investment. Consider whether there are ways to maximize the ROI: Is there a way to drive down the costs? Is there a way to boost the return?

Explore Low-Cost Learning Opportunities

Learning something new doesn't always require a massive financial or time investment. If possible, it's best to "test" your interest before committing to a big monetary investment up front. Today, more than ever, low-cost learning opportunities are readily available—if you know where to look. How can you find learning opportunities that let you try before you buy?

There are many ways to explore learning new things without spending much money. One of the fastest and easiest ways to learn is informally, through free resources, on the job, and through personal connections.

- **Open educational resources.** Open educational resources are free or low-cost materials—such as books, videos, and online courses—that are broadly available. These materials are as effective as traditional materials and are perceived positively by instructors and learners.[2]

- **Informal learning opportunities.** Informal learning opportunities are experiences that happen on the job, during volunteer work, and through shared experiences. Engagement in informal learning opportunities improves learners' attitudes, knowledge, skills, and performance.[3]

- **Learning from others.** Learning from others, such as friends, coworkers, or connections, can also be a valuable way to initiate learning. It can be better to learn, initially, from generalists rather than specialists.[4] It's possible that generalists can relate more broadly to other people's experiences and initial understanding, and specialists can contribute to deeper learning later.

- **Sponsored learning.** Many localities, nonprofits, associations, and companies offer learning programs that can be no or low cost. It's always worthwhile to investigate what opportunities may be available to you—right in your neighborhood or by your employer.

These kinds of learning may not always award learners a credential; however, they can give you enough exposure to something to determine whether you want to continue learning formally.

Simple Strategy: Start Looking for Learning Opportunities

You can easily find resources that help you explore a new interest, field, or topic with little to no expense. This is a great way to "try before you buy." To get started:

1. **Find resources.** Put together your own free learning experience using a mix of library or used books, YouTube videos, social media posts, and podcasts.

2. **Find events.** Find and attend live events such as meetups, conferences, volunteer opportunities, community interest groups, and courses offered through community centers, libraries, and community colleges.

3. **Consider those you already know.** Do you have friends, coworkers, neighbors, relatives, or other contacts who could provide you with guidance? Add these folks to your list; they are invaluable subject matter experts.

Don't Dismiss the Value of Real-World Experiences

One of the best ways to learn, not surprisingly, is by engaging in real, authentic work. These experiences form the backbone of so many important life skills that you learn, from taking care of yourself to taking care of your family and communities. And authentic experiences provide all the ingredients to put new knowledge and skills directly into practice.

Real-world experiences are even more powerful when paired with more academic or theoretical learning. Behavioral, cognitive, and other skills improve when combined with more traditional learning programs.[5] The ideal blend, then, is to find learning experiences that combine more theoretical learning with real-world learning opportunities. As you look to learn new things, consider how you can blend real-world learning (perhaps through work, internships, or mentoring) with more theory or skill-based learning (perhaps through free resources, microcredentials, or degree-based programs).

Simple Strategy:
Find Real-World Learning Experiences

If you don't have time to engage in a formal internship, externship, clinical, or apprenticeship, don't worry. There are numerous real-world experiences that are less formal. To get started:

1. **Focus on reality.** If you are investigating courses, microcredentials, or degrees, consider prioritizing those that incorporate real-world learning opportunities.

2. **Complement your learning.** If you are engaging in real-world learning, such as learning something new on the job, complement it with free or low-cost resources or a microcredential.

3. **Seize opportunities.** If you are taking courses or pursuing a degree, find opportunities for real-world learning, such as volunteer work, job shadowing, or a formal internship or apprenticeship.

"Stack Up" Smaller Credentials

Have you ever wanted to earn a degree but then thought that it would take too long or too much of your time? Today, there are a variety of alternatives to traditional degrees. Some of these apply or "stack" toward a degree, just as you might stack bricks together to form a building. These are known as microcredentials, or short ways of beginning to learn something without taking an entire program or degree. Typically, a microcredential requires you to take a few courses to earn a badge, certificate, or certification. Often, they can be completed in a few weeks or months. Many microcredentials provide the skills to advance to a new or better job. Increasingly, microcredentials have become a common way for employers to identify that a candidate possesses specific skills.[6] In fact, many microcredentials are low cost or free, enabling learners to dip their toes into something new without significant investment.

Good microcredentials are:

- **High quality:** They meet industry standards or accreditation requirements.

- **Effective:** They provide data on learner satisfaction, success, and career outcomes.

- **Qualifiers:** They prepare the learner to take an exam or for licensure.

- **Stackable:** They can be applied toward another learning experience or degree.

Simple Strategy:
Identify Valuable Microcredentials

Today, stackable microcredentials are readily available if you look for them. Nearly anyone can complete a short certificate or certification. To get started:

1. **Start searching.** Conduct an internet search for a microcredential. Consider using the terms *badge*, *diploma*, *certificate*, and *certification*, as these are common types of microcredentials that are shorter than a full degree.

2. **Assess career implications.** Consider whether any of the microcredentials lead to professional licensure. If so, you'll want to be sure that the microcredential truly qualifies you for work in the field.

3. **Determine if they stack.** For those microcredentials that capture your interest, determine whether they "stack" into an associate's, bachelor's, or master's degree. If they do, you might appreciate that later, if you want to continue learning more.

Find Belonging and Community

A strong sense of belonging contributes to achievement. When you consider learning opportunities, some feel like a great fit and others simply don't. Choosing a learning program that doesn't match your interests, abilities, or cultural values can have a negative impact on your success, but choosing one that aligns with your goals, perspectives, and values can take you far indeed.

Experts believe that what we might call "fitting in"—being matched to the right institution, academic program, and community—can contribute to success.[7] When learners, especially those who are underrepresented, perceive a cultural mismatch, it can increase cortisol levels, indicating a stress response.[8] These sorts of mismatches aren't things that you easily adjust to; cultural mismatches often persist throughout the length of one's program of study.[9]

A team of researchers wondered exactly what impact that sense of belonging has on the learning process. They found that when college students experienced a sense of hope and belongingness, they had improved academic self-efficacy; that is, they felt more confident in their abilities.[10] Similarly, researchers studying undergraduates on academic probation found that increased hope and belongingness were associated with significant improvements in academic achievement and larger increases in hope correlated with larger increases in academic performance.[11] A sense of belonging is also correlated with higher motivation and engagement.[12] So, if you feel that you do better work when you "fit in," you're exactly right.

Simple Strategy: Aim for Belonging

With a little effort, you can select learning experiences that are a good cultural fit and foster your sense of belonging. To get started:

1. **Consider your needs.** When you are considering a learning experience, ask yourself how well you might fit in or belong based on your life experience, prior knowledge, and values.

2. **Look at the evidence.** Don't base your judgment on fears or biases; rather, look for actual evidence. What are the learner

demographics? What support is offered to learners? What does it feel like if you attend an informational session or visit?

3. **Keep looking.** If you don't feel like you fit in, don't give up. Look for organizations, activities, or communities that would enable you to feel a sense of inclusion and belonging.

The Cumulative Effect

Have you ever contemplated starting something new but then put it aside because it seemed too big or too expensive? Maybe you realized that there would be a hidden cost to learning, or you hoped to find more enjoyable options in real-world communities of practice. That's where seizing the opportunities all around us comes in. Any single strategy in this chapter can help you weigh different opportunities, and together, they can help to put you on a path for success.

Imagine that you want to learn a new hobby that might one day open the door to a small business, like vegan baking. Your mind goes immediately to a formal learning course, but you are dismayed by the expense. You decide that there must be other options, so you begin to curate low-cost and free resources, such as used books, free videos, and community workshops at your local grocery store. You practice at home, cooking for friends and relatives, knowing that these real-world challenges are helping you acquire valuable skills. Still, you yearn to enroll in a formal learning program and learn with the guidance of a strong curriculum and team of expert bakers. You start by registering for a short microcredential—a vegan baking certificate—and find the experience so rewarding (and so effective) that you ultimately decide to invest in the more expensive degree, understanding that it also provides courses on establishing a business and networking opportunities with successful bakers worldwide. Along with your fellow students, you realize that these folks will form a valuable community of practice, helping you to build a vegan baking business complete with a bakery, catering business, and your own courses. One day you realize that you're not only a much better baker, you're also better at sizing up the opportunities around you.

This example isn't a series of coincidental choices—they're part of a measured plan designed to support learning. This plan includes things like considering the return on investment, exploring low-cost learning opportunities, finding real-world experiences, and finding belonging and community. These strategies can be even more impactful when layered with others, creating a plan that's tailored to your growth.

Take Action: Make Your Own Plan

Throughout this chapter, you discovered how to weigh and seize learning opportunities. Learning something new often requires time, money, energy, and a careful analysis of the return on investment. Learning doesn't need to involve a formal program, course, or class. There are many things you can learn by curating your own resources, some of which are very low cost or entirely free. Real-world experiences are powerful ways to learn that enable you to learn important associated skills that are often valuable in real life and in the workplace. The best approach is to pair formal learning experiences with real-world learning for the best of both worlds. Microcredentials are short badges, certificates, or certifications that take less time than earning a degree. They enable you to earn a credential that lets employers know that you possess certain skills. One important part of considering any new learning experience is determining whether it's a "fit" for you. Feeling that you "belong" is positively related to your overall motivation, engagement, and achievement and can prevent you from dropping out.

Take a moment to reflect on the ways you typically undertake a new learning experience. After contemplating the following questions, develop a simple plan to seize learning opportunities and consider sharing it with someone who is supporting your learning. If you need more support, be sure to read Chapter 18 on building a robust learning network. For additional resources, visit www.already-smarter.com.

- When it comes to learning something new, do you spend time comparing costs, considering the return on the investment, and contemplating how much time something is likely to require?

- When you're thinking about learning something new or improving your current knowledge, how do you find free or low-cost learning opportunities?

- Who are the connections in your life that may enable you to learn something new in the real world?

- What kinds of microcredentials might help you acquire skills—quickly?

- What beliefs, values, and communities might be important for you to see reflected in a learning experience?

CHAPTER 6

Master Your Time and Energy

R egardless of whether you want to advance your career, finish a required course, or follow a lifelong passion—like learning to sing—your success depends upon your ability to learn something new—and to learn it *productively*. Yet many of us slow ourselves down by wasting time and energy.

This is something I used to really struggle with: *maximizing* my time. And while many people report being familiar with time-management strategies, many still feel strapped for time and don't know how to use time to their advantage.[1] Over the years, I have met numerous others—especially college students and early career professionals—who share this challenge. I have worked with them to learn to master their time and energy in ways that drive their lives forward. In my coaching practice, I have noticed how maximizing time can open the door to greater energy and momentum.

This chapter can help you explore strategies for making the most of your time. It introduces five well-supported approaches that may help you optimize your schedule and complete learning tasks. With a bit of strategizing, you might find yourself becoming more efficient and productive as you change how you manage your time and energy.

Before you begin this chapter, think about how managing your time and energy could help you progress through learning experiences and ultimately contribute to your bigger aspirations.

- What are some of the ways you have tried optimizing your time? Have they worked?

- Why might time and energy management affect your learning performance?

- How might time and energy management help you achieve some of your larger aspirations?

Manage Your Time Closely

The aim of time management is to use time effectively and increase the quality (and sometimes quantity) of activities performed in a limited time. You can almost think of time management as a way to expand or grow one of life's most limited resources: time. It makes sense, then, that time management may be an important part of life. But does time management pay off when it comes to learning?

Researchers in the Netherlands surveyed 758 learners between the ages of nineteen and seventy-one and found that learners who managed their time and effort had the best academic performance.[2] Other researchers found that learners benefit from both being knowledgeable about time management and practicing time management techniques; however, learners who practice good time management tend to benefit more.[3]

In addition, learners who perceived themselves to be in control of their time reported greater satisfaction with their jobs and lives, less ambiguity over their work, fewer feelings of being overloaded, and less job-related and physical tension.[4] Good time-management practices help you feel in control of your time, satisfied with how you spend it, and healthier and more balanced. Poor time management can increase your sense of stress.[5] Being in control requires you to determine how you want to spend your time, manage your time wisely, and set boundaries to protect your time.

Simple Strategy: Make Time for Time Management

Not only can you optimize your time, you can make *more* time. But you need to start by understanding how you are using the time you have. To get started:

1. **Find categories.** Identify the biggest categories that your life tasks fall into. For example, caring for family, working, sleeping, commuting, exercising, and relaxing. Be as detailed as you can with each category.

2. **Track actual time.** For one week, track how much time you spend on each category. At the end of each day, log how much time you spent in each area.

3. **Remove and reduce.** Look for ways to optimize your time. Which things could you remove or reduce to make more time for learning? Be specific.

Tweak the Time You Learn

Have you noticed that you may have more energy, more focus, and more interest at certain times of day? Maybe you feel more alert midmorning or more tired midafternoon, or maybe you have timed your caffeine consumption around common points in the day when your energy lags. Often, this is tied to your circadian rhythm—the body's internal clock that runs every twenty-four hours.

The circadian clock—that is, how the time of day affects your body and mind—also affects your cognition and memory formation.[6] However, choosing the best time of day to learn is a bit more complicated. Researchers asked subjects to perform a simple memory task at two different times: morning and afternoon. They found that the subjects had better recall in the morning.[7] Indeed, waking up earlier is related to higher grades.[8] And learning during daytime hours is more effective than learning later in the evening or nighttime, with the ideal time to learn being afternoon.[9] In short, it appears your performance may be improved by rising early, and your memories may be sharper in the morning, but that afternoons are ideal for learning.

Simple Strategy:
Align Learning with Your Internal Clock

With a bit of thoughtful scheduling, you can match your learning activities to your internal clock. To get started:

1. **Rise early.** Consider trying to become a "morning person," which is often related to higher performance.

2. **Focus in the morning.** If you can, consider taking courses or assessments in the morning, when your recall is typically stronger.

3. **Learn and review a bit later.** Afternoons are often a good time for learning activities, especially compared to evenings, when you might engage in lighter reviews.

Use Calendars to Organize Time

Do you use a calendar? Not just to find out what the date is, but to plan your time? Many people rely on their calendars for appointments, classes, or work-related meetings but rarely rely on them to organize their days and weeks—especially with the kinds of specific activities that support learning.

A calendar can be a powerful learning tool. Experts who studied the use of a calendar tool found that learners who used one improved their time-management skills and, consequently, their academic performance.[10] But when it comes to scheduling time for learning, how much time is the *right* amount of time? Researchers in Germany studied more than 1,000 people aged sixteen to sixty-five to determine how the time they spent on a learning task affected their performance. They found that the impact of time varied depending upon the difficulty of the task and each individual's skill level. While there is no one-size-fits-all amount of time that you should spend studying, spending more time on a task helps you perform better when you are learning something new or difficult.[11] That said, using a calendar can help you better understand the actual time things take and begin to manage your time more realistically.

Simple Strategy: Use Your Calendar to Structure Your Learning

You can begin to use (or improve how you use) a calendar to structure and optimize your time and improve your learning. The key, however, is to use a calendar properly to both schedule your day and then stick to that schedule. To get started:

1. **Include everything.** Plan out your ideal week, including all your responsibilities: family, work, commuting, and leisure.

2. **Make time to learn.** Insert time for learning, selecting times that work for you and that you are likely to stick with; better yet, make sure these are aligned to your circadian rhythm.

3. **Tweak things.** Make a bit of extra learning time each day or each week. For example, swap out one or two other events to make more time to learn.

Bypass Procrastination

Procrastination—putting things off until later—undermines learning in numerous ways. Procrastination causes you to postpone goals and learning opportunities, sometimes permanently. When you procrastinate, you lose valuable learning time, therefore eroding how much and how well you learn. Procrastination also sparks your anxiety and inhibits your sense of control.

Often, procrastination stems from delaying doing something that is perceived as unpleasant. A procrastination expert has found seven qualities that tend to make tasks seem averse and like something you should put off. These include tasks you perceive as boring, frustrating, difficult, ambiguous, unstructured, unrewarding, and unmeaningful.[12] Procrastination may be caused by a desire to avoid these adverse states. Unfortunately, by procrastinating, you experience relief from these negative emotions, which rewards your procrastination and perpetuates the tendency to procrastinate further.[13]

To avoid procrastination, you need to become better at *intentionally tolerating* negative states, such as boredom or fear of failure, and consciously reminding yourself of your ability to withstand these emotions.[14] And, if possible, you should select tasks that interest you, tap your intrinsic motivation, include collaboration, and are well managed, as these are easier for you to complete.[15]

It may also be helpful to explore the reasons why you procrastinate. Adopt strategies such as time management, problem-solving, learning techniques, sleep hygiene, and goal setting. Then develop a "contract" to complete something you would typically procrastinate.[16]

Simple Strategy: Stop Procrastinating

Anyone can stop procrastinating with a bit of practice. To get started:

1. **Stop unwelcome tasks.** When possible, don't undertake learning activities that you find boring, frustrating, difficult, ambiguous, unstructured, unrewarding, or unmeaningful.

2. **Make them enjoyable.** When you must undertake such tasks, try to find ways to make the tasks more interesting or enjoyable, such as working on them with a partner.

3. **Find your tolerance.** If you cannot make a task more enjoyable, acknowledge these negative emotional states and remind yourself that you can tolerate these states.

Squeeze in Microlearning

Many of us spend considerable time on our mobile phones. What if you could turn this habit into learning time? While you may typically use your phone to engage in social media, text friends, and consume content, there are also powerful ways that these devices can help you seize microlearning moments.

Microlearning—dividing learning into small chunks that can be completed in a short amount of time—can improve the effectiveness and efficiency of learning.[17] Mobile-based microlearning delivers small chunks of learning and shorter learning activities that can enhance autonomy, competence, relatedness, and satisfaction.[18] YouTube videos, for instance, can be used for microlearning.[19]

Social media, if used intentionally, can enable microlearning experiences. Experts found that following the social media of classmates, especially if in the same program, can foster feelings of belonging to a community and create opportunities for career networking.[20] Social media also enhances language learning.[21] In this way, social media can help you gain fluency with the words and phrases related to a learning experience.

Simple Strategy: Learn Through Your Phone

You can use your mobile device to squeeze in a bit of extra learning during your spare time. To get started:

1. **Get connected.** Connect and communicate with classmates on social media to foster a sense of connection to others who have similar goals and interests.

2. **Choose the right content.** Select videos, podcasts, and posts that further your learning goals.

3. **Listen up.** Find content related to what you are learning on podcasts or in audiobooks, and squeeze it into the spare time you might normally spend commuting, exercising, or walking.

The Cumulative Effect

Have you ever put the effort into learning something new but found yourself unable to get started or just plain short on time? You might have thought, *how can I possibly fit another thing in*, or *I'll start this later*. That's where mastering your time and energy comes in. You may find that each tool in this chapter helps you *manage* your time, but combined, they may help you *maximize* your time.

Imagine you want to conquer a big dream, like becoming a professional vocalist and taking your show on the road, but you keep putting it off. Despite feeling "time poor," you still want to pursue your interest in learning how to sing—and to sing well. You begin using your calendar more consistently to block time for learning, strategically selecting times when you can focus. Then you begin to align your learning to your natural body clock, finding that you absorb things more effectively in the afternoon and making time to review what you learned the following morning. At long last, you decide to tackle your tendency to procrastinate, simply telling yourself that you have managed uncomfortable tasks before and can do so again. The hardest part is just getting started. You also find an accountability buddy to help you stay on track. Most importantly, you realize how much additional learning you can fit into your day by using your phone to squeeze in some microlearning—videos, apps, and podcasts—rounding out your learning in fun, engaging ways. As you begin to better manage your time, you start noticing that you're feeling a bit less stress and somewhat more in control. Finally, you notice how strong your voice has become, and you credit it, in part, with strong time management.

The choices in this example aren't random—they're part of a thoughtful plan intended to support your learning. This plan includes things like managing your time closely, tweaking the time you learn, using calendars to organize time, bypassing procrastination, and squeezing in microlearning. The true strength of these tools may come when combined with others you've learned to build a more personalized learning routine.

Take Action: Make Your Own Plan

In this chapter you learned about the value of time management. Time management improves performance and satisfaction, reduces stress, and predicts academic achievement. This may mean aligning learning tasks with certain times each day; for example, taking tests in the morning and practicing in the afternoon. Using a calendar improves both time management and performance and helps avoid procrastination. Procrastination leads to further procrastination, but if we do find ourselves procrastinating, two of the best ways to overcome it are to remind ourselves that we can tolerate unpleasant tasks and to enlist others to work with us. Our phones can also be a secret ingredient to squeeze in learning when we are short on time, if used to view microcontent or connect with fellow learners.

Take a moment to reflect on how you value, spend, and manage your time and whether you are using your time wisely. After contemplating the following questions, develop a simple plan to master your time and energy and consider sharing it with someone who is supporting your learning. If you need more support, be sure to read Chapter 18 on building a robust learning network. For additional resources, visit www.already-smarter.com.

- How does your ability to manage time affect how well you learn new things or your success when you enroll in courses?
- What might the ideal time of day to learn be for you?
- How might using a calendar help you to learn, do, and become more?
- How might you overcome any tendencies to procrastinate?
- How can your social media connections and the content you consume support your learning and life goals?

CHAPTER 7

Start Strong by Building Familiarity

As the saying goes, sometimes the hardest part of anything is just getting started. Of course, this can pertain to starting something big, something small, or something in between—like taking a couple of real estate courses. When it comes to beginning something new, many of us have a rocky start, failing to properly orient ourselves to the environment, experience, or even just the materials, which can contribute to a sense of disorientation, disconnection, and discouragement.

As a learner, I used to feel like I was rushing at the last minute to find parking, locate a classroom, or even just log into an online course—never mind reading a syllabus or reviewing a textbook. This is actually surprisingly common, with 85 percent of people surveyed reporting that they don't routinely take time to prepare.[1] As an instructor, I helped learners get prepared simply by taking steps to familiarize themselves with a learning environment or experience so that it is less daunting and more comfortable. Many learners I have worked with are surprised at how simple (and valuable) it is to have a strong start.

This chapter can help you feel more comfortable as you begin a new learning experience—an important step in getting started. It introduces five valuable strategies that may help make learning environments and experiences feel more approachable. With a few adjustments, you might find yourself shifting from feeling uncertain to more at ease as you familiarize yourself with the expectations and experience.

Before you begin this chapter, think about how spending time familiarizing yourself with a learning experience could help your confidence, success, and larger goals.

- What are some of the ways you have tried to get prepared or oriented in the past? Have they worked?
- Why might getting familiar with an experience affect your learning performance?
- How might getting familiar with things in general affect your big dreams?

Get Oriented to Build Familiarity

Have you ever gone to a new workplace, navigated a new campus, or logged in to a new online event and suddenly found yourself confused, stressed, and just plain disoriented? These feelings can impede your success and fill you with self-doubt. In the worst of cases, you may experience "stage fright" and flee the new experience without even getting started. How can we overcome these feelings before they overwhelm us?

One way to establish a "soft start" is to orient yourself. Researchers studied nearly 4,000 students who were learning online. They found that learners who participated in an orientation boosted their self-efficacy; that is, their confidence in their learning ability.[2] Similarly, another study found that those who attended an online orientation earned a higher grade point average (GPA) and had superior completion than those who did not.[3]

These simple acts of getting oriented can make a big difference. For example, if you're heading to a cooking class and you have the chance to drive by the location in the days before, do it. Or, at least, map it in advance to familiarize yourself with the route and the time it takes to get there. Taking advantage of an orientation, whether it's an orientation to a new learning environment or an online tutorial that shows you how to get started, is a wise way to begin. And if there isn't an orientation, consider creating your own by exploring the learning environment. Perusing a learning environment in advance, understanding what is expected of you, and meeting a few friendly faces can help you feel more confident and comfortable about what's to come.

Simple Strategy: Orient Yourself

Even if you can't join an official orientation ahead of a learning experience, you can always create your own self-orientation. To get started:

1. **Sign up.** If an institution, program, or learning provider offers any kind of orientation, take it. These are great opportunities to learn more and meet people.

continued

2. **Orient yourself.** If there is not a formal orientation, consider creating your own. This may include reviewing course documents, previewing digital spaces, exploring physical spaces, or asking former learners to describe the experience and its requirements.

3. **Bring your questions.** Before you join an orientation, create a list of questions that you have. Even if you don't ask them, just having them in mind will help you make the most of the orientation.

Understand the Expectations

A big part of learning something new is understanding what good performance looks like. When you undertake a new learning endeavor, whether it's a formal degree program, an online course, or a required training, it may be tempting to dive right in. The challenge, of course, is that you may not be *prepared* for the experience, causing learning to become another one of life's stressors. But there are a couple of things you can do before beginning to make sure that you understand the course expectations and are able to do your best.

In a traditional course, the best way to understand expectations is to review the syllabus and read the learning objectives. Together, these items provide a comprehensive overview of what you are expected to learn and do. A *syllabus* is an outline of the subjects, requirements, and policies for a course, and *learning objectives*—often found in the syllabus—are brief statements that indicate what you are expected to learn, know, or do after taking a program, course, or learning experience.

Learners who study—ahead of being quizzed on—their course syllabus have a much better understanding of what to expect from a course and what is expected of them.[4] The learning objectives stated on the syllabus help learners narrow their focus and better direct their learning.[5] These goal statements help prime your brain so that you know exactly what you are trying to do.

Even if you are setting out to take an art class at your local community center, take time to review any documents that approximate a syllabus and objectives. Together, these are like guideposts on a path: They keep you pointed in the right direction and tell you exactly where you are going. If you begin to read each of these, you'll know what you need to do to be successful and exactly what you are going to learn.

Simple Strategy: Understand What's Expected

Setting the right expectations about any learning experience is an easy first step in the right direction. To get started:

1. **Read the syllabus.** If your learning experience includes a syllabus, review it carefully, and take the syllabus quiz if one is provided (or quiz yourself, if there is not). If there's not a formal syllabus, review the course description or any associated documentation.

2. **Review the objectives.** Many learning experiences provide a list of learning objectives around which the experience is focused. Don't ignore these. Take a few minutes to review the objectives, as they will help prepare you for the experience.

continued

3. **Scan the assessments.** If there are no objectives, but there are assessments, review those ahead of the experience.

Find Signals to Spot What's Important

When you are driving, traffic signals, car signals, and map signals help you navigate to your destination quickly and without incident. Over time, using them becomes so habitual that they may become entirely automatic. In learning experiences, other types of signals operate in much the same way. So how can you spot these signals to help you learn?

In learning science, the *signaling effect* is when you use cues to help you spot information. Researchers reviewed almost fifty years of research on signaling and found that it helps you direct your attention, learn faster, and retain more.[6] By focusing your attention, signaling reduces the cognitive load—making complex information easier to digest.

You can also use text-based signals when you read. Researchers analyzed forty-four studies on text structure and found that analyzing the layout of text directly affected how well learners comprehended the information within that structure.[7] Visual signals, which draw your attention to titles, headings, and other features, help you better understand the structure of text and the relationships between ideas. Next time you read something, consider scanning for these features to build a mental map before you begin.

> ## Simple Strategy:
> ## Spot Signals—or Make Your Own
>
> Finding signals is a fast way to understand how information and experiences are structured to help you learn more easily and quickly. To get started:
>
> 1. **Look for signals.** Pay attention to signals. These may include icons, visuals, or other indicators that guide your attention.
>
> 2. **Scan the text.** Scan the text structure—such as headings, subheadings, and bold words—to foster understanding.
>
> 3. **Annotate.** Create your own signals and text cues by annotating texts and notes in ways that will readily help you spot certain things (such as things you need to review or know).

Lean on Your Prior Knowledge

Learning is rarely something that happens on a blank canvas. Often, you possess some type of prior knowledge about a topic. In some cases, your prior knowledge is extensive. When it is, you are building upon your expertise and experience, which makes things a bit easier. In other cases, your prior knowledge is quite sparse, forcing you to draw on whatever limited connections you can make.

According to Julie Dirksen, author of *Design for How People Learn*, "Learning experiences are like journeys. The journey starts where the learner is now and ends when the learner is successful."[8] But to get started, it's helpful to understand where you are—in short, to orient yourself. She explains that the people "who understood and remembered the most" were those who knew a bit before they got started: "They were able to understand and retain the information specifically because they already had a mental picture."[9]

Considering what you already know boosts both understanding and memory. Prior knowledge within a subject area is strongly related to successful new learning, as well as your judgment about that learning, such as how well it's going.[10] Having prior knowledge of something seems to activate the brain in ways that make building new memories easier.[11]

Combining prior knowledge with curiosity is even better. Together, they can increase the effectiveness of understanding and applying feedback.[12] And if you lack prior knowledge, curiosity can enhance learning and help bridge that gap.[13]

So, if you are taking your first painting class, think about what you know about painting already—things you may have learned from painting a room or going to an art museum—and ask yourself what you are most curious to learn about.

Simple Strategy:
Tap Your Prior Knowledge

If you are sorely lacking in prior knowledge of a subject, don't worry. You can cultivate your prior knowledge with a little effort. To get started:

1. **Consider what you know.** Connect topics to your prior knowledge by actively asking yourself: What do I already know about this topic? Make a short bulleted list.

2. **Engage your curiosity.** What about this topic are you most curious about? Create a list of questions that you might ask an expert.

3. **Find answers.** Build your prior knowledge—and answer your questions—by conducting a quick internet search.

Spend Time Exploring Tools and Platforms

Now more than ever, technology is an important resource to enhance learning. Increasingly, learning involves an abundance of resources, many of which are enabled by technology: online courses, ebooks, course websites, social media groups, videos, games, podcasts, and mixed reality. Navigating each of these can add to the cognitive load of a course; that is, to the amount of mental effort required. How can you use technology in ways that improve your mood and performance?

The good news is that technology can help many learners. For example, students who learned in a technologically enhanced, active environment performed better than learners who took the exact same course in a traditional setting.[14] However, feelings about technology are directly related to its effectiveness. Researchers analyzed 186 studies on how technology-based learning affected student emotions. They found that positive emotions, such as enjoyment, were correlated with the usability, support, and achievement that the tool provided.[15] In other words, *helpful* technologies generate positive emotions, while frustrating technologies may make you question your abilities.

It's also important to be aware of how to use the best tool for any specific task. Experts studied the reading differences among print materials, handheld devices, and laptops and found that learners performed reading tasks better with print materials, followed closely by laptops and lastly by handheld devices.[16] Of course, this varies greatly depending upon the exact nature of the task and the person doing it, but it does remind you to carefully match your learning tool to your learning goal.

Simple Strategy: Select the Right Tools

Select tools that are easy to use and that you enjoy using—and, importantly, use them for the right purposes. To get started:

1. **Create online.** Use a laptop if you need to spend time creating, writing, or navigating a complex online environment.
2. **Watch tablets.** Use a tablet if you are watching media, playing a game, or reading.
3. **Check phones.** Use a phone for shorter interactions, such as checking emails or checking your grades.

The Cumulative Effect

Have you ever been on the verge of learning something totally new but felt apprehensive because you didn't know what the institution, program, or course would be like or if you would feel comfortable with it? You worried, *will this be a good fit for me?* That's where starting strong by building familiarity comes in. On their own, the strategies in this chapter can help you get more comfortable learning something new, and combined, they can accelerate your growth.

Imagine you want to learn something that you're not totally bought into, like how to sell real estate as a side hustle or, maybe, a whole new career. You find a real estate class and take a few moments to understand what the experience involves—where it happens, what's required, and what materials you'll need—which boosts your comfort and your confidence. You review the program description, syllabus, and learning objectives, and you scan through some of the online reviews from other students to see what you might expect. Once you have the materials, including a coursebook, you scan the table of contents and chapters, noticing signals about the topics you will be learning in headings, bold terms, and callouts. You review the tools you will be using, including an online learning portal, an app, and a WhatsApp thread. Recognizing that your prior knowledge and curiosity are helpful ways to activate your brain and mind, you also take time to reflect on what you already know and some of your big questions about real estate, compiling these into two lists. All of this preparation hasn't just equipped you to embark on a real estate career; it has taught you how to prepare for almost anything new that comes your way.

These aren't haphazard choices—they're part of an intentional plan to support your learning. This plan includes things like getting oriented to build familiarity, understanding expectations, finding signals to spot what's important, leaning into your prior knowledge, and spending time exploring tools and platforms. Used together with other strategies, the techniques in this chapter can help shape a learning journey uniquely effective for you.

Take Action: Make Your Own Plan

In this chapter, you explored the role that getting familiar with a learning experience can play. Getting oriented, reviewing learning objectives, finding signals, tapping prior knowledge, and exploring technology are all aspects of getting (and staying) familiar with a learning experience and paving the way for success. A good orientation boosts self-efficacy, which boosts performance. Learning objectives narrow our focus on what matters most. Signals direct our attention so that we can learn faster and retain more. Tapping prior knowledge activates our brains and builds our memories. And becoming familiar with technologically enhanced, active environments enables superior performance.

Take a moment to reflect on how you typically orient yourself to a new learning experience. After contemplating the following questions, develop a simple plan to start each learning experience strong and consider sharing it with someone who is supporting your learning. If you need more support, be sure to read Chapter 18 on building a robust learning network. For additional resources, visit www.already-smarter.com.

- Have you ever struggled to find your way to a learning location or through an online environment? How did this affect your motivation and your satisfaction?

- What might you do before a new learning experience to set yourself up for success?

- What kinds of signals have you relied upon when learning something new?

- How has your prior knowledge affected new things you are trying to learn?

- Has technology helped or hindered your learning?

CHAPTER 8

Drive Your Learning

S ome of your aspirations—like learning glassblowing with hopes of displaying the finished piece in a gallery—may seem bigger than others (like learning how to use a new software program in your job). However, they all require some degree of learning—and the ability to learn *effectively*. Yet many of us struggle to learn effectively—or at least efficiently—because we simply don't know the basic steps for managing our learning.

At school, I was taught many things, but never the simple steps of regulating my learning. As a result, I often engaged in poor learning strategies only to make limited progress and ultimately to get stuck. This is actually quite common; more than 80 percent of those surveyed reported that they don't routinely regulate their learning.[1] As a learning and leadership coach, I have worked with people to explore ways to get unstuck by learning the simple steps to managing their learning processes. In working with learners, I am often amazed at how far a bit of self-regulation can go.

This chapter can help you explore simple steps for regulating your learning. It introduces a flexible process that you may find useful in a variety of learning experiences throughout your life. With effort and practice, you might feel more in control of your learning, shifting from feeling daunted to becoming increasingly more disciplined.

Before you begin this chapter, think about how your approach to managing or regulating your learning could help you achieve your learning goals and your life aspirations.

- What are the techniques that you currently use to regulate your learning?

- Why might managing your learning process improve your learning performance?

- How might managing your learning process help you reach your aspirations?

Step 1: Get Meta

Learning something new requires you to think not only about whatever you are learning but also about your learning process itself. That means reflecting on your broader interests, specific goals, and possible strategies. You might ask yourself: How important is this to me, and how much time do I want to spend learning it? You might consider why you ultimately want to learn something—and if that outcome is likely. And you might consider options for learning it: hiring a coach, watching YouTube, or taking a class. Without even knowing it, you might also consider what has or hasn't worked for you in the past. But does all of this thinking about learning ultimately help you learn?

Thinking about learning is at the core of improving it. A team of researchers reviewed ninety-five interventions to find out which helped learners the most. They found that one thing seemed common to all the interventions: metacognitive instruction.[2] That phrase simply means helping people think about their learning. Metacognitive strategies seem to help you learn not only for more immediate purposes, such as taking a test, but also for the longer term.[3]

Metacognition is critical to your ability to manage, or regulate, your learning. And the ability to self-regulate by selecting certain strategies has a large effect on academic achievement, regardless of exactly which type of strategy is used, the type of course it is used in, and the level of study.[4]

There are at least six models of self-regulated learning, commonly known by the names of the scholars who have developed them: Zimmerman; Boekaerts; Winne and Hadwin; Pintrich; Efklides; and Hadwin, Järvelä, and Miller.[5] While you could adopt any of these, the chapters that follow will focus on one of the most well-accepted and enduring models, known as Zimmerman's Cyclical Model. This model involves three phases: forethought, performance, and self-reflection.[6] Each will be discussed in more detail in this chapter.

Simple Strategy: Think About Your Thinking

Everyone can get better at their metacognitive strategies just by becoming aware of their thinking and learning and reflecting on what works and what doesn't work. To get started:

1. **Consider what's difficult.** Think about the things that make thinking, learning, or doing more difficult for you. These might include being tired, being hungry, or being distracted. Then consider how to minimize these things.

continued

2. **Consider what's easy.** Think about the things that make thinking, learning, or doing easier for you. These might include prioritizing specific times of the day, using certain tools or technologies, or eating or drinking certain foods or beverages. Then consider how to maximize these things.

3. **Consider new strategies.** Think about the new things that you might try because of this book. These might include changing your mindset, using sleep more effectively, or practicing in certain ways. Then consider how to adopt these things for the best effect.

If you aren't sure which things make learning easier or more difficult, don't worry; there are plenty of new strategies you can learn in the chapters ahead!

Step 2: Prepare Yourself

You may find that, all too often, you jump into learning experiences without pausing to prepare yourself. Just as you might research a destination and pack your belongings before going on a trip, you'd be wise to prepare for a learning journey. Preparation is an important precursor to embarking on learning something new and it's the first step toward effective self-regulation. But how do you go about preparing?

According to Dale Schunk and Barry Zimmerman, authors of *Self-Regulated Learning: From Teaching to Self-Reflective Practice,* "Academic self-regulation is not a mental ability, such as intelligence, or an academic skill, such as reading proficiency; rather, it is the self-directive process through which learners transform their academic abilities into academic skills."[7] According to Zimmerman, the first step in self-regulation, analogous to preparation, is called "forethought." The forethought phase consists of two types of behaviors: analyzing the learning task and contemplating your motivations to engage in it.[8]

- **Analyzing the task.** Analyzing the learning task includes setting goals for what you would like to accomplish and taking time to plan how you might achieve your goal. For example, you might set two goals and the strategies you'll need to adopt to accomplish each.

- **Contemplating motivations.** Contemplating your motivations involves connecting this goal with your beliefs about your abilities, your expectation to achieve a positive outcome, and your interest in the task itself or its value to your life.[9] For instance, you might consider that you have learned many things like this before, you will succeed with practice, and this will improve the quality of your life.

Importantly, forethought is the phase where you should consider the best strategies for learning something. Some of these strategies may come naturally for you, while others may seem novel. With any luck, you'll have picked some of these strategies up in this book. In any case, you'll benefit if the strategies you select align with your interests and motivations. In other words, they'll simply be things that you enjoy doing.

Simple Strategy: Find Forethought

Everyone should exercise a bit of forethought before learning. To get started:

1. **State your goal.** Set goals for what, specifically, you would like to accomplish, even if the goal is simply reading a chapter or making time for a practice session.

2. **Consider your motivation.** Contemplate your motivations by asking yourself how the learning experience or task will improve your knowledge, relationships, or life.

3. **Select your strategies.** Consider which strategies—including those within this book—might best help you to undertake (and accomplish) your learning.

If goals, motivations, and strategies sound unfamiliar, return to these concepts in other chapters.

Step 3: Monitor Your Performance

Learning is the active process of changing yourself using new knowledge, new skills, and new abilities. It requires you to consider how well you are performing and adjust your performance accordingly. This is how you improve at practically anything: learning a new language, picking up a sport, or pursuing a long-held dream. But what's the best way to go about monitoring yourself?

According to Zimmerman, the second phase in self-regulation is called the "performance phase." This consists of maintaining self-control and consciously observing yourself.

- **Maintaining self-control.** There are many tips for maintaining self-control, such as blocking time, minimizing distractions, requesting help, and creating consequences for yourself if you don't follow through.

- **Observing yourself.** There are a couple of ways to observe yourself. The first is by actively thinking about your learning and asking yourself, *How am I doing?* The second is by recording yourself and watching the video recording afterward.[10] What's important is to be an active observer of your performance, especially in areas of improvement.

Maintaining self-control and practicing self-observation work closely together. As you implement things to maintain control and advance your learning, your observational techniques allow you to determine what is working—and what needs to be modified. In other words, you are getting near-immediate feedback on your strategies and progress, allowing you to make modifications and changes in real time.

Simple Strategy: Focus on Your Performance (and How to Improve It)

There are many things you can do to improve your performance; that's what this book is all about. To get started:

1. **Set yourself up for success.** To achieve high performance, schedule learning time, minimize as many distractions as possible, and identify the best ways to readily get help when you need it.

continued

2. **Observe your effort.** Remain aware of your effort, progress, and performance, and adjust as you go—taking time to repeat or redo things as needed.

3. **Watch yourself.** Consider video recording yourself, even if you are just reading. Then, when you go back and observe yourself, note things that you may not have been aware of, such as how often you looked away, checked your phone, or reread pages.

Step 4: Reflect, React, and Reconsider

Only by reflecting on performance can you begin to improve it. Self-reflection is a critical part of learning—and it's the third phase of Zimmerman's model. It allows you to really think about what you have learned, how it may benefit you, and what you need to improve on. But, in the rush to complete learning tasks and projects, it's an easy step to skip. Unfortunately, this limits the learning experience—it's like leaving a movie before the ending.

According to Zimmerman, there are two important aspects of self-reflection: The first is a judgment around your performance and the second is a reaction to that judgment.

- **Judgment of performance.** When making a judgment, such as *I did a good job* or *I did a poor job*, it's important to consider what the judgment is attributed to. For instance, if you did a poor job, why? Were you disinterested, tired, or distracted?

- **Reaction to judgment.** When reacting to that judgment, consider your attitude: How is this affecting your mood? It's important to express satisfaction with your effort, even if you are unhappy with the result. Self-reflection allows you to consider how you need to improve. It's the time to ask yourself: What could I do better? How could I improve my learning skills? Which other techniques could I incorporate?

It may be helpful to adopt "systematic reflection." This is a process where you start by asking why you did something a certain way, then consider what may have happened if you had done things differently. Then give yourself feedback on both the outcome you achieved and the process you used.[11] Of course, systematic reflection is more effective for people who are interested in improving their learning—in other words, people who are using this book.[12]

Reflection is particularly important when we encounter failure. When undertaking any learning experience, it's important to pause to reflect on how the inevitable moments of failure are affecting you and what you might do differently. It may sound trite, but failure helps you learn.[13] If you have experienced failure, one of the best ways to boost your performance is to reflect on both your correct and incorrect actions.[14] Focusing on what you did correctly—not just incorrectly—may make you feel psychologically safer and enable you to go forward.

If you are reflecting on your performance throwing pottery, for example, be honest when you look at the completed vase. If it's lop-sided, ask what happened—and *why* it happened. Then ask yourself if your attitude or behavior played a role (maybe you were distracted or tired). And take a few minutes to acknowledge what you did well. Remember, one bad performance doesn't make a bad potter.

Simple Strategy: Reflect Effectively

Self-reflection is a skill that anyone can acquire. To get started:

1. **Be honest.** Judge your performance by asking yourself, *How did I do?*

2. **Look for causes.** Determine what caused or affected your performance by asking yourself, *What caused me to perform well or poorly?*

3. **Contemplate your attitude.** Consider your attitude by asking yourself, *How did my attitude about learning this affect my performance?*

Step 5: Notice Your Evolution

With time and practice, you can become a natural self-regulator. While self-regulation may sound straightforward enough, rarely does it come naturally. It's important to recognize that becoming better at self-regulation is a process. And you may become an expert self-regulator in one domain but still struggle in another. As with all things, you improve the more you practice.

According to Zimmerman, there are four stages you pass through when you are learning something new and using your self-regulated learning techniques.[15]

1. **Observation.** This is one of the simplest ways to begin to improve: *Watch* an expert perform the task.

2. **Emulation.** This involves trying to do something in exactly the same way that an expert does by copying their behavior, technique, and style as closely as you can. You might adjust your environment to match theirs, your habits to match theirs, and even your outlook to match theirs.

3. **Self-control.** This step involves practicing the skill independently. Try to do it on your own, but in an environment that is structured and safe—maybe even with an expert there to help you out if you get stuck.

4. **Self-regulation.** The last step is to try the skill in different settings—without help.

In all these phases, you need to invest cognitive and metacognitive resources in addition to dealing with the original learning task.[16] This just means that you need to think about your learning while you do the work related to learning. There are no shortcuts to ultimate success.

Simple Strategy: Become a Skilled Self-Regulator

You can become a highly effective self-regulated learner. You'll get better and better at analyzing, preparing, and reflecting, and you'll become a much better and faster learner. To get started:

1. **Identify where you are.** Consider where you are in your self-regulation cycle: Are you observing, emulating, in control, or self-regulating?

continued

2. **Begin to shift.** Consciously begin shifting yourself from observation to emulation to self-control and finally self-regulation, remaining conscious of where you are.

3. **Take your time.** Don't try to move too quickly; accept that the phases may take weeks, months, or years to accomplish. The important part is aiming for better self-regulation.

The Cumulative Effect

Have you ever undertaken something new and, not knowing where to start, just dove in rather than being strategic and thoughtful about the experience? Lacking a plan, you may have gotten quickly confused, overwhelmed, or simply stuck. That's where driving your own learning comes in. Each method outlined in this chapter can help you improve your learning, yet it's the combined sequence that can help you become a strong self-regulator.

Imagine that you are excited to learn something new and fun—maybe a new creative pursuit like glassblowing. You're about to take your first class, and you're tempted to jump right in, but that hasn't served you well in the past. This time, you take a more thoughtful approach, starting with forethought. You begin by asking yourself why you want to learn this, what might be most challenging, and what you might need to be successful. Then you begin the actual work, during which you focus on your effort and make microadjustments as you go. Once you've finished, you don't just put all the supplies away and admire your work; instead, you take time to reflect. You contemplate what worked well and what could've worked better—and, importantly, what you might do differently next time. Each time you go to class, you get better at moving through these phases, and you find that you are shifting from being an observer to a true self-regulator—a skill you can apply to any learning situation, not just glassblowing.

This sequence isn't arbitrary—it's part of a purposeful plan intended to support your learning. This plan includes things like preparing yourself, monitoring your performance, reflecting on opportunities for improvement, and noticing your own evolution. As you work through this book, notice how the strategies can complement one another, with each one adding to your personalized approach that grows stronger over time.

Take Action: Make Your Own Plan

This chapter focused on metacognition and self-regulation—two related aspects of managing one's learning process. Metacognitive techniques help us think about our learning and enable us to better self-regulate. While there are many models of self-regulation, Zimmerman's model is one of the simplest and most referenced and involves three steps: forethought, performance, and self-reflection. We become better self-regulators by observing, emulating, controlling, and then ultimately regulating our learning.

Take a moment to reflect on how you manage your learning. After contemplating the following questions, develop a simple plan to manage your learning and consider sharing it with someone who is supporting your learning. If you need more support, be sure to read Chapter 18 on building a robust learning network. For additional resources, visit www.already-smarter.com.

- How might you prepare for a new learning experience?

- How might you attend to your performance while you are learning?

- Why might it be helpful to periodically reflect on your successes and struggles?

- What is the last thing you learned that took some time to master—and what stages did you go through?

PART III

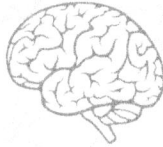

Engage Actively

Learning is not a passive endeavor. Once you've established a clear intention to learn, you need to begin the actual process of learning—and engaging productively in that process. All too often, you may find yourself going about learning in haphazard ways, relying on habits or outdated practices that may make learning less effective and more arduous. You need to actively engage in practices that will not only help you learn but also make learning more enjoyable.

The third part of this book is about doing the work of learning something new. This part includes four chapters focused on improving your mental stamina, building your memory, embracing experiential learning, and developing a practice routine. These sections will help you adopt the strategies to do the real work of learning: focusing, building memory, and adopting active learning and thoughtful practice routines. These are the skills that make learning a successful endeavor.

CHAPTER 9

Train Your Focus Like a Muscle

A chieving anything of value in your life—from walking a dog to starting your own doggy day care business—may require you to learn many things and to learn them *clearly*. Yet many of us struggle to find our focus, especially among the sheer number of distractions that compete for our attention.

In my life, I have struggled with this too, especially in our world of constant texting, instant messaging, and posting. Evidently, I'm not the only one who has battled my focus; when asked, the majority of people indicated they would like to improve their focus.[1] Over the years, I have worked with people to explore ways to overcome distractions and improve their ability to focus. Simply being able to focus can be an important step toward accomplishing everything from daily tasks to big dreams.

Importantly, this chapter does not specifically address attention deficit disorder (ADD) or attention deficit hyperactivity disorder

(ADHD). These conditions can significantly affect attention, focus, and learning. If you suspect you may have ADD or ADHD, it is important to seek evaluation, guidance, and support from a qualified medical professional.

This chapter can help you develop an essential learning skill: focusing. It introduces six evidence-based strategies that may help improve focus on both immediate tasks and long-term learning goals. With consistent practice, you might find yourself shifting from feeling distracted to becoming more deliberate—treating your focus like a muscle that you can strengthen and that will, in turn, strengthen you.

Before you begin this chapter, think about how learning to focus better could help you improve your learning performance—and your life performance.

- What are some of the ways you have tried focusing? Do they work?

- Why might your ability to focus affect your learning performance?

- How might your ability to focus contribute to your interests, career, and other goals?

Create Spaces for Productivity

One of the best things we can do to maintain our focus is learn in spaces that enhance that focus. Our physical learning environments contribute to the cognitive load of the learning experience.[2] *Cognitive load* is the burden put on your thinking, not just from learning but from the surrounding environment. For example, a noisy, distracting, uncomfortable environment adds to the difficulty of whatever you are trying to learn.

Interestingly, researchers found that people were 32 percent more productive if they designed their own spaces.[3] They also found that spaces with greenery, actual plants or pictures, contributed to higher productivity than bare spaces.[4] Plants in particular contribute to productive environments.[5] When you're creating a learning space, make it active. Yes, *active*. That means that you can *actively* engage in the learning process, using furniture, materials, and technology, almost like your own personal learning studio. For example, researchers who studied chemistry learners found that poorer-performing learners earned higher grades if their classroom had group tables or flexible chairs that facilitated movement.[6]

Noise affects your environment, concentration, and performance. However, listening to white noise, such as the soft hum of a fan or gentle static, can improve cognitive performance. White noise is a soft, constant background noise that blocks out other noises. In one study, learners who listened to white noise during a vocabulary lesson recalled more words correctly.[7] There may even be a link between white noise and memory formation. Researchers recently concluded that white noise may be helpful in enabling learning for those with memory problems due to aging.[8] And white noise isn't just limited to soft humming sounds. Nature sounds—such as the sound of flowing water—may also enhance cognition and concentration.[9]

Lighting may also affect learning and mood.[10] You can learn by using either natural or artificial light; however, having adequate levels of vitamin D helps with cognition, therefore being near sunlight, which supports vitamin D production, may be especially beneficial in darker seasons.[11] Researchers also found that people felt less tired in brighter light; the least positive in low, cool lighting;

and remembered more in brighter, cooler lighting.[12] Brighter, cooler lighting also seemed to improve concentration.[13] When it comes to learning, stick with cooler, brighter, natural lighting if you can.

Paying attention to temperature in your learning space will help you manage and improve your learning. Experiencing heat during a learning activity is not only uncomfortable and distracting, but it also inhibits learning.[14] But that begs the question: Is there an ideal temperature for learning? Researchers have tried to answer this exact question. Finnish researchers found that productivity among adults was at its highest at a temperature of around 22°C (which equates to 71.6°F).[15]

Experts found that the color of a room plays an important role in your mood, well-being, and performance. They analyzed forty-five studies over a thirty-year period and found a few general themes. Green tends to evoke the most positive emotional response; white can cause fatigue, apathy, and the highest error rate; red can improve cognitive performance but cause excitement and anxiety; blue can enhance creativity; and neutral colors can increase productivity.[16] Of course, this may vary by culture, age, and personal preference, as well as your ability to see colors.

Simple Strategy:
Enhance Your Learning Environment

Even if you don't have access to a dedicated learning space, or if you are generally lacking in space altogether, there are still things you can do to choose spaces that will optimize your learning. To get started:

1. **Make space.** Make or select a quiet, dedicated space. If you can, design the space yourself and try to include plants,

pictures, and items that motivate you. Make or select a space that is active by considering how the furniture and materials enable you to actively engage in the learning process.

2. **Enhance the sound and lighting.** Consider adding a white noise soundtrack—this could be in the form of a fan, a white noise machine, or a white noise app on your phone— and situate yourself near a natural light source or select bulbs that are bright and cool for lamps in your learning space.

3. **Control the temperature and color.** To maximize your learning, learn somewhere with a temperature close to 71°F or 72°F. Consider incorporating supportive colors into your learning space, including neutrals to enhance productivity, blue to spark creativity, and green to evoke a positive mood. Regardless of what colors you ultimately choose, make sure they are personally motivating and meaningful to you.

Single-Task for Focus

Dedicating time to learning can be difficult, especially among family, work, and other commitments. You may try to combine learning with other tasks: learning on the treadmill, learning while commuting, or learning while watching children. And even if you do manage to carve out time to learn, it may be tempting to keep technology nearby, perhaps listening to music or a podcast, half-watching a television series, or frequently checking social media. How does all this multitasking affect your ability to learn?

Multitasking only makes learning more challenging than it needs to be. To put it plainly: Multitasking is nearly impossible unless a behavior is very simple or completely automatic. For those behaviors that are *not* completely automatic, you are rapidly switching between tasks, attending first to one, then to another in rapid succession. This switching disrupts the main task and may cause you to make mistakes.[17]

Dividing your attention among more than one task may seem easy, but it impedes performance. In fact, dividing your attention during the encoding phase of memory, when you are first observing or learning something, interferes with your ability to remember it.[18]

For example, studies that examined the relationship between learners' media use during class and their GPA revealed that using social media or texting during class seemed to be associated with a lower overall GPA.[19] Just listening to music, watching television, and checking social media are all behaviors that make your job as a learner more difficult and less successful.

Simple Strategy: Stop Trying to Multitask

Although you live in a world where multitasking is incredibly common, you can learn how to stop this habit and focus your energy on what you are learning. To get started:

1. **Single-task.** Don't multitask unless a behavior is completely automatic, especially when you are learning something new.

2. **Maintain attention.** Remember that most behaviors are not completely automatic, even if you think that they are, but instead require some degree of your attention.

3. **Separate yourself.** Identify the things that trigger you to multitask, such as your phone, being near the television, or

studying when your friends or family are home, and physically separate yourself to avoid getting distracted.

Maintain Attention and Alertness

The ability to pay attention, whether you are watching a demonstra-
tion or reading a book, is critical to learning. Attention allows you to
take new information in, and working memory allows you to understand it. However, attention is easily fragmented, especially when
you become fatigued or distracted. And these days, with so much
coming at you, your attention may feel under siege. How might your
attention—or lack of attention—affect your ability to learn?

Attention is related to your overall alertness, with too little
arousal producing boredom and too much producing anxiety. When
you are learning in a traditional setting, you are typically in a state
of low to medium alertness. However, during heightened states,
say during an exam, this increase in alertness may improve performance.[20] However, it's not possible to always stay in this focused
state of alertness. Human attention wanes over time. Considerable
cognitive resources go into mental activities.[21] Mental fatigue sets
in, especially after a period of work that requires high concentration,
and this leads to distraction, slower reaction times, and incorrect
responses. The exact timing of when your attention begins to wane
varies, depending upon individual motivation and the task itself.[22]

Fortunately, there are things you can do when you feel your attention slipping. Taking a short power nap of just seven to ten minutes
helps recharge your brain.[23] If you have access to the outdoors, a short
nature walk will also allow you to shift attention to what's called "soft
fascination," during which thoughts are less taxing.[24]

Simple Strategy: Maintain Your Attention

With a little effort, you can remain alert and maintain your attention. To get started:

1. **Take a walk.** Take a short walk outside and enjoy being in nature.

2. **Go soft.** Turn your attention, briefly, to "soft fascination," or lighter thoughts that are less demanding. Instead of thinking of problems or challenges in your life, reflect on lighter things like a streaming show you are watching, a book you are reading, or a trip you hope to take.

3. **Remotivate.** Use this time to visualize your immediate or longer-term goals. Be as specific as possible in your visualizations and how you might feel once a goal has been reached.

Clear Your Mind

Concentration is the ability to stay absorbed in one activity, such as listening or reading. It is related to your ability to block out distractions, including the distractions from your very own mind, such as thoughts that may intrude and preoccupy you. Have you ever tried to focus, only to find your mind returning to other thoughts? If this describes you, you might want to begin practicing *thought suppression*. People who are good at suppressing thoughts tend to have fewer anxious thoughts and good working memory capacity.[25] This may mean suppressing specific thoughts, replacing nagging thoughts with different ones, or clearing the mind of all thoughts.[26]

Suppressing specific thoughts is called *direct suppression*, which involves pushing a memory out of mind. Replacing one thought with another is called *thought substitution*, which requires retrieving an alternate memory or creating an alternate thought.[27] For example, if you are taking swimming lessons but find yourself fixated on fears related to water, refocus on your technique.

Another alternative is to undertake demanding work. For example, researchers primed sixty hungry participants to think about chocolate and then asked them to avoid thinking about chocolate and, instead, focus on a complicated task. They found that engaging in demanding tasks may be a successful strategy for diverting attention.[28]

Simple Strategy: Suppress or Replace Pesky Thoughts

You can manage thoughts that threaten your attention. To get started:

1. **Spot thoughts.** Notice when distracting, nagging, or consuming thoughts come to mind.

2. **Stop thoughts.** Actively push the thoughts out of your mind by saying or thinking *I'm not going to think about this right now.*

3. **Replace thoughts.** Replace the thoughts by either refocusing yourself on a task or substitute thought—for example, things that you are grateful for or a goal you are working toward.

Take Powerful Microbreaks

While powering through something may seem attractive, well-timed and well-used breaks produce better results. When you do any difficult work—exercising, landscaping, or building something—do you try to keep going for extended periods of time or do you schedule breaks? If you're like most people, you probably take breaks. And if you don't take breaks—well, you probably should.

Several studies have analyzed the effects of different types of breaks on workers, adult learners, and children.

- Workplace researchers surveyed seventy-one employees for two weeks and found that taking "cognitive microbreaks"—short breaks to relax or socialize—were related to an improved attitude and better performance. This was particularly true for those who were less engaged.[29]

- College researchers also found that taking three five-minute exercise breaks during a fifty-minute video lecture promoted attention, resulted in superior learning, and increased understanding more so than other types of breaks.[30]

- Researchers found that children reported that not only were play breaks "very fun," but they helped them learn better.[31]

Consider using your next break to take a walk, do something physical, or just play a game for a few minutes.

Simple Strategy: Break It Up

When you're endeavoring to learn something new, it's easy to incorporate cognitive microbreaks. To get started:

1. **Plan breaks.** Incorporate breaks, especially if you are just learning something or have less familiarity with something.

2. **Enjoy breaks.** Use microbreaks to relax and socialize (not to do other work) to foster a better mood.

3. **Have fun.** Consider sprinkling play breaks throughout your day to do something that you enjoy.

Daydream to Unlock Learning

Have you ever felt your mind begin to wander while you're working on something? Maybe, if you are doing something that doesn't require close attention, you begin to think of other aspects of your life. Mind-wandering is a normal part of the human condition. But how does daydreaming affect learning?

Daydreaming during learning is very common. Indeed, 90 percent of learners daydream while doing coursework; about half of them daydream about actual events that have taken place in their lives and a large proportion report still being able to concentrate on learning tasks. Thus, the *right kind* of daydreaming may help you interact with your thoughts and improve brain functioning.[32]

Daydreaming can degrade your performance unless it's done the right way. There are two types of mind-wandering: deliberate and spontaneous. Deliberate mind-wandering is intentional whereas spontaneous is not. These activate your brain in different ways and, therefore, have a different impact on your thinking.[33] If you're unsure which type you are engaging in, monitor your level of surprise. When you deliberately mind-wander, you have a conscious moment where you begin thinking about something of interest. When you spontaneously mind-wander, on the other hand, you don't have a distinct moment of initiation, and when you realize your mind is wandering, you may feel surprised or irritated.[34]

When engaging in cognitively demanding work, deliberate daydreaming, especially when focused on solving problems, may foster creativity and better problem-solving skills.[35] It can help you achieve positive results, such as enhanced mood, creativity, and decision-making.[36]

Simple Strategy:
Stop Daydreaming—or Do It Right

If you find that you're a daydreamer, take heart. Daydreaming the right way may benefit your learning. To get started:

1. **Stay present.** If your mind-wandering is impeding listening or learning, bring it back to the present moment.

2. **Solve problems.** If you are doing work that is boring or redundant, try focusing your mind on problem-solving. This may include contemplating how you might do the work differently, more effectively, or more efficiently.

3. **Daydream.** If you are working on something challenging, take a "daydream break" during which you think about alternate ways to solve the problem or complete the work.

The Cumulative Effect

Have you ever put effort into learning something new but felt unfocused, distracted, or scattered? Maybe you have felt like your attention was divided among so many things that they all jumbled together. That's where training your focus like a muscle comes in.

Each strategy in this chapter can help you focus, and together, they can have a cumulative effect.

Imagine that you want to start your own small business, like a doggy day care company, but there's so much to learn that you feel increasingly scattered. You know that your environment—and your mind—can be your worst enemies. So you begin by making your learning space conducive to learning: light, bright, and just the right temperature. Then you eliminate distractions so you can more easily single-task and design your schedule to maintain your attention by taking frequent, planned breaks. An argument you had with a friend keeps intruding on your thoughts, so you calmly redirect your attention to the most difficult and consuming parts of your learning, like setting up your revenue plan. During the more routine parts, you allow yourself to daydream—but about creative ways to improve your business even more. As your doggy day care begins to take shape, your enthusiasm for the business grows. You think to yourself, *not only am I good at working with dogs, I'm also much better at focusing.*

These strategies aren't accidental—they're part of a measured plan intended to support your learning. This plan includes things like creating spaces for productivity, single-tasking for focus, maintaining attention and alertness, clearing your mind, taking powerful microbreaks, and daydreaming to unlock learning. Consider how these practices could be combined with others in this book to form a powerful, personalized learning approach.

Take Action: Make Your Own Plan

This chapter explored the role of focus and attention. Trying to learn means trying to focus, and that involves managing distractions, attention, and our minds. Multitasking only works for automatic behaviors, so eliminate distractions to improve your concentration. If you sense your attention is wavering, restore it by napping, walking, or shifting attention to something else for a few minutes. If intrusive thoughts continue to crop up, try pushing them out of mind, focusing on other things, or doing something that requires your focus. Cognitive microbreaks give our brains a rest and improve our attitudes, performance, engagement, and learning. Or, if you can't step away for a break, "problem-oriented" daydreaming may enable creativity, problem-solving, and decision-making.

Take a moment to reflect on your attention and if there are opportunities for improvement. After contemplating the following questions, develop a simple plan to improve your focus and consider sharing it with someone who is supporting your learning. If you need more support, be sure to read Chapter 18 on building a robust learning network. For additional resources, visit www.already-smarter.com.

- How might you make your environment more conducive to learning?

- What might you do to minimize distractions and maximize your focus?

- How might you better sustain your attention?

- How might you manage intrusive thoughts, worries, memories, and self-doubt that affect your ability to concentrate?

- How can you use planned breaks to help you complete something difficult, do something better, or be more productive?

- Do you think that letting your mind wander has hurt your ability to concentrate, learn, or remember things? Or has it helped preoccupy you while you complete boring or redundant tasks?

CHAPTER 10

○———————————————○

Make Your Memory
a Superpower

S ome of the most exciting opportunities in your life may push you to learn. You may find yourself learning a new language to seize an opportunity to spend a few days, weeks, or months in another country. Such an experience can hinge on your ability to learn not just a language but also culture, customs, and currency—and to learn all of this in a way that sticks in your memory. Yet many of us find ourselves easily forgetful, believing we have weak or poor memories.

This certainly describes me: From a young age, I just assumed that my memory was somehow faulty, not realizing that I was simply not using it properly. In fact, few people prioritize their memories; only three percent of those surveyed routinely used memory techniques to learn.[1] That's a shockingly low number, given the centrality of memory to learning. As both an instructor and a coach, I have worked with people to explore ways to take meaningful steps to improve their memories, unlocking what seems like additional brainpower. In my experience, there is more we can do to improve our memories than we may realize.

This chapter can help you strengthen your learning by improving how you manage your memory. It introduces five research-based strategies that may help enhance retention and recall of what you study. With persistence, you might find yourself moving from feeling rusty to having better recall of what you learn.

Before you begin this chapter, think about how learning to improve your memory could support your learning process and other areas of your life.

- What are some of the ways you currently support your memory—especially when you are learning something new?
- Why might strengthening your memory skills affect your learning performance?
- How might strengthening your memory skills help you achieve some of your larger aspirations?

Build Working Memory

In your day-to-day life, you may find yourself remembering oddities from your past but failing to recall things you studied for years or more. A song or jingle may come to mind easily, if not intrusively, yet facts learned in fourth grade are impossible to recall. These experiences may leave you questioning your memory or leave you aghast when others seemingly remember more. When it comes to learning, memory plays an important but often invisible role in your performance. However, understanding how memory works can be the first step toward improving it.

Developing memory involves several processes: encoding new information, holding it briefly in short-term memory, manipulating it in working memory, consolidating it into long-term memory, and then retrieving it as needed. Because this process happens over and over, memory is constantly changing. Memory is reformed and transformed after initial encoding and updated based on new experiences.[2]

Working memory is important when it comes to learning, because holding information in working or short-term memory enables you to "use" and "reason" with it.[3] The research indicates that you may be able to "train" your working memory and that this promotes brain plasticity—which means neural pathways change, grow, and make new adjustments.[4]

Working memory can be improved by alleviating concerns about your incompetence. Instead of attributing the difficulty of learning to yourself, begin attributing it to the complexity of the experience itself. This intervention improves working memory span and overall comprehension.[5] In other words, it's perfectly okay to say "learning is difficult work"; just resist the temptation to think, *because my memory is so bad*. If you can frame things this way, you will learn and remember more.

Simple Strategy:
Understand How Memory Works

By understanding how your memory works, you can begin to improve it. To get started:

continued

1. **Know how it works.** Be conscious that memory involves encoding new information, holding it in working memory, and then consolidating it into long-term memory.

2. **Imagine growth.** Understand that your brain has "plasticity," and imagine your neural pathways changing and growing.

3. **Embrace improvement.** Remind yourself that difficulty learning or remembering is not related to your innate abilities and that you can improve both memory and learning.

Find Novelty to Spark Learning

Have you ever noticed that you tend to recall exciting events—vacations, adventures, thrills—much more easily than everyday things? You may be able to recall the details of a meal you had a decade ago but not the lunch you made yesterday. This is because your brain prefers novelty. And novelty helps you remember things.

Doing new things, in new places or in new ways, sparks new memories. Researchers believe that people may remember objects and experiences that are new or unexpected.[6] In fact, memory systems are especially tuned to detect contextual or unexpected novelty, which can trigger a dopamine reaction and pupil dilation as part of learning and attention.[7] This reaction may be one of the reasons people enjoy going to new places and experiencing new things.

One key aspect of novelty is the degree to which something is unexpected or surprising.[8] Going on field trips is a common way of incorporating novelty into learning, but researchers have found that while a little novelty can spark learning, too much seems to impede it.[9] Simple changes in your approach to working or learning can go a long way. For example, jobs that involve frequent novelty or task changes may enhance brain plasticity.[10]

Simple Strategy: Introduce Novelty to Heighten Learning

You can find or introduce novelty in learning experiences to heighten your learning. To get started:

1. **Find new experiences.** When choosing learning experiences, select experiences that have some element of novelty.

2. **Incorporate novelty.** If a learning experience lacks novelty, such as reading a book, pair it with something new: a new food, beverage, smell, object, person, or place.

3. **Learn in new ways.** Try learning in a new way (especially if you are struggling with something).

Use Cues to Support Recall

Have you ever noticed that you may recall scenes from a movie or series but are not able to recall things you studied or read? What causes you to remember some things but forget so many others? Fortunately, there are strategies you can adopt to strengthen your memories.

Making clear associations with new information helps you better recall it later. Just the process of focusing on enhancing your working memory has been shown to improve performance.[11] Using memory strategies—like connecting a new word with a familiar word and image—helps you retain two to three times more facts.[12] Memory training can reshape the brain's networks to resemble more closely those of "memory athletes." Just six weeks of memory training elicited improvements that lasted up to four months.[13]

One of the most powerful strategies is developing "cues." Memory cues are words or visuals you associate with new information that helps you recall it.[14] Cues often associate facts and concepts with language, symbols, and images that trigger a memory.[15] While it may be tempting to adopt memory cues that have been developed by others, generating your own can make information more understandable, place it into long-term memory, and help with retrieval.[16]

As you build your long-term memory around a subject, you can begin to rely on a mental framework for organizing knowledge and experience, called *schemas*, for easy access and retrieval to short-term memory cues. These associations allow you to focus on more complex aspects of a task and explain why experts get progressively faster at processing information and solving problems[17] and why waiters can remember long lists of orders without writing them down.

Simple Strategy:
Develop Meaningful Memory Cues

Anyone can associate things they are learning with simple cues, especially if they are relevant and meaningful. To get started:

1. **Create a cue.** Associate what you are learning with a relevant cue, such as an object, symbol, word, or phrase.

2. **Make it meaningful.** Make sure that the cue is personally meaningful to you. For example, don't use a generic word

cue; use a more personal cue such as the name of a friend or pet or familiar place.

3. **Visualize it.** Ensure that the cue sparks a visual in your mind that you can readily picture.

Make Simple Sketches a Superpower

Do you ever find yourself doodling when you're in a course or a meeting? Or maybe you like to sketch out your ideas and plans to help visualize them. Doodling and sketching may be meaningless random scribbles that are a way to pass the time, or they might be related to what you're learning and how you think.

In fact, the simple act of sketching enhances memory. Drawing to-be-learned information boosts performance of learning words and definitions better than many other memory techniques.[18] Drawing items may even help with later recognition better than writing words out.[19] Drawing is particularly effective for older adults; therefore, drawing pictures may be a way to enhance memory performance.[20]

Drawings can be made even more powerful if you add signals that help boost your attention. For example, research subjects who saw pictures of faces that coincided with a target square had better long-term memories of those faces.[21] The trick, however, is that the target must be presented at the same time as the image, not before or after.[22] If you are studying something that requires memorization, such as a diagram or map, you might try drawing a simple signal, like an arrow pointing to the parts of the diagram or map you need to remember.

Simple Strategy: Sketch to Enhance Learning

Even if you doubt your artistic abilities, anyone can draw a sketch, diagram, or signal to help them remember more and learn better. To get started:

1. **Sketch it.** Make sketches of the information you are learning.

2. **Make sketches memorable.** The sketches don't need to depict exactly what you are learning, so long as they are meaningful to you or spark your memory.

3. **Emphasize important parts.** Add signals to those sketches, such as arrows, labels, or target squares, so that when you review these later you are prompted to recall important details.

Remember the Right Way

When it comes to remembering things, there are many techniques you can use. Many of these come quite automatically. For example, you might try rereading something; repeating a name, phone number, or address; or rehearsing a procedure or technique. But just how effective are these tactics when it comes to building memory?

Using strategies like repeating (such as reading something several times), refreshing (such as thinking about something after it is gone, like a phone number), and elaborating (such as adding details to a picture in your mind) during the encoding phase can enhance memory performance. Repeating and refreshing primarily benefit working memory, while elaboration is particularly effective for improving long-term memory.[23] However, there are many nuances to how effective these techniques are.

- Rereading helps immediate recall and comprehension but does not help with delayed recall.[24]
- Refreshing may maintain short-term or working memory but not necessarily contribute to longer-term memory.[25]
- Rehearsing things over and over in your mind may also not be as effective as you believe.[26]

In general, repeated study combined with sleep *does* ensure that memory is stable and long-lasting.[27] And retrieval practice—the process of taking tests—promotes long-term memory and, importantly, the application of that material to new problem-solving.[28]

Simple Strategy: Repeat Right

Repeating things can help you learn if you repeat in the right ways. To get started:

1. **Repeat.** Repeat things, such as a phone number, that you need to recall soon.
2. **Reread.** Reread things, such as directions, to support immediate understanding.
3. **Recall.** Use repeated study and frequent recall to shift information from short-term to long-term memory.

The Cumulative Effect

Have you ever tried to learn something new but struggled to remember even simple things that you just read or saw? You might have even wondered if your memory was getting worse. That's where making your memory a superpower comes in. While any one strategy in this chapter can help you remember things better, bringing several strategies together may foster even greater memory benefits.

Imagine that you want to learn something that opens up opportunities—like learning a new language so you can travel, study, or work abroad—but remembering some of the phrasing is proving tricky. Before you even begin learning, you consciously review your knowledge of memory formation. You think about the process of encoding, holding, consolidating, and retrieving information. Then, as you plan your learning journey, you begin to incorporate a few subtle but important supportive techniques, including finding novel ways to learn like changing tasks, studying in new environments, and learning with new people. For particularly difficult material, you begin producing memory cues that help you to connect the new material to what you already know. You keep a sketchbook where you can create visuals—diagrams, images, and processes—along with clear signals and labels. Finally, you skip the things that don't work well in favor of those that do, like quality sleep, spaced practice, and frequent quizzes. As you become more and more fluent in the new language, you notice something else: Your memory is much better than you had believed. You wonder what else you might start remembering now that you know how to support your memory.

The techniques used in this example aren't scattershot choices—they're part of a deliberate plan intended to support your learning. This plan includes things like building short-term memory, finding novelty to spark learning, using cues to support recall, making simple sketches a superpower, and retrieving things the right way. The strategies here are part of a much bigger picture; when linked with others in this book, they can help create beliefs, behaviors, and environments that truly support you.

Take Action: Make Your Own Plan

In this chapter, you learned how your memory works and how you can improve it. Developing memory involves encoding, consolidation, and retrieval. Sometimes we mistakenly believe we have poor memories, when in actuality we aren't enabling ourselves to remember. Our brains prefer new objects and experiences, which enhance brain plasticity. We can also produce meaningful cues to build associations between new and known information. Drawing new information also improves performance, especially if we incorporate signals to draw our attention to salient features. Repeating, rereading, and rehearsing may help short-term and working memory, and repeated study over time, combined with frequent quizzing, supports long-term memory.

Take a moment to reflect on your memory and some of the practices that may be helping maximize it. After contemplating the following questions, develop a simple plan to improve your memory and consider sharing it with someone who is supporting your learning. If you need more support, be sure to read Chapter 18 on building a robust learning network. For additional resources, visit www.already-smarter.com.

- What do you do to try to remember things and to improve your memory in general?

- Do you enjoy going to new places, trying new things, and meeting new people? Do you tend to find new situations more exciting and more memorable?

- How do you make associations between things you know (songs, simple words, symbols) and things you try to remember?

- Do you doodle, sketch, or draw things? If so, how might this affect your thought process?

- How might rereading, repeating, and rehearsing help you remember things?

CHAPTER 11

Embrace Powerful Experiences

Sometimes your goals may seem super exciting—like creating a sustainable farm in your backyard—but learning to do something in service of those goals (like reading about soil conditions) can seem tedious and boring. This is where we go wrong: choosing lackluster ways of learning, where we quickly lose interest, and shying away from powerful, transformative experiences.

Even today, I find myself prioritizing the easy options, like reading and listening rather than getting out in the world. But while so many of us love exciting experiences, we may find ourselves settling for easier options—reading, watching, listening—rather than truly immersing ourselves in learning. And even those who do engage in rich learning experiences might not know how to engage in a way that promotes effective learning, growth, and change.[1] In my time as a coach, I have worked with people to explore ways to embrace powerful, and sometimes unconventional, learning experiences in service of their larger aspirations and goals. Many learners I have supported are surprised by how much more they learn when they engage in powerful learning activities.

This chapter can help you learn about the power of experiential learning. It explores five high-impact ways to make your learning come to life. With effort and an open mind, you might become more active and adventurous in your approach to learning.

Before you begin this chapter, think about how active, experiential learning could support your learning, satisfaction, and larger life goals.

- What have you learned *actively*—and did it stick?

- Why might active and experiential learning affect your performance?

- How might active and experiential learning help you achieve some of your larger aspirations?

Get Active to Learn More

Throughout history, learning has been an active process. For generations, humans learned a great many things by actively engaging in hands-on work. Today, *active learning* refers to learning methods where you are actively involved in the learning process, whether through hands-on practice, collaboration, project-based work, or simply taking the lead in your learning. Active learning differs from more passive forms of learning, such as reading, watching, and listening—although, with a few tricks, these can each be made more active, too. The big question is: Does active learning help you learn?

A team of researchers wanted to know just how much of a difference active learning really makes. In this technology-filled world, is active learning still necessary? Or can you read, watch, and listen instead? They evaluated more than 225 published research studies and compared traditional lecturing to active learning in science, technology, engineering, and math—often abbreviated as STEM subjects. What did they find? On average, active learning improved exam scores by 6 percent. That may not sound like much, but it can be the difference between moving from a C to a B or a B to an A. They also found that active learners were much less likely to fail their courses.[2] In short, active learning works now just as well as in the past.

Simple Strategy: Adopt Active Learning Strategies

You may not be in a course or learning a subject that seems to lend itself to active learning. However, you can improve your learning by adopting some active learning strategies. And these strategies may make it a more enjoyable experience as well. To get started:

1. **Take notes.** At a minimum, taking notes makes a passive activity into a more active one. Instead of just reading or listening, you are engaging by taking notes.

2. **Draw concept maps, diagrams, or models.** Help your mind organize information by drawing a concept map, which connects different concepts with lines and arrows; creating a diagram, which shows how things relate; or drawing a schematic, which shows parts of a whole. These are powerful ways to make learning more active.

3. **Teach someone else.** Find a partner and learn together. Just ensure this is allowed and not considered cheating or plagiarism.

Interact for Strength in Numbers

Collaborating with others is one of the best ways to actively improve performance. One of the hallmarks of active learning is learning together, through human interaction. Such interaction may be facilitated through collaboration, where two or more people support each other on independent work, or cooperation, where two or more people work closely together on shared work. But does human interaction help you learn?

Pairs and groups often perform better than individuals do alone. Groups can do a better job recalling details, problem-solving, and even playing video games. Experts believe that this is due to the pooled knowledge of the group, as well as taking others' perspectives into consideration and learning from observing members of the group.[3]

However, collaborative learning can be challenging because it adds cognitive load by making participants rapidly switch between multiple speakers and perspectives. But it does help participants retrieve, correct, and reinforce their prior knowledge and extend their working memory capacity.[4] It is even more powerful if it is used with a group size of four or fewer and when focused on a single topic rather than a series of topics.[5]

Many of these benefits also extend to remote teamwork, also known as computer-supported collaborative learning (CSCL). CSCL benefits individual learning processes and also boosts motivation and self-efficacy.[6] CSCL improves knowledge gain, skill acquisition, and student perceptions, with the computer enabling better group task performance and social interactions.[7] CSCL can be a powerful tool for practicing processes.[8] Even CSCL that is delivered on a mobile device may support meaningful improvements in learning.[9]

If you can't find a small group of people to learn with, a single study buddy will do. Students who studied with a buddy found the interaction worthwhile and recommended the practice for future courses.[10] But just *studying* with someone doesn't necessarily do the trick. Peer learning is most effective when you try to reach agreement. Working toward consensus—such as sharing the same response to a question—enables peer learning to be effective.[11]

Simple Strategy: Interact Intentionally

With the rise of the internet, online learning, and social media, interacting with others is easier than ever, regardless of what you are learning. To get started:

1. **Find a partner.** If you are learning something new, find someone to do it with.

2. **Keep it small.** If you have a group, try to keep it to four or fewer, if possible.

3. **Reach agreement.** Take feedback seriously and consider trying to reach agreement.

Flip Your Learning

Technology has enabled us to learn nearly anywhere, anytime. No longer do we need to go to classrooms and lecture halls as we once did to listen, watch, and learn. As a result, time spent learning in physical spaces can be informed by what you have learned before entering them. This is commonly called "flipped learning" because more passive, independent learning typically happens before more active, collaborative learning.

Flipping the order in which you do certain things can help you maximize their effects. Flipped learning involves learning something on your own *before* attending an in-person or live learning experience. It's sort of like doing homework before class rather than after class. Compared to traditional, lecture-based learning, it produces gains in learning, engagement, and satisfaction.[12]

Researchers around the world have found additional benefits. Korean researchers found a significant improvement in motivation, self-directed learning, and learning achievement.[13] Turkish researchers also found that flipped learning improved motivation and metacognition—or how one thinks about their learning.[14] Norwegian researchers also found that flipped classes improved learning.[15] And these types of improvements were found regardless of how long flipped learning lasted.[16]

Simple Strategy: Flip Your Learning

Anyone can flip their learning by just preparing or planning for a learning experience. To get started:

1. **Prepare yourself.** The key to flipped learning is going to a learning experience prepared.

2. **Get ahead.** Wherever possible, read, watch, or listen to materials ahead of an in-person event so that you are prepared or briefed.

3. **Bring ideas and questions.** Summarize what you have learned and bring questions about things you may not understand.

Go Beyond "Learning by Doing"

There's nothing in life quite like having a great experience. Whether it's a special event, an evening with friends, or a weekend away, experiences stay in your mind and memories. Some learning experiences are highly experiential and leave a lasting impression. But what effect do these experiences have on learning?

Learning by doing is a long-standing and effective approach. As David Kolb writes in the groundbreaking book *Experiential Learning: Experience as the Source of Learning and Development*, the "learning process must be reimbued with the texture and feeling of human experiences shared and interpreted through dialog and with one another."[17] He continues: "Learning methods that combine work and study, theory and practice provide a more familiar and therefore more productive arena for learning."[18] Experiential learning gives you a chance to complete projects and tasks just as they might occur in real life. It's the classic way to "learn by doing." Students learn more through experiential learning, or learning through experience, than through traditional learning methods such as lecturing.[19]

But what constitutes experiential learning? According to researcher Thomas Howard Morris, it involves five themes:[20]

1. Learners are actively involved participants, not just watching something from the sidelines.

2. The knowledge they are learning is situated in time and place, not vaguely disconnected from a point in time or location.

3. Learners engage in novel experiences that are new to them or their lived experiences.

4. The experience allows learners to inquire into real-world problems that need to be solved.

5. Each experience involves self-reflection that requires learners to pause and consider what they have learned.

For example, watching a video about air pollution is not experiential learning, but visiting a neighborhood to help solve a problem related to air pollution and then reflecting on that experience could be a powerful form of experiential learning.

Simple Strategy: Embrace Experiential Learning

Experiential learning is one of the oldest ways of learning. To get started:

1. **Be active.** Be an active participant in your learning by working on real projects and tasks. This may mean working on a project for an employer or for an organization that will evaluate and provide feedback on your work.

2. **Mind the context.** Make sure what you are learning is related to the context in which you are learning it. For example, if you live in the Midwest and are studying climate change, your experiential work should be on the impacts of those changes in the city, county, or state that you are in so that you can understand the effects firsthand.

3. **Find novelty.** Engage in novel experiences related to real-world problems, followed by reflection. The experience should be new for you—not something you do routinely—and you should reflect on what you experienced and how it affected you.

Embody and Situate Your Learning

Have you ever found yourself learning something new by mimicking the body motions or techniques of an instructor or expert? Or going to a certain place—maybe a gym or museum—to enhance your learning? You're not alone. Certain movements and environments help many people learn more effectively.

Some researchers support the concept of *embodied cognition*—when thinking is enhanced, supported, or connected to body movements.[21] Embodied cognition can support learning and, in children, help with short-term memory and vocabulary.[22] Similarly, *situated cognition* is often connected to unique contexts, based on appropriate tasks, and includes active learning and reflection.[23] These learning theories are popular among those who study how people learn skills that require movement, such as playing an instrument, participating in a sport, or learning a skill in the health professions.[24] Together, embodied and situated cognition emphasize the importance of using our bodies and environments to help us learn.

Simple Strategy: Use Your Body to Learn

You can use your body to learn—just consider it an extension of your brain. To get started:

1. **Observe movements.** If you are learning something new, observe your body movements and those of experts.

2. **Practice movements.** As you practice, try to perform any relevant movements as part of the learning process, adjusting for accuracy and based on feedback.

continued

3. **Incorporate movements.** Even if what you are learning doesn't require movements, consider incorporating some that might help you remember key facts or vocabulary, such as tracing your finger along the boundaries on a map to learn geography.

The Cumulative Effect

Have you ever tried to learn something new but found that the learning experience fell flat, felt boring, or was just plain tedious? Worse, these experiences just didn't seem to "stick." That's where embracing powerful experiences comes in. Although each of the active learning techniques in this chapter can bring learning to life, a combination can amplify the effect.

Imagine that you take up something that requires hands-on work, like organic gardening or sustainable farming, but reading and watching videos just aren't cutting it. You realize that you want to—no, you need to—get your hands dirty. You start by getting just a bit more active by taking notes, sketching diagrams, and engaging in forums. Then you go all in by working with a friend or neighbor and experimenting. But before each session, you structure your own flipped learning experience where you each watch a video or read an article, and then give it a try. Enjoying hands-on gardening, you begin volunteering at a garden center and taking some of the workshops they offer. During these, you follow along with the gestures and behaviors that you want to be able to mimic later. One day it dawns on you how far your gardening skills have come—and how valuable powerful learning experiences can be.

These strategies aren't random—they're part of an intentional plan to support your learning. This plan includes things like getting active to learn more, interacting for strength in numbers, flipping your learning, going beyond learning by doing, and embodying your learning. Think of this chapter as one piece of a puzzle; when combined with the strategies in others, they can form a personalized learning journey.

Take Action: Make Your Own Plan

This chapter explored learning by doing. Active learning, such as completing projects, performing procedures, and simulating real work, can make a big difference in your learning. One way of learning actively is by learning collaboratively. Working in pairs and groups improves attitude, performance, and achievement—especially if we drive toward consensus. Active learning is enabled by being prepared for a learning experience. The preparation that comes with flipped learning improves our awareness, engagement, and performance, while also making us feel more motivated and satisfied. Experiential learning gives us a chance to learn as we might in real life, if we select the right experiences in the right contexts. Embodied and situated cognition are when thinking is enhanced, supported, or connected to body movements and environments that help us acquire skills.

Take a moment to reflect on the kinds of learning activities you typically engage in. After contemplating the following questions, develop a simple plan to embrace powerful learning experiences and consider sharing it with someone who is supporting your learning. If you need more support, be sure to read Chapter 18 on building a robust learning network. For additional resources, visit www.already-smarter.com.

- How might you engage in more active learning activities?

- How might you get more support and interaction in a learning experience?

- How might you plan to prepare before you set foot into a classroom, training, or hands-on learning experience?

- Do you find that you learn better when something is very hands-on?

- How might you improve your performance by using your body or environment?

CHAPTER 12

Design a Precision Practice Routine

N o matter what you are hoping to achieve—from painting your walls to producing an oil painting for your local arts scene—you won't achieve it without some practice. This is particularly true if you are dreaming of doing something that requires some level of precision or expertise that only comes with sustained practice. Yet many of us think *trying* is the same as *practicing*, unaware of how to establish a practice routine.

It took me years to realize that trying something can just as easily turn you off to it, whereas a practice strategy contributes to long-term success. But, when asked, more than 80 percent of respondents didn't routinely establish a practice strategy when learning something new.[1] In my work as a learning and leadership coach, I have enjoyed helping people to explore ways to establish practice strategies to achieve things that they never expected. Again and again, I'm reminded that people who lack progress are often lacking a practice strategy.

This chapter can help you understand how intentional practice contributes to skill acquisition. It introduces five evidence-backed strategies for practicing more effectively, which may help you make progress toward your goals. With diligence and consistency, you might find yourself moving from uncertainty to precision as you build a strong practice routine.

Before you begin this chapter, think about how devising a personalized practice strategy could help you sharpen new skills and advance your big dreams.

- What are some of the ways you typically practice—do they work?

- Why might a practice strategy affect your learning performance?

- How might a practice strategy help you achieve some of your larger aspirations?

Practice Deliberately to Hone Skills

Have you ever set out to deliberately practice something? Maybe you set aside time to focus on your tennis serve, or reserved a space to practice golf swings, or found someone to help you play the piano. *Deliberate practice* is a formal term for this kind of focused practice— it refers to performing an activity with the clear intention of personal improvement. The question is: But how does it actually work?

Sometimes deliberate practice is done alone, other times it is with guidance from an expert. A skilled teacher can communicate learning goals in ways that the learner can understand during practice. The teacher arranges practice activities to target the goals and provides immediate feedback, while the learner can make repeated, revised attempts that gradually approach mastery.[2] And if you cannot work with a dedicated coach or trainer, take heart: You may be able to work with a robot. Researchers found that combining robotic guidance with unassisted practice in teaching aspiring golfers how to putt provided at least short-term learning improvements.[3]

Deliberate practice is considered useful for enhancing performance in games, music, and sports.[4] Whether you're learning to play an instrument, participate in a sport, or complete a complex task, deliberate practice may help you get better.

Simple Strategy: Practice Deliberately

With a little effort and perhaps some guidance, you can engage in deliberate practice. To get started:

1. **Seek guidance.** Find someone who is skilled at whatever you want to deliberately practice. Ask them to guide you through the activity, step-by-step.

2. **Request feedback.** As you perform the activity, ask for—and incorporate—their feedback by making small, intentional adjustments.

3. **Reflect.** At the end of the deliberate practice session, take notes on what you did well and what you want to improve for the next time.

Block Practice for Complex Procedures

Have you ever tried doing something over, and over, and over again? Maybe you practiced free throws, tennis serves, or golf swings. Maybe you rehearsed a scene or song for a performance. Or maybe you baked a dessert repeatedly until it was completely perfect. This kind of repetitive practice is called *blocked practice*, and it helps improve accuracy and fluency.

Blocked practice allows you to practice one skill at a time in a focused block before moving on to another skill. Massed practice is very similar; the key difference is that massed practice involves a single session without any breaks.

Blocked practice has been shown to help with software training—especially during the learning process itself—and massed practice helped with visual training (like deciphering dental images) and physical training (such as throwing a softball).[5] Compared to other types of practice, massed practice may be easier to stick with, while blocked practice may result in greater fluency with a task.[6] If you're considering perfecting something, try practicing the most difficult parts in blocked repetition.

Simple Strategy: Practice in Blocks

Anyone can engage in blocked or massed practice; the key is simply sticking with it. To get started:

1. **Ask if it fits.** Consider what you are trying to learn: Is it a complex process or skill? If so, it's a candidate for blocked or massed practice.

2. **Devise the best strategy.** If you need to learn one specific technique, then choose blocked practice to repeat it over and

over. If you need to learn several techniques, then consider massed practice, where you perform each task back-to-back.

3. **Select the right time.** Select a time of day when you're rested, focused, and have enough time to adequately repeat the technique or procedure with a few planned microbreaks.

Space Out Practice over Time

Have you ever found yourself learning something bit by bit, spaced out over the course of days, weeks, months, or years? Maybe you've improved your ability to sing over years of practice. Or maybe you have perfected your technique at the gym by working with a trainer for several months. Spacing practice out over an extended period of time can improve your results.

Spaced or distributed practice involves reviewing or revisiting learning materials or activities multiple times over a longer period. This involves multiple, sometimes shorter, learning sessions, each of which can involve massed practice. Spaced practice may relieve cognitive load by providing a rest period in between sessions.[7]

People who have a higher ability in the first place are more likely to space out their studying. However, the benefits of spacing things out, or even taking short breaks to space things out, were the greatest for those with lower ability levels and a lower likelihood of completing a task.[8] Spacing practice seems to lead to more significant gains for novices.[9] For example, spacing out studying helped people learn a new language, including improving both immediate and subsequent recall and overall accuracy.[10]

Simple Strategy: Space Out Practice

Spacing out practice sessions can help you learn something over an extended period. To get started:

1. **Pick a skill.** Determine which skill you'd like to learn that might benefit from spaced practice, especially those skills that are new to you.

2. **Develop a schedule.** Devise a spaced practice schedule over the course of several days, weeks, or months.

3. **Get further apart.** Since your performance is likely to improve, space the sessions progressively further apart over time. For instance, you may start with a daily schedule, then shift to a weekly schedule, and ultimately end with a monthly schedule.

Interleave to Distinguish Differences

Have you ever learned about one thing by comparing it to another? Perhaps you've compared the process of baking bread to baking vegan bread, or compared the way it feels to play a ukulele to the way it feels to play a guitar. There are some learning topics that benefit from a very specific kind of practice where you actively distinguish among things that are similar but not identical, for example, two types of wine, two X-ray images, or two sets of directions. You may have gone back and forth, looking first at one then the other, to distinguish exactly what was different.

Interleaved practice is a great way to improve your ability to spot subtle differences. This practice helps learners to compare, contrast, and discriminate among topics.[11] Interleaving allows you to discern slight similarities or differences, especially where understanding those nuances is key to your learning, such as variations in the anatomies of animals, medical procedures applied in an emergency, or how language is used in different contexts.

Interleaved practice involves studying exemplars from different categories with one rule: No two exemplars from the same category can be studied consecutively.[12] Researchers have found that interleaving is best for learning material that is more similar between categories, less similar within categories, and somewhat complex.[13]

Simple Strategy:
Interleave Your Practice

Interleaving helps discern how to do things that are slightly different. Interleaving may sound tricky, but anyone can do it. To get started:

1. **Focus on differences.** Determine if what you are learning would benefit from interleaving. Are you learning about fine-grain differences that require you to discern between two or more similar things? Be mindful to select different practice elements—for example, types of processes, procedures, or techniques.

2. **Establish a schedule.** Set up an interleaving schedule that alternates between the different elements. Make sure you are alternating between the different elements so that you have an opportunity to discern the differences.

continued

3. **Make things progressively harder.** Consider placing things that are more obviously different at the beginning of your practice schedule and more similar progressively toward the end, so that it becomes increasingly difficult to identify the nuances.

Practice Randomly to Build Flexibility

At some point in your learning process, you'll be past the basics and into more nuanced skills and decisions. Many complex processes require a variety of techniques, depending upon the techniques or responses needed. This is the perfect place for something called *random practice* (and the related technique of variable practice). These approaches involve a practice schedule that includes frequent, and sometimes unpredictable, task changes. This way, you're constantly adjusting your behavior.

Random practice is a technique whereby you practice different skills in an unpredictable order, and *variable practice* is a technique where you practice the same skill under varying conditions. Variable practice strategies result in a higher level of learning for motor skills, possibly because these may be more deeply encoded in the brain.[14] For example, when learning to play the clarinet, random practice performers played significantly faster.[15] Similarly, researchers who studied high school baseball players found that random practice improved hitting performance on both the dominant and nondominant sides.[16]

In tasks like these, the benefits of random practice may be due to what's called the contextual interference effect (CIE), which is when a random schedule requires more cognitive activity to discern and react to subtle nuances.[17] Random practice for volleyball players, for instance, resulted in more refined control over specific parameters of a volleyball serve.[18]

You may use random practice when learning something that requires subtle, unique responses due to the circumstances, such as catching a softball, painting a portrait, or learning how to respond to a patient in therapy. Researchers have found that random practice is effective for longer-term retention and may be better when incorporated later in the learning process.[19]

Simple Strategy: Practice Randomly

Incorporating random practice into your routine only requires finding a few spare minutes, though that can be the trickiest part. Consider practicing while you're waiting for someone else, while in transit, or when you unexpectedly have free time. This is the best time for random practice. To get started:

1. **Consider if it's the best fit.** Determine if what you are learning would benefit from random practice. Does it require you to perform differently based upon the unique context?

2. **Select the right environment.** Establish a practice environment that enables random practice. This may mean going to a space that allows you to work with different individuals under different circumstances.

3. **Find a partner.** Ask a friend, classmate, or tutor to present you with scenarios that require unique reactions or responses.

The Cumulative Effect

Have you ever worked on getting better at something, but you weren't improving even though you were practicing? Day after day, week after week, even month after month, you may have felt like your learning had hit a plateau. That's where designing a precision practice routine comes in. Individually, each approach in this chapter can improve how you practice; together, they can launch your performance into hyperdrive.

Imagine that you want to challenge yourself with a precision skill, like oil painting, but practicing here and there doesn't seem to be paying off. Then a light bulb goes off: You need a practice strategy. You decide to begin with deliberate practice of specific skills with an expert painter offering feedback. Following each of those sessions, you add in blocked practice, where you repeat certain types of color blending over and over, but you space these sessions out to about twice a week. Monthly, you decide to interleave similar brush stroke techniques so you can compare the results and deeply understand the nuances. And for fun, you randomly practice everything you are learning with a friend, just to keep things interesting. After two months, a friend remarks on how far you've come, and you realize how much your painting—and your ability to practice anything—has improved.

These choices aren't haphazard ones—they're part of a purposeful plan intended to support your learning. This plan includes things like practicing deliberately to hone skills, blocking practice for complex procedures, spacing out practice over time, interleaving to distinguish differences, and practicing randomly to build flexibility. The cumulative effect is powerful: Integrating concepts from this chapter with those from others can amplify your success as a learner.

Take Action: Make Your Own Plan

This chapter dove into the old saying: *practice makes perfect*. But there are numerous ways to practice, including deliberate, spaced, blocked, interleaved, and variable practice techniques. Deliberate practice involves revising our performance to gradually improve. Blocked practice produces repetition that helps us master complex processes. Spaced practice helps us acquire new skills over time. Interleaved practice helps us alternate between multiple, similar things. And random and variable practice enable us to react to a variety of unpredictable circumstances. By incorporating multiple modes of practice, we can gain great fluency and skill.

Take a moment to reflect on your approach to practicing something new. After contemplating the following questions, develop a simple plan to design a precision practice routine and consider sharing it with someone who is supporting your learning. If you need more support, be sure to read Chapter 18 on building a robust learning network. For additional resources, visit www.already-smarter.com.

- When was the last time you set out to practice something because you wanted to improve?

- Try to recall a time you practiced something through nonstop repetition or drills. What made this effective (or ineffective) for you?

- Can you think of something you got much better at because it was spaced out over a long time?

- Was there ever a time when you learned two things that were very similar but with subtle differences? How did you do it?

- What kinds of activities do you think might benefit from practicing in random or variable ways?

PART IV

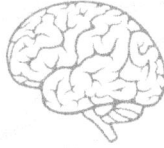

Optimize the Mind-Body Connection

L earning is not just about using your mind. Once you've begun to actively learn, you can optimize your learning by nourishing, moving, and resting your body in ways that support your mind, brain, and behavior. It's easy to separate the work you do on your mind from how you support and use your body. In fact, leveraging the mind-body connection can be a powerful way to enhance learning.

The fourth part of this book is about nourishing your body and mind and using your senses. This part includes four chapters focused on activating learning through wellness, resting well to learn well, using all of your senses, and building robust learning habits. These chapters will help you support your learning by using both your brain and your body. The beverages, exercise routines, rest, sensory experiences, and habits you engage in can be pivotal to a sound learning practice—and go a long way toward establishing successful learning.

CHAPTER 13

Activate Your Body for Peak Learning

Y ou may find that your big goal, and the learning needed to achieve that goal, seems like something you can do simply by reading a book or sitting at your computer. Maybe you want to learn stock trading to build a high-growth portfolio; this may seem like something you can simply learn if you find the right information. This is where many of us go wrong: We undermine our ambitions by not considering the mind-body connection and how we can use our muscles to improve our minds. Many of us learn more slowly because we rarely involve our bodies in the learning process (unless we are learning something physical).

In all my years of learning, this is probably one of the few learning strategies I have focused on the most. Still, more than 80 percent of people surveyed reported not regularly engaging their bodies in ways that support their learning—missing a huge opportunity for improved performance.[1] In my career as a coach, I have worked with people to explore ways to optimize their learning by doing something they start to love: managing their overall health and wellness. Activating your body can be a valuable step toward activating your learning.

This chapter can help you explore ways to enhance learning through activities that may not seem directly related to traditional study methods. It explores five important ways to prime your body—and brain—to learn more effectively. With a few simple actions, you might find yourself feeling more balanced and ready to learn at your best.

Before you begin this chapter, think about how leveraging your body to improve your mind could make you more successful in learning and in life.

- What are some of the things that you do for your body and mind purely to be healthy?
- Why might your wellness habits affect your learning performance?
- How might your wellness habits help you achieve some of your larger aspirations?

Stay Hydrated for Thinking and Learning

Hydration is critical for health. If you've ever been dehydrated, you may have felt tired, lightheaded, and (of course) thirsty. These feelings impair your ability to focus and disrupt the learning process. Being dehydrated, even just a bit, can impair your thinking.[2] Dehydration has negative effects on mood, memory, and attention—and the simple act of rehydration improves memory, attention, and reaction times.[3]

Researchers in Malaysia found that cognitive function was much higher among learners who were hydrated.[4] The effects of hydration have other benefits that indirectly affect your ability to learn. Being hydrated can even boost your mood, especially for those who may not be able to easily regulate their water consumption.[5] Being in a good mood is the perfect mental state for learning.

When it comes to hydration, not all beverages are created equal. For example, drinks that are mild diuretics may also prompt your body to expel water. Healthy drinks, such as water, boost performance.[6] Water is the gold standard for keeping you well-hydrated and, therefore, enhancing performance and mood. Drinking certain juices can also bestow both immediate and longer-term benefits. Three of the most researched juice varieties include pomegranate, grape, and good old-fashioned orange juice.

- Drinking pomegranate juice consistently for four weeks improves brain activity, including verbal and visual memory.[7]

- Drinking grape juice improves cognition and mood, specifically reaction time on a measurement of attention, and enhances feelings of calmness.[8] Drinking it daily for three to four months seems to improve memory function in complex tasks that may endure over time.[9]

- Drinking orange juice, which is rich in flavonoids, may enhance cognition for as many as six hours in healthy adults.[10] It enhances blood flow to the brain in young adults.[11] Frequent consumption of flavonoids is associated with improved cognition. Drinking orange juice daily for eight weeks has been shown to be beneficial for older adults.[12]

Simple Strategy: Stay Properly Hydrated

For many, remaining hydrated is easily within reach. You just need to make sure you drink the right things and consume them often enough. However, not everyone lives in a place where clean drinking water is readily available. To help, consider supporting organizations and efforts that safeguard clean water and help deliver it to communities and people in need. To get started:

1. **Be aware.** Recognize the signs of dehydration, including brain fog and confusion.

2. **Choose water.** When you're even mildly dehydrated, prioritize drinking water and healthy drinks over beverages that further dehydrate you. If you can, bring water with you to learning experiences, especially if an experience is lengthy, warm, or outdoors.

3. **Consider juice.** Drink orange juice to enhance cognition. Drink pomegranate juice to improve verbal and visual memory. Drink Concord grape juice to improve your mood and feelings of calmness.

Drink Coffee, Tea, and Cocoa to Power Learning

Coffee, tea, and cocoa are three of the world's most common and beloved drinks. The sheer variety of these hot, healthy, and tasty concoctions has turned them from simple staples into a sophisticated science. Many people turn to these beverages to start their day, wake up, or give themselves an energy boost. But how do they affect your mind, memories, and learning?

If you like coffee, you're in good company. To determine whether coffee helps you learn, let's begin by looking at one of its core properties: *caffeine*. Drinking caffeine can indeed improve physical performance, such as participating in endurance or power sports.[13] However, the effects of caffeine on brain function are not quite as clear. It seems to depend upon the *amount* of caffeine someone drinks. Low to moderate doses of caffeine seem to improve cognition, including alertness, attention, and reaction time.[14] At moderate doses, caffeine also results in improved memory and coordination. In high doses, however, caffeine may compromise learning and spike anxiety.[15] While there are many ways to consume caffeine, it seems that coffee, specifically, may have brain benefits. Moderate coffee drinking seems to enhance cognition in older adults.[16] This may be related to coffee's reported ability to safeguard the brain by providing some kind of protective effect against later cognitive impairment.[17] Some research has even indicated that coffee might reorganize the functional connectivity of the brain, enabling better thinking and functioning.[18] If you are a caffeinated coffee drinker, it may be better to support your habit than to skip it when you are trying to learn something new, as cravings have been shown to impair memory. Specifically, cravings interrupt your ability to monitor your accuracy during tests.[19]

If you're a tea drinker, you're not alone. Humans have been drinking tea for thousands of years. Could tea be a panacea for learning? Green and black teas contain caffeine as well as the amino acid L-theanine. These teas have been shown to improve performance on tasks that require people to shift their attention from one thing to another and remain alert. L-theanine has the added effect of promoting relaxation, sustained attention, memory, and distraction suppression.[20] Green tea in particular may be beneficial for the brain. This may be because *catechins*, the type of flavonoids in green tea, are powerful antioxidants that fight neurodegeneration.[21] Catechins enhance cognitive function and may decrease brain plaques and neuroinflammation.[22] They may even prevent and treat neurodegenerative diseases.[23]

If you enjoy cocoa, you'll be happy to hear that drinking it enhances your attention and reduces the errors you might make due to inattention.[24] Similarly, after consuming cocoa flavanols, young adults experienced better cognitive performance.[25] Cocoa appears to improve general cognition, attention, processing speed, and working memory—and may even help compensate for a poor night's sleep.[26] Cocoa and chocolate have measurable neurocognitive effects and may prevent the onset of age-related cognitive impairment and its progression.[27]

Simple Strategy: Consume Wisely

Consuming coffee, tea, and cocoa are relatively easy ways to boost learning performance, if you find the "right amount" to keep yourself alert and focused. To get started:

1. **Get alert with coffee**. If you choose to drink coffee, drink a low to moderate amount, as more may erode memory and learning and spike anxiety. As caffeine can boost alertness, attention, and reaction time, try drinking it just ahead of a learning experience. And if you drink coffee regularly, avoid skipping it when you are learning as the cravings may distract you.

2. **Concentrate with tea.** Drink tea when you want to enhance your concentration and attention. Black and green teas provide the benefits of caffeine with the added calming quality of L-theanine. Steep it for just two to three minutes to avoid bitterness.

3. **Focus with cocoa.** Grab a cup next time you're looking for a treat that can help you focus your attention. Find high-quality (preferably low or no sugar) cocoa powder. Add the cocoa to hot water, steamed milk, or plant-based milk, or add a bit of cocoa to smoothies, oatmeal, or cereal.

Exercise (for) Your Mind

In recent years, there has been a preponderance of evidence around the benefits of aerobic exercise. Raising your heart rate through jogging, walking, biking, and other sports is often attributed to heart health, weight management, and stress reduction. However, recent research has also drawn connections to the mind, brain, and mood. How do you think aerobic exercise affects your ability to learn new things?

Experts have studied both the regularity of cardiovascular exercise (whether it is chronic or acute) and the intensity (whether it is high or low). Of course, some people do a mix. For example, you may undertake chronic low-intensity exercise, such as daily walks, and acute high-intensity exercise, such as the occasional run.

Researchers reviewed seventeen studies to look at the effect of chronic (ongoing) and acute (single session) exercise in adults and found that both types improve memory function.[28] Chronic aerobic exercise leads to improvement in executive function, which is related to planning, judgment, and reasoning.[29] Additionally, even shorter-term aerobic exercise—defined as three times a week for one hour for about three months—can reduce the cognitive results of aging and boost brain health in adults.[30]

In terms of intensity, high-intensity cardiovascular exercise might result in more cognitive gains.[31] Among adolescents, working memory significantly improves when they engage in high-intensity exercise, such as sprinting, compared to lower- or moderate-intensity exercise, such as walking, jogging, or stretching.[32] But moderate exercise, particularly in the morning, also seems to enhance working memory as well as executive function.[33] And exercises that require some degree of coordinated movement, such as jumping rope, improve cognitive function, especially with longer durations.[34]

Resistance training may also make your brain stronger. When you think of resistance training, you might think of weightlifters who are focused entirely on building muscle. However, resistance training has many positive benefits for your brain, such as preventing neurodegenerative diseases.[35] Resistance training improves cognitive performance and executive function, which means it improves your planning, reasoning, and decision-making abilities.[36] Even just two sessions per week promoted memory and reduced brain atrophy among older females.[37]

Imagine that you could shift the timing of your exercise routine to enable yourself to learn more or remember what you are learning more effectively. Could the timing of exercise matter? A team of researchers set out to answer this question. They reviewed twenty-five studies on this topic and found that acute or intense exercise had the greatest impact on memory, when performed before memory encoding, such as the moment you see a new object, or during early memory consolidation, such as the time immediately after seeing the object.[38] Therefore, it would be best to exercise just prior to a learning experience or just afterward for greatest effect.

Simple Strategy: Exercise for Your Mind

You can boost your learning by exercising, even if just for a few minutes several days per week. To get started:

1. **Create a schedule.** Establish a routine of regular moderate exercise, such as low-intensity walking, preferably in the morning. If your doctor approves, consider occasionally accelerating your pace or adding in short sprints. At regular intervals, perhaps once a week, include some kind of coordinated exercise, such as jumping rope.

2. **Aim for twice.** With your doctor's approval, engage in resistance training at least twice a week for fifteen minutes. Try to incorporate exercises using just your body weight, such as lunges, push-ups, and planks, so you can continue your practice even if you can't get to the gym. Rapidly cycle through a sequence of resistance exercises to add an aerobic element, as discussed earlier.

3. **Schedule your routine.** Consider scheduling your exercise routine immediately before a learning experience or immediately afterward. If there's something difficult you're trying to master, consider sandwiching it between two exercise sessions. If you can help it, avoid trying to study while you are exercising, as this can add to the cognitive load and diminish your performance for both.

Stretch for Attention, Cognition, and Memory

Humans have long benefited from two ancient forms of exercise: yoga and Tai Chi. These powerful poses, combined with breath work and concentration, have been shown to enhance more than just your body and spirit. How do you think that they can contribute to improved attention, cognition, and memory?

Researchers analyzed fifteen research studies on the effects of yoga on cognition, finding that yoga had the greatest effect on improving attention and processing speed, followed by executive function, with acute yoga improving memory.[39] Yoga enabled significant improvement in the manipulation and maintenance of working memory.[40]

Even gentler mind-body exercises like Tai Chi have been shown to improve cognitive performance and function, especially among people older than sixty.[41]

Simple Strategy: Start a Simple Practice

You can enjoy yoga or Tai Chi, even if it's just a few gentle poses that you practice every day. To get started:

1. **Find resources.** Consider adopting a yoga or Tai Chi practice, leveraging free online resources.

2. **Design your own sequence.** If you don't have the time or resources to go to yoga or Tai Chi classes, simply adopt a short sequence of poses that you enjoy doing.

3. **Time it.** Aim for just ten to thirty minutes per day.

Let Your Mind Flourish Outside

Where is the best place to exercise? While it's tempting, not to mention convenient, to exercise in your home, gym, or yoga studio, it may be worthwhile to step out into the world, especially if you have access to a park, hiking trail, or other green space. Communing with nature, even briefly, bestows untold benefits that include supporting your cognitive function, memory, and well-being. How might nature help you learn?

Taking a walk in nature is a simple way to improve performance. Nature benefits your mind and brain. Spending time in nature may support your sense of overall well-being and your personal growth.[42] Importantly, it also improves your cognitive functioning.[43] Experts found that as little as ten minutes of sitting or walking in nature improved well-being for college-age learners.[44]

In fact, for older adults, the very act of walking is associated with executive function, memory, and processing speed, and having a faster walking pace is associated with less year-over-year decline in cognition.[45] Brisk walking produces significantly better cognitive performance.[46] Daily walking resulted in a 38 percent lower risk of dementia, and daily gardening was nearly as high, resulting in a 36 percent lower risk of dementia among men.[47] Gardening activities produced specific improvements in brain nerves and cognitive function.[48] Of course, these kinds of improvements vary by individual and are influenced by many factors, including environmental factors like air quality; nevertheless, they do demonstrate the benefits of exercise on our minds.

Simple Strategy: Go Outside

Even if you live in a city, you can usually find public park space or create your own indoor garden with plants, images, and nature sounds. To get started:

1. **Get out.** This may include sitting outside, gardening, walking, or hiking, depending upon your fitness level.

2. **Make it last.** Try to engage with nature for at least ten minutes each day.

3. **Bring nature in.** If you cannot get outside, surround yourself with plants or create your own indoor garden, complete with nature sounds and natural light.

The Cumulative Effect

Have you ever tried to buckle down and learn something, but you couldn't seem to do it because you felt fatigued, foggy, or unfocused? That's where activating your body for peak learning comes in. While each strategy in this chapter can help you prepare your body for learning, weaving them together can create a foundation for deeper learning.

Imagine that you want to develop something that feels complicated, like devising your retirement investment strategy, but you're feeling sluggish. You increase your hydration and even add in a bit of strategic caffeine a few minutes before you start studying, sometimes alternating between tea or cocoa to enhance your focus. You also establish an exercise routine: a half hour of resistance training twice a week to sharpen your investment decision-making, timed just before or after your learning sessions. You join a yoga studio and take classes whenever you're feeling energy-poor and add in a weekly nature walk as well, using the time outside to contemplate your overall investment options. All of this helps your focus, functioning, and energy. After about three months, you realize how healthy you feel—and how far your investment strategy is taking you. Now that's a win-win.

These activities aren't completely arbitrary—they're part of a thoughtful plan intended to support your learning. This plan includes things like staying hydrated for thinking and learning; drinking coffee, tea, and cocoa to power learning; building your resistance to build your mind; stretching for attention, cognition, and memory; and letting your mind flourish outside. The more you blend these strategies with others in this book, the more you can form personalized learning habits that truly work for you.

Take Action: Make Your Own Plan

In this chapter, you learned about the role your body can play in learning, starting with one thing that humans cannot live without: liquids. When you are trying to learn something new, make sure to avoid dehydration, optimize your caffeine intake for alertness, and consider a mug of cocoa, cup of tea, or glass of juice to boost your overall cognition. Similarly, it's no secret that exercise is important for our bodies, our health, and our longevity. But only recently have the connections between exercise and brain health, memory, and cognition been studied. The findings indicate that adopting the right exercise routine can also help you achieve your learning goals. Cardiovascular exercise and resistance training both benefit your brain, mind, and performance. Yoga improves cognition, attention, processing speed, executive function, and memory, and Tai Chi enhances cognitive function and performance. Spending time in nature supports your well-being, growth, and thinking.

Take a moment to reflect on some of the small things that may go a long way toward learning. After contemplating the following questions, develop a simple plan to activate your body for peak learning and consider sharing it with someone who is supporting your learning. If you need more support, be sure to read Chapter 18 on building a robust learning network. For additional resources, visit www.already-smarter.com.

- Do you consume enough water or juice every day?

- How might coffee, tea, or cocoa help or hinder your ability to learn and perform?

- How might exercise help your thinking, learning, and memory?

- Do you practice yoga or Tai Chi? If so, do you notice mental clarity, enhanced energy, or other benefits that may improve your concentration, thinking, and learning?

- Do you have access to parks, beaches, hiking trails, or even just a small garden? If so, how might you leverage these spaces to help you learn more and achieve your goals?

CHAPTER 14

Sleep Smartly and Strategically

W hether you want to get a job, take the next step in your career, or launch a profitable business—or just learn something for fun, like how to swim—your goals depend upon being able to learn something new and commit that learning to memory. Yet many of us inadvertently inhibit our learning because we underestimate and misunderstand the ways in which sleep affects learning.

As someone who struggles with insomnia, this is the learning strategy that I have struggled with the most and perhaps learned the most about. While information on the importance of sleep is becoming increasingly available, only one in five people surveyed routinely applies sleep-based strategies to their learning process.[1] I have helped people consider ways to maximize their learning (and feel more rested while they do so) by adopting strategic sleep habits.

In my coaching relationships, I have noticed that prioritizing sleep can pay dividends in learning and in life.

This chapter can help you incorporate sleep as a key component of your learning process. It explores five research-based ways to make sleep the secret weapon for learning and success. With a bit of effort, you might find yourself feeling more refreshed and ready to retain new information by optimizing your sleep habits.

Before you begin this chapter, think about how optimizing your sleep could help you progress through learning experiences and ultimately improve the quality of your whole life.

- What are some of the ways you adjust your sleep when you're learning something new?
- Why might sleep-based strategies affect your learning performance?
- How might sleep-based strategies contribute to your career, life, and larger goals?

Sleep Before and After Learning

Most people spend between a quarter and a third of their lives asleep. That may seem like a waste of time or, on the other hand, like a wonderful reprieve from the stresses of daily life. Regardless, it's a biological necessity, as sleep allows both body and brain to recharge. But how can you tweak your sleep habits to maximize the power of your mind?

It may not surprise you that you learn better after a good night's sleep.[2] However, sleep doesn't just help you remain awake and alert *during* learning; it also helps you retain information *after* learning.

Neuroplasticity—your brain's ability to form and reorganize connections—is not only happening while you acquire new information but also during the "offline" periods afterward, such as post-learning sleep.[3] Neuroplasticity is thought to be generated by sleep.[4] Newly acquired information is transformed into long-term memory during sleep, almost like charging your phone.[5] While you sleep, your brain is busy processing, storing, and building memories.[6] Therefore, sleeping after learning plays an important role in building memories—whether you sleep immediately afterward or later that evening.

Simple Strategy: Sleep to Learn

Even if you have trouble sleeping, there are things you can do to improve your sleep and use periods of sleep to enhance your learning. To get started:

1. **Think ahead.** Start by making sure you're rested ahead of any important learning experience.

2. **Take a nap.** Consider closely following learning with a period of sleep, such as a nap.

3. **Prioritize sleep.** Prioritize sleep the night after learning something to help your brain retain it.

Avoid Sleep Deprivation

Sleep deprivation inhibits concentration and performance. You may know what it's like to trudge through the day after a bad night's sleep, feeling tired, irritable, distracted, or forgetful. Nevertheless, many have become accustomed to chronic sleep deprivation due to too much stress, too little time, or just poor sleep hygiene. How does sleep deprivation affect your ability to learn?

Sleep deprivation affects both speed and accuracy of cognitive capabilities, causing lapses in attention and reaction time and degraded short-term and working memory.[7] According to experts at the National Institute of Neurological Disorders and Stroke, sleep is required to support the brain pathways that enable learning and memory formation; without sleep, it's harder to concentrate and respond.[8]

There are two types of sleep deprivation: 1) total sleep deprivation, where you are up an entire night or more without any sleep and 2) partial sleep deprivation, where you don't sleep enough for several nights in a row. How do each of these affect learning and performance? Not surprisingly, total sleep deprivation impairs attention, memory, and decision-making, while partial sleep deprivation tends to just affect attention.[9] However, several nights of chronic sleep restriction (about five hours or fewer per night) can be as damaging as a single night of complete sleep deprivation.[10] And cumulative, partial sleep deprivation degrades overall working memory capacity, making it more difficult for you to hold information in your mind that you need for learning.[11]

Simple Strategy: Develop a Sleep Schedule

With a little practice, you can do your best to improve the amount and quality of your sleep. To get started:

1. **Be consistent.** Establish a consistent sleep schedule.

2. **Get the minimum.** Get at least five hours of sleep per night.

3. **Make it up.** If you fall short one night, make sure you prioritize sleep the next.

Nap to Boost Alertness

Taking a nap is one of life's little pleasures. Sometimes you set out to take a nap; other times, you find yourself nodding off when you are deeply relaxed. Regardless, napping seems to be a part of the human condition. But how do naps affect learning, and how might you harness them to help you learn more?

Well-timed naps deliver powerful results. A seven-to-ten-minute nap boosts alertness afterward, and both short and long naps can help your mind. Brief naps of just five to fifteen minutes provide a near-instant benefit that can last from one to three hours, while longer naps of more than thirty minutes can boost cognitive performance for several hours. Taking a full hour-long nap really speeds up your brain processing.[12] What if you need a nap but can't take one? In that case, at least take a rest break. Short breaks can serve as a countermeasure against poor performance.[13]

Simple Strategy: Nap to Learn

Get napping. Naps of all lengths help your mind, brain, and performance. To get started:

1. **Be alert.** If you are feeling drowsy, take a seven-minute nap to boost alertness.

2. **Boost your performance.** Take a brief nap (fifteen minutes) to increase your performance for up to three hours or an even longer nap (thirty to sixty minutes) to increase your performance for a longer period.

3. **Improve your memory.** Consider sandwiching a learning experience between two naps: one to increase your alertness and one to help your brain consolidate memory.

Use Sleep to Space Out Learning

Sleep is a function that breaks your life into separate days. For most people, going to bed marks the end of one day, and getting up marks the beginning of another. This cadence creates a structure by which things—work, school, interests—are naturally spaced out. What if it turned out that this spacing of time benefited your ability to learn?

Learning new skills is enhanced by the time that passes when you take breaks or space out things. However, learning skills that require conscious effort, like playing an instrument or sport, are enhanced not only by the very act of spacing learning but also by the amount of sleep you get *during* that time. Your performance improves between practice sessions when you separate the sessions with a good night's sleep.[14] Research also indicates that some skills, such as learning to discriminate among things, can be enhanced by being followed by a sixty-to-ninety-minute nap.[15] When you're learning something new, space it out with sleep.

Simple Strategy: Space Learning with Sleep

Sometimes, all you need to do to improve your learning is to space it out. To get started:

1. **Add sleep.** Incorporate periods of napping or sleep into your learning or practice schedule.

2. **Space learning.** If you are learning a new skill, space learning with several full nights of sleep.

3. **Nap in between.** If you are learning to discriminate among similar things, follow each with a brief nap.

Boost Memory During Sleep

Sleeping may seem like a time when you turn your senses off. Certainly, you limit particular senses, such as eyesight, by closing your lids, blocking out light, and using eye masks. But your senses don't stop. What if you could leverage your senses during sleep to help you learn or remember better?

Sleep helps your memories consolidate what you learned before you went to sleep. Memory processing during sleep may be boosted by stimulating the brain through sensory cues, such as pairing a specific smell with learning and then enabling that smell again during slow-wave sleep,[16] which lasts the first sixty to ninety minutes during the first hours of sleep.[17] This is related to the notion of pairing cues from the initial learning experience with later recall.[18] For example, if you are learning how to surf on vacation and then you go back to your hotel room, sleeping with the windows open so that you can smell the ocean might further stimulate your brain and enhance your abilities the next day.

Simple Strategy: Reactivate Your Memory

You can reactivate your memory by incorporating scents. To get started:

1. **Observe scents.** Take note of the scents that may be associated with a learning experience. For example, learning to swim may be associated with chlorine, learning to horseback ride may be associated with hay, and learning to cook may be associated with spices.

continued

2. **Incorporate real scents.** Consider creative ways to (safely) pair the smell that you associate with a learning experience with a nap or the beginning of a sleep routine. This may be as simple as napping with the windows open or as difficult as bringing a bit of the outside world into your napping environment. Just be careful not to use candles or other items that may be unsafe during sleep.

3. **Pair scents.** If a particular learning experience doesn't have any remarkable scents, consider introducing one subtly. For example, a bit of lavender oil on your shirt sleeve during an online course and a bit of the same lavender oil on your pillow when you sleep might just do the trick.

The Cumulative Effect

Have you ever enrolled in a course and expected—as anyone would—that you might begin to see improvement, yet you didn't? Your learning wasn't sticking, and worse yet, you felt tired, unalert, and depleted. That's where sleeping smartly and strategically comes in. Any of the strategies in this chapter can help you leverage sleep to learn more, but layering them together can help sleep become a critical aspect of your success.

Imagine that you finally decide to improve something that you've always felt bad at, like swimming, but it's slow going. Then your instructor mentions that you seem a bit tired—which is true—and suggests that you prioritize sleep. You realize, not surprisingly, how much a good night's sleep helps improve your performance. But as you tweak your sleep routine, you notice other improvements. When you learn right before you sleep, it tends to stick a bit more. And when you can't get a full night's sleep, a seven-to-ten-minute nap before your lessons helps quite a bit. On Saturdays you adopt a power technique: swimming in the morning, taking a sixty-to-ninety-minute nap later, and then mentally reviewing your techniques later in the day, a sequence which seems to really strengthen your abilities. You even try incorporating some subtle memory cues into your sleep, like ocean sounds, hoping that may give you a bit of an edge. Then one day you realize swimming isn't as daunting as you had expected. And you realize another hidden benefit: just how rested you have been feeling.

These aren't accidental choices—they're part of a deliberate plan intended to support your learning. This plan includes things like sleeping before and after learning, avoiding sleep deprivation, napping to boost alertness, using sleep to space out learning, and boosting memory during sleep. Pulling together strategies from multiple chapters can result in a more holistic, thoughtful way to approach your learning.

Take Action: Make Your Own Plan

Throughout this chapter, you discovered the critical role that sleep plays in cognition and learning. Sleep helps us remain alert during learning and helps our brains consolidate our experiences into long-term memory for later recall. Being deprived of sleep degrades our attention, decision-making, memory, and accuracy. Napping can correct this deficiency by speeding up brain processing and boosting alertness. Sleep also allows us to naturally space things out, which is one of the reasons sleeping may help us learn. By spacing learning out with a sixty-to-ninety-minute nap and triggering our brains with scents associated with learning, we can learn new skills more effectively.

Take a moment to reflect on your sleep habits and the role sleep plays in your performance. After contemplating the following questions, develop a simple plan to use sleep as a learning strategy and consider sharing it with someone who is supporting your learning. If you need more support, be sure to read Chapter 18 on building a robust learning network. For additional resources, visit www.already-smarter.com.

- How important is sleep to you? Do you have a solid sleep routine and get enough sleep each night?

- How do you think getting too little sleep affects your concentration, learning, and memory?

- How might taking a nap help you think, learn, and do more?

- How do you think sleeping in between practice sessions affects your ability to learn and remember new things?

- Do you think that you might be able to tap into your senses while you are sleeping?

CHAPTER 15

Engage Your Senses to Learn Deeply

W hen you are about to step into new territory to follow a dream, make a pivot in your life, or take an interest to the next level—like learning how to sail to join an ecotourist sailing crew—you might prioritize your mind, brain, and memory and give little thought to your senses. Yet many of us don't learn deeply because we only rely on our brains and don't recognize the power of our senses.

In my life, it took some time to recognize the value of using my senses, but when I finally did, it magnified my ability to learn. Perhaps because these are under-recognized as learning techniques, only one in ten people surveyed use these strategies in their normal learning process.[1] As a coach, I have worked with people to explore ways to engage their senses to learn deeply. In working with learners, I am often struck by how little attention we give to these powerful learning tools.

This chapter can help you learn using sensory-based learning strategies. It explores five evidence-based ways to "turn up" your learning power by engaging multiple senses. With practice, you might find yourself learning in a deeper, more immersive way as you incorporate sensory-rich approaches.

Before you begin this chapter, think about how your senses could help you learn more fully and help you achieve career and life goals.

- What are some of the ways you use your senses when you learn?

- Why might using your senses affect your learning performance?

- How might using your senses help you achieve some of your larger aspirations?

Find Positivity and Humor

Some days, positivity doesn't come naturally. It can be easy to see the glass as half empty or to find yourself entertaining worst-case scenarios. And when your mind goes to these darker thoughts, you may journey down a rabbit hole of bad news and worrisome thoughts. How do moods like these affect your ability to learn?

Your mood can influence how you feel, what you attend to, and how much you remember. In short, your mood either paves the way for learning—or stands in the way of it. Emotional information captures your attention, but which types of emotions capture attention in ways that enhance learning?[2]

When you are happy, your attention broadens to include more things—for example, you may notice many things in your surroundings.[3] Happy moods enable cognitive processes, such as memories and reasoning, whereas negative moods tend to inhibit these processes.[4] For example, sad music, compared to happy music, prompts more mind wandering.[5] And people who experience depression report less confidence in their performance.[6]

In general, it's best to prime yourself to have a happier mood, but there can be some risks. Positive moods may also open you up to being more gullible: falling for misleading information, uncritically accepting messages, and believing meaningless information.[7] If you are struggling with your mood, look for humor. Finding humor in things can improve your learning performance by attracting your attention, reducing anxiety, and decreasing stress hormones.[8] In this way, humor can be the antidote to negative feelings that impede learning.

Simple Strategy: Manage Your Mood

You can adjust your mood. To get started:

1. **Use gratitude.** To improve your mood, list five things for which you are grateful.

2. **Play music.** If you are feeling down, listen to a song or playlist that makes you happy.

3. **Smile.** Try simply smiling for a few minutes or recalling a joke or circumstance that made you laugh.

Inhale Strategically

Have you ever smelled something that instantly triggered a memory from your past? Maybe it's the smell of cookies baking, an ocean breeze, or a perfume that a relative used to wear. Smells can be deeply connected to your memories. How, then, can your sense of smell affect your learning?

Smells help with memory and learning. Your olfactory system, also known as your sense of smell, may play more of a role in your cognition than you realize. Respiration—the simple act of inhaling and exhaling—is connected to brain activity, mood, and cognition.[9] Research suggests that when people concentrate on tasks, nasal inhalation may increase brain activity and performance accuracy. In other words, the very act of inhaling purposefully may enhance your learning.[10]

Our senses of smell are closely associated with visual-spatial orientation—what we perceive around us—and our memories of these things.[11] This is because smell and spatial memory are connected to overlapping brain areas that affect one another.[12] What this means, for example, is that smelling pine trees, the ocean, or rain may help you understand your surroundings, place yourself within them, and recall them more vividly.

You can use this to your advantage in learning by enabling your own steady inhalations and triggering your sense of smell. For example, just smelling coffee has been shown to be a possible way to enhance several cognitive processes, such as the ability to hold attention, the quality and speed of memory formation, and sense of alertness.[13] Recent research from the University of California has shown that enriching the olfactory system with an odorant diffuser for just two hours each day improved cognition by a whopping 226 percent among older adults.[14]

Simple Strategy: Smell to Learn

You can use nasal inhalation and your sense of smell to enhance your awareness, learning, and memory. To get started:

1. **Observe smells.** Notice (or introduce) smells in the environments where you are learning.

2. **Inhale steadily.** Focus on steady inhalations while you are learning.

3. **Brew coffee.** Consider triggering cognition by smelling coffee or using a diffuser.

Focus on Facial Expressions

Facial expressions, including your own, may help you learn more. Have you ever noticed others (or even yourself) making expressions when doing something? Maybe you've seen people wrinkling their foreheads when reading a book or biting their lips when working out a tough problem. How might such expressions help you learn?

Facial expressions are more than involuntary muscle contractions; they help you concentrate and even learn. Exhibiting subtle negative facial microexpressions—such as squinting, furrowing the brows, or making a slight frown—through a learning experience is associated with a higher likelihood of learning for those who already have some prior knowledge.[15]

Interestingly, one of the most valuable expressions may be frowning. Frowning seems to enable sustained attention.[16] If you are trying to learn something more complex, it may be a good idea to put on a "learning face." Such expressions seem to generalize across tasks that require different types of problem-solving, decision-making, and learning.[17]

But what about the expressions of those who are instructing or tutoring us? People perform better when their tutor's facial expressions match the content.[18] For example, if a tutor is emphasizing something sad, scary, or funny, adopting the appropriate facial expression helps their students learn.

Simple Strategy: Express More to Learn More

You can consciously adjust your expressions to help you learn more. To get started:

1. **Find expressive people.** If you choose a tutor, find one who is expressive or emotive.

2. **Change your expression.** When you are learning, adopt a learning expression.

3. **Frown.** Maintain a slight frown to better focus your attention.

Use Gestures to Grasp Meaning

When someone is teaching you something new, do you pay attention to their gestures? Maybe they're showing you how to make a recipe, play a sport, or create something, using their hands to imitate a shape, simulate a motion, or point something out. These gestures are probably helping you much more than you realize. Could gestures be the secret to learning new things, such as languages?

There are two types of gestures: *deictic* and *iconic*. Deictic gestures draw our attention to a specific person, place, or thing by pointing, nodding, or gesturing toward it. Iconic gestures help us understand meaning based on their similarity to an action, such as using your hand to simulate typing on a phone and saying, "I'll text you later" or pretending to type on a keyboard when talking about writing. The gestures can help everyone—but they are especially helpful for people who are learning new languages by enabling longer retention of both information and actions.[19] By attending to these gestures, we learn more. This may sound intuitive, but it indicates the importance of focusing on the people who are helping us learn.

And the benefits go beyond just watching people gesture; they can carry over to simulated or technology-based instruction. When learners interact with pedagogical agents such as avatars, gestures, and facial expressions make them appear more humanlike and increase learning outcomes.[20] And in video lectures, the instructor's pointing improved learners' performance more than other types of cues.[21] Imitating these types of gestures while learning can be helpful, too. Imitating gestures that teachers make improves long-term recall of the material.[22]

Simple Strategy: Just Gesture

You can incorporate gestures into your learning experiences, or pay better attention to other people's gestures, to learn more effectively. To get started:

1. **Observe gestures.** Pay attention to the gestures that your instructors, your tutors, or other experts make.

2. **Imitate gestures.** When you can, imitate meaningful gestures in real time or later.

3. **Add gestures.** When you study on your own, add gestures, such as pointing to relevant pieces of information in a diagram or passage.

Make Eye Contact for Better Recall

Next time someone is teaching you something, pay closer attention to their eyes. Are they looking at you? Are they looking at what they are doing? For sighted teachers, chances are that they are doing both, although you may not have consciously noticed. How might this be subtly affecting your ability to focus on and remember what they are teaching you?

A little bit of eye contact can go a long way. Watching people's eyes improves your emotional connection, interest, and reaction.[23] Receiving direct eye contact from an instructor seems to improve learning and subsequent recall. However, observing eye contact exchanged *among others* may actually decrease recall. Eye contact seems to target to the intended recipient of the message, boosting memory for that person while potentially decreasing performance for those who are excluded.[24]

The benefits of eye contact even hold true online and over video. Learning is enhanced (on video) by the instructor's presence, including their real-time drawing and direct eye contact.[25] For example, learners benefited from watching video lectures that enabled them to observe where the instructor was looking on a recorded slide presentation.[26]

Simple Strategy: Look 'Em in the Eye

If you're sighted, you can use eye contact to enable your learning. To get started:

1. **Make eye contact.** Position yourself somewhere where whoever is teaching can easily make eye contact.

2. **Find faces.** If you are learning remotely, use resources, such as live webcasts or recorded videos, that show the instructor's face and eyes rather than text or voice alone.

3. **Be aware.** If an instructor or tutor is making eye contact with others, but not you, compensate by incorporating other learning strategies into your experience.

The Cumulative Effect

Have you ever found yourself well into a learning experience, but you just didn't feel like you were getting all that much from it? You may have wondered, *is there something I'm doing wrong?* That's where engaging your senses to learn deeply comes in. While each technique in this chapter can help you to engage your senses, their combined use may turn your senses into a superpower.

Imagine that you've been invited to join something that you want to prepare for, like a sailing excursion, but your sailing class doesn't seem to be improving your skill. You realize that you can't always see the instructor, and you make sure you're positioned near enough to him that you can see his expressions and gestures, which helps you notice certain information. Observing where he looks, like at equipment or instruments, helps you learn. You remember that when you're happy, you're more focused, more confident, and less stressed. So when you are reading about sailing and watching videos of techniques, you do so in environments, like coffeehouses, that boost your mood and have scents that enhance attention and memory. And when you're on the water, you inhale through your nose to improve your focus and accuracy. Suddenly, you think sailing doesn't seem so hard—and neither does learning (when you know how to use your senses).

These choices aren't scattershot—they're part of a thoughtful plan intended to support your learning. This plan includes things like finding positivity and humor, inhaling strategically, focusing on facial expressions, using gestures to grasp meaning, and making eye contact for better recall. When these strategies are combined with others from this book they can multiply, each building upon the others in complementary ways.

Take Action: Make Your Own Plan

In this chapter, you learned how your senses, emotions, and body language can help you learn. Feeling happy or more positive expands attention and clears thinking, and a bit of humor allows for better focus and reduces stress. Breathing and smelling improve brain activity and allow for better understanding and remembering what was learned. Observing and making expressions help us better understand what we or others are doing. Monitoring and mimicking gestures help us learn techniques and procedures. And maintaining eye contact improves comprehension and recall. Engaging in learning opportunities that are positive, supported by scents, and taught by expressive instructors who encourage you to mimic their gestures and see their eyes all help make learning more effective.

Take a moment to reflect on your emotions, senses, and expressions. After contemplating the following questions, develop a simple plan to engage your senses for deeper learning and consider sharing it with someone who is supporting your learning. If you need more support, be sure to read Chapter 18 on building a robust learning network. For additional resources, visit www.already-smarter.com.

- How have your emotions affected your ability to concentrate, think, and remember?

- Do you associate smells with specific times, places, and events?

- How might your facial expressions—or those of others—may be helping your performance?

- Do gestures help you learn? How could you use gestures to improve your learning?

- Does making eye contact or following people's eyes help you learn?

CHAPTER 16

Automate Your Success with Smart Habits

Imagine that you are standing on the threshold of a big dream—maybe achieving a savings goal so you can take a break and travel the world—but this hinges on learning how to save, and saving in ways that become *automatic*. In this case, your big dream may actually be undermined by some other habits: spending too much money shopping online, eating out, or paying for subscriptions that you don't even use. Yet many of us learn more slowly because we are unaware that learning is competing with other deeply ingrained habits.

As a learner, I used to let my bad habits—watching television, snacking, checking my phone—interrupt my big dreams. And I'm not alone; when asked, the majority of those surveyed said they would like to build better habits.[1] In my coaching practice, I have worked with people to explore ways to replace bad habits with smart habits. Many clients are surprised to find that modifying a few habits can go a long way toward improving their learning.

This chapter can help you examine ways to modify, replace, or foster habits that support learning. It introduces five well-supported strategies that may help strengthen your learning process and support your goals. With the right strategies, you might find yourself feeling more intentional and successful as you develop habits that align with your larger ambitions.

Before you begin this chapter, think about how modifying old habits and building new ones could help you improve your learning and ultimately contribute to other life goals.

- What are some of the ways you have tried modifying or building habits—have they worked?
- Why might smart habits affect your learning performance?
- How might smart habits affect your larger life and big dreams?

Build Learning Habits

Some of the things you seek to learn are about starting new behaviors: learning to meditate and continuing the practice every morning, learning to swim and going to the pool after work, or learning Mandarin and practicing it daily. This type of learning requires you to not only make learning itself habitual but to make *what you are learning* habitual. How can you make learning so habitual that it becomes automatic?

Habits are surprisingly complex behaviors. To the person performing them, habits just feel like normal, everyday behaviors. However, there are six unique attributes of behaviors that become habits. They start with a goal, are triggered by an event, are developed through repetition, become automatic, are reinforced, and take time.[2]

The best way to form a habit, according to researchers, is to address each of the attributes:[3]

- Develop a conscious goal or intention.

- Piggyback your goal onto a regular event that is already automatic (for example, studying while you have your morning coffee).

- Repeat them every day.

- Evaluate how automatic behaviors affect you by asking, *How is this helping me?*

- Reinforce the habit by introducing positive rewards, such as praise, self-praise, or following it with an enjoyable activity.

- Be consistent over time for eighteen days to thirty-six weeks.

If you can follow most—or better yet, all—of these six steps, you'll develop new habits in no time.

Simple Strategy: Change Your Habits

If you want to, you can change or adopt any habit. To get started:

1. **Set goals.** Align new habits with broader goals, interests, and purposes.

2. **Make time.** Build learning habits into your schedule or attach them to things you already do (for example, learning

continued

for forty-five minutes every morning or while having your morning coffee instead of reading the news).

3. **Find support.** Work with others who are trying to adopt or change the same habit and celebrate as you make progress.

Trigger Habits with Minimal Effort

Habits are routine behaviors that can be hard to break and easy to trigger. Triggers spark a behavior or response without requiring much thought, intention, or control. Habits are triggered automatically, almost like impulses. Smelling cigarette smoke may tempt you to pick up a cigarette if you are a former smoker, tasting a dessert may pull you off a diet, and opening a textbook may prompt you to begin highlighting text.

How can incorporating triggers help you adopt new habits? Developing a new habit requires consciously initiating actions by developing new triggers. Over time, these deliberate actions can become automatic.[4] Think about all the triggers that perpetuate habits in your life. Take, for example, a coffee habit: It may be triggered by time of day, smell of coffee, feeling tired, sight of a coffee shop, or any number of other elements. You can make your learning strategies into habits, too, by connecting them with triggers. For instance, simply picking up a book could trigger you to begin taking notes. Before long, you may begin repeating new learning behaviors automatically.

Simple Strategy: Use Triggers

Building triggers into your habit-formation routine can begin to make habits automatic. To get started:

1. **Establish new triggers.** Consider the best triggers for a new habit. What do you do daily that might "prompt" you to begin or make it easier to begin?

2. **Piggyback habits.** Is there something you already do that you could "piggyback" the new habit on top of? For example, if you take a daily walk, could you use this time to reflect on your progress toward a goal?

3. **Remove old triggers.** Consider removing triggers that may impede the development of your new habit. Are there things that trigger you to do things that are counterproductive to your new habit that you can remove from your life or day-to-day environment?

Consider How Environment Triggers Habits

You are, in many ways, a product of your environment. Your hobbies and habits are often directly related to the place where you live and the environment you live in. This may complicate your ability to adopt new habits and change existing habits. How can you modify your environment to introduce new habits and learn new ways of being?

You may have more luck instituting a new habit if you change your environment to better suit it.[5] When it comes to your immediate environment—say, your workplace or a specific room in your home—this may mean adding things that help you learn or removing things that hinder your learning. However, these changes may go beyond your immediate environment into the places within your community, neighborhood, or city. Swap out a bar for a coffee shop, a noisy café for a library, or change your route to work to begin to associate your life with the things you need for inspiration or motivation.

For example, let's say you're trying to learn how to rock climb but find that you rarely take the time to practice. If you habitually stop by a bar on your drive home from work for happy hour with your colleagues, you may change the route to take you by a location that may benefit your learning—a rock gym, a bouldering wall, or a recreational center. These sorts of locations may trigger habits you are trying to build or help you stop unwanted or unproductive habits.

Simple Strategy:
Modify Your Environment

While adopting or changing habits may seem overwhelming, modifying your environment may be one concrete step you can take to make progress. To get started:

1. **Change environments.** Consider changing your home or study environment. How can the space in which you live, work, and study help you eliminate bad habits and start good habits?

2. **Change spaces.** Consider changing your use of public or community spaces. Are there public spaces that trigger bad habits or that might help cultivate new habits?

3. **Change routes.** Consider changing your route or path. How you get to work, school, or other locations may trigger habits. How might you adopt new habits if you altered the way you move around in your community?

Swap One Habit for Another

Do you have an old habit that you'd like to eliminate? Or is there something you do that may be taking time away from your goals? Maybe you find yourself spending too much time on social media, streaming services, or gaming. What if you could use this time to advance your life, career, or personal goals?

Don't just try to add new habits; also try swapping out old habits for new ones. In fact, one common way to transform old, undesirable habits into new ones is to identify the cue that triggers the habit you are unhappy with and replace the old, undesirable response with a new, positive one.[6] This may sound simple, but there are two key challenges: accurately identifying all of the triggers that prompt the undesired behavior and consistently changing your response over time. For example, if seeing your phone triggers you to check social media, you might replace that behavior with watching a short YouTube video that supports your learning. Then, bit by bit, begin minimizing the time spent on social media and expanding the time you spend learning.

Simple Strategy: Substitute a New Habit for an Old One

You can swap old habits for new ones. To get started:

1. **Decide what to stop.** Select something that you want to stop doing. This may be something that takes up too much of your time each week.

2. **Identify prompts.** Consider what triggers that habit and prompts you to do it.

continued

3. **Establish replacements.** Find replacement habits that are similar enough that they may have common triggers: reading on the couch instead of watching TV on the couch, or surfing YouTube on a learning topic rather than surfing social media.

Form a Habit in Just Days (or Weeks)

The key to habit formation is perseverance over time. You may have tried adopting habits in the past, only to lose your resolve after a few days or weeks. Maybe you lost interest, motivation, or just plain stick-to-itiveness. All too often, new habits go by the wayside before they become entrenched in our lives. How long does it take for a new habit to stick?

Researchers wanted to investigate how habits are formed in everyday life. They began recording the activity of ninety-six volunteers. Each volunteer chose an eating, drinking, or other behavior to carry out daily. They found that the time it took for the task to become a habit ranged from 18 to 254 days (or about thirty-six weeks). This research indicated that forming a habit varies considerably among people and among tasks. One of the keys to changing habits, therefore, is simply sticking with a new behavior, which means that some things may take a bit longer to "stick" than you might like.[7]

Simple Strategy: Be Patient

Don't get discouraged if a new habit takes time to form. It *will* form if you stick with it. To get started:

1. **Set a sprint**. Plan new habits in eighteen-day sprints.

2. **Check progress**. After eighteen days, analyze your progress and ask yourself how you can improve. Each sprint will get easier.

3. **Stick with it**. Keep your long-term goals in mind, and don't fret if it takes the better part of a year to form the new habit: It will happen.

The Cumulative Effect

Have you ever wanted to learn or do something healthy that would become completely habitual, yet you found that some of your unproductive habits kept creeping back in, undermining the new ones you wanted to create? That's where automating your success with smart habits comes in. You might start with just one habit formation technique, but using multiple strategies together can cement powerful new habits.

Imagine that you want to learn something that will become habitual, like managing your finances, but some of your current habits get in the way. First, you set out to understand how habits are formed: by setting a clear goal, finding a reliable trigger, repeating the habit often, reflecting on its benefits, reinforcing it, and staying consistent. Then you link your new habit to something you already do, like listening to a financial podcast on your morning commute. You realize that your frequent happy hours are working against your financial goal, so you replace them with trips to the gym, where you can watch videos about the day's economic news while on the treadmill. This helps you to save money while you contemplate strategies for investing it. And when you backslide, you remember that new habits take time—and become easier once you see the benefits. Before long, you find that you haven't just built a financial habit, you've also learned how to build and swap habits, which will benefit many of your future goals.

These aren't random choices strung together by chance—they're part of a purposeful plan intended to support your learning. This plan includes things like building learning habits, triggering habits with minimal effort, considering how environments trigger habits, swapping one habit for another, and forming a habit in a few days or weeks. Now you can consider making your learning journey even more powerful by adding tools from other chapters to further produce a strong cumulative effect.

Take Action: Make Your Own Plan

This chapter tackled the complicated topic of modifying habits—things you do automatically. There are six things needed to form a habit: developing a goal, triggering the habit, repeating the habit often, reflecting on the benefit of the habit, reinforcing it, and remaining consistent. We can use triggers to establish new habits if we find things to piggyback a habit onto and eliminate old habits by changing our environments. We can also trade one habit for another by making old triggers ignite new habits. Despite what you may have heard, there is no magic amount of time to form a habit. In general, it takes anywhere from eighteen days to thirty-six weeks.

Take a moment to reflect on how you might make learning a lifelong habit that comes naturally. After contemplating the following questions, develop a simple plan to automate your success with smart habits and consider sharing it with someone who is supporting your learning. If you need more support, be sure to read Chapter 18 on building a robust learning network. For additional resources, visit www.already-smarter.com.

- What bad habits you could replace with a learning habit?

- How might incorporating triggers help you adopt new learning habits?

- How might you change your environment to make learning more of a habit?

- Are there things in your life that you would like to stop doing to begin making space for other things?

- How long do you usually need to do something before it becomes automatic?

PART V

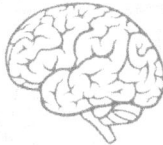

Resolve to Evolve

L
earning takes resolve and ongoing improvement. Once you've come to believe in yourself, set your intention, actively engaged in learning, and used your body to further optimize your learning, it may seem like there's nothing left to do. Unfortunately, that's not how learning works. More often than not, you need to continue to improve your learning strategies, adopt new technologies, and lead others on their learning journeys. This willingness to change and adapt is at the very heart of the learning process.

The fifth and final part of this book is about continuing to evolve your learning mindset and skills. This part includes four chapters focused on amplifying your learning, enlisting the support of others, embracing future technologies, and championing learning for others. These chapters will help you fine-tune and improve your approach to learning. By adopting more learning practices, building a community of practice, using emerging technologies, and becoming a learning leader, you can continue to improve your learning and better support other learners.

CHAPTER 17

Maximize Your Learning

I n life, there are a few traits we possess that may give us an advantage, such as a sense of humor, ability to empathize, or quick reaction time. Yet we forget that we have these superpowers when we begin learning something new. Better yet, there are a handful of learning techniques that similarly provide us with an advantage.

Many of us don't know how to fine-tune and maximize our learning with these specific techniques. If you are like me, you may have heard about them and then dismissed them, favoring familiar techniques that may be less effective. In my experience as a coach, I have consulted with people who are keen to explore ways to adopt techniques that fine-tune their learning. Sometimes adopting just one or two targeted learning strategies can make a big difference.

This chapter can help you fine-tune your learning and accelerate your success. It explores seven evidence-based ways to elevate your learning practice and accelerate your success. With the right techniques, you might find yourself reaching new levels of growth as you maximize the return on your learning efforts.

Before you begin this chapter, think about how a few specialized techniques might help you boost your learning as well as a few important goals.

- What are some of the learning tricks or techniques you have tried—did they work?
- Why might a few specialized techniques fine-tune your learning performance?
- How might one or two favorite techniques help you achieve some of your career or personal goals?

Take Notes the Right Way

If there is one thing that you've probably already done to enhance your learning, it's taking notes. Taking notes has long been one of the most tried-and-true ways to support learning. But does note-taking work, or is it just a waste of time and paper? The very act of writing down notes (not to mention later referencing them) can help with memory formation. Writing and drawing by hand activate certain regions of the brain that are important for memory and encoding new information.[1]

While it may be tempting to type your notes on your laptop, you might want to think again. While typed notes may be beneficial for organization, accessibility, and even speed, they may not be the best for learning. Research shows that handwritten note-taking is often more effective than electronic note-taking.[2] In general, researchers found that people who take handwritten notes remember more than people who type their notes.[3]

The only thing that may be better than handwritten notes is hand-drawn sketches. Researchers found that when you draw, the brain exhibits neuronal activity that is conducive to learning and that taking traditional notes, combined with visualizations such as sketches, symbols, or simple diagrams, facilitates learning.[4]

Simple Strategy: Take Effective Notes

Taking notes is one of the simplest things you can do to facilitate learning. To get started:

1. **Be strategic.** Consider the best way to take notes for a specific learning experience. Is there a document you might add your notes to, such as a printed guide? Or would you prefer to take notes using a laptop? In some circumstances, for example, doing something experiential, you might prefer to use your phone and associate your notes with photos. Before a learning experience begins, decide exactly how you will capture notes.

2. **Add symbols.** Incorporate drawings, diagrams, or meaningful symbols into your note-taking.

3. **Review your notes.** Immediately after the learning experience, review your notes and make sure that they still make sense, and make modifications or corrections as needed. Then go back and review them periodically to refresh your memory.

Map Out Concepts

Have you ever made a pros and cons list? Or produced a map that shows where one place is relative to another? Maybe you have created a shopping list with items grouped by the stores you need to purchase them from. If so, you've used *concept maps*, which are visuals or diagrams that show how concepts are related. Concept maps help you clarify relationships and organize your ideas. How can you use these types of maps to help you learn?

Developing and using concept maps supports learning regardless of the discipline or subject that you are trying to learn.[5] This means that they are effective no matter if you are learning to fish, learning to fly, or learning to write. However, *creating* your own maps provides a greater benefit than simply studying maps made by someone else.[6] Start your concept maps from scratch and make them meaningful to you.

Concept maps can take many forms: tables, flowcharts, timelines, or visuals that show categories, ways to solve a problem, steps in a process, or connections among things. Crime series often show the ultimate concept map: an entire wall with photos, clippings, and maps that help detectives piece together the relationships among various aspects of a crime.

Simple Strategy: Create a Concept Map

Anyone can create a concept map. It's simply a diagram that shows how you believe the concepts are related. To get started:

1. **Develop a map.** As soon as you start learning something new, begin to develop a concept map that indicates relationships among important concepts.

2. **Use tools.** Consider using a whiteboard or sticky notes so that you can easily modify concept connections as you learn more.

3. **Incorporate color.** Use colors to indicate specific types of connections. For example, black lines might signal direct connections, and red lines might convey indirect connections.

Work Through Examples

If you're trying to do something new—bake a cake, repair a leaky tire, or do a home repair project—have you ever searched online for a video that walks you through it? If so, you've looked for something that researchers call a *worked example*. Worked examples help you understand the steps needed to solve a problem.

By studying examples, you can learn procedures and anticipate errors. Worked examples show exactly how a problem is solved, similar to an online recipe that goes step-by-step. Worked examples may have a learning advantage over other types of problem-solving, especially for novice learners who benefit from seeing direct examples by others.

Worked examples help with one very important aspect of learning: error anticipation. This important skill enables learners to anticipate errors before they make them.[7] The benefits for worked examples don't seem to be equal for all steps in the problem-solving process, though. They tend to be most valuable for the most difficult steps. So if you don't have time to review or perform the "entire" example, at least focus on the hardest part.[8]

Simple Strategy:
Work Through Worked Examples

We can all leverage worked examples to learn more and to learn more *quickly*. To get started:

continued

1. **Find an example.** When you are learning something new, try to find a step-by-step worked example of how to do it. Worked examples are easy to find on the internet, but be sure to find one that is high quality and accurate.

2. **Make an example.** If you cannot find a worked example, but you know an expert or more skilled peer, ask them to make one. Better yet, consider making one yourself with their supervision.

3. **Focus on difficulty.** Focus your attention on the most difficult steps in the process or the steps that continue to trip you up.

Explain Things to Yourself

Do you talk to yourself? Perhaps you have found yourself trying to make sense of something by explaining it to yourself in your head. This self-talk is similar to what researchers call a *self-explanation*. How can you use self-talk to help you think things through and learn more?

Self-explanation is, just like it sounds, explaining something to yourself. Simple as that may seem, it is powerful to consider how one thing may be related to another, or a way to paraphrase something complex, predict a hypothesis, or summarize a procedure. Explaining things aloud helps form new associations and clarify relationships. And using self-explanation techniques during learning and problem-solving has been shown to improve performance.[9]

There is a learning advantage to explaining things to yourself rather than relying solely on expert explanations. By doing so, you're retrieving prior information from memory and elaborating on it with new information, thereby forming new associations and meaning.[10] Just make sure that your self-explanation is, of course, correct. And if your explanation is incorrect, make sure to work on it until you can restate it accurately.

Simple Strategy: Explain Things to Yourself

Self-explanations are easy ways to contemplate and reinforce concepts. To get started:

1. **Explain aloud.** When you learn something new, take time to explain it to yourself as though you were explaining it out loud to someone else.

2. **Make it short.** Practice your explanation until it is short and concise. Think about it as an elevator speech: How might you explain something in a single sentence?

3. **Elaborate.** Ask yourself to elaborate on one element of your explanation: "What's the most important thing about this?" or "What's the most commonly misunderstood aspect?"

Journal for Learning

Writing about things will help you clarify your thinking. If you've ever had a journal or diary, you may have noticed that the very act of writing things down can help you sort out your thoughts, understand your feelings, and make decisions. When you use writing to help you learn, it's called *writing to learn*. Writing to learn is a process by which learners use writing as a tool to learn various subjects, such as health care, business, and hobbies. How exactly does writing help you learn?

Writing to learn enables you to focus on what you believe you know, what you are learning, and how you can improve. It is not meant to be polished, high-stakes writing; rather, it is intended to help you think through your understanding of new concepts, connections, or relationships. Even writing a simple summary, for example, enhances comprehension.[11] Researchers at Arizona State University and the University of Utah reviewed fifty-six studies on the effects of learning across subjects as diverse as science, social studies, and math—subjects you don't necessarily associate with writing. What did they find? Writing enhances learning in every subject. They also found that this holds true across grades and ages.[12] Importantly, writing to learn is different from note-taking. When you write to learn, you are focusing on improving your understanding of a concept. When you take notes, your goal is simply to record information as accurately as possible.

Simple Strategy: Write to Learn

Even if you consider yourself a bad writer or if you don't like writing, you can still benefit from writing to learn. It's a simple process that anyone can adopt to help learn something new or difficult or to improve performance. To get started:

1. **Consider what you already know.** Take a few minutes to write down what you already know about a subject or skill as well as things you would like to know more about.

2. **Summarize what you learned.** This can be a few short sentences or phrases listing or summarizing main points, ideas, concepts, or techniques. Jot down how this relates to your

prior knowledge, program of study, or career. How are these learnings relevant, and why are they important?

3. **Reflect on areas to improve.** State what you need to learn or improve—or what might be most confusing. Be as clear as possible about areas for improvement, gaps in your understanding, or perceived deficiencies. Indicate how you will go about doing this learning or improvement. Write down what you will read or review, whom you may ask for help, and other strategies you may use—such as devising a practice routine, soliciting feedback, or finding a peer tutor.

Lean In to Testing

Tests often evoke feelings of stress and anxiety. They may conjure up stressful images of silently taking a written test or working through an important timed assessment. Or for many of us, the memory of seeing a poor grade after a much-dreaded exam. But what if you found out that the very process of taking tests was good for your memory and learning?

Tests do not simply check learning; they promote it. According to Peter C. Brown, Henry Roediger, and Mark McDaniel, authors of *Make It Stick: The Science of Successful Learning*, "One of the most striking research findings is the power of active retrieval—testing—to strengthen memory, and that the more effortful the retrieval, the stronger the benefit."[13] They write: "The act of retrieving learning from memory has two profound benefits. One, it tells you what you know and don't know, and therefore where to focus further study to improve the areas where you're weak. Two, recalling what you have learned causes your brain to reconsolidate the memory, which strengthens its connections to what you already know and makes it easier for you to recall in the future."[14] Testing, it turns out, is a powerful way to learn.

The *testing effect* is the learning benefit that comes from testing. Tests force you to retrieve information from your memories, and this process strengthens the memory of that information.[15] In short, retesting yourself on previously studied information enhances your long-term memory.[16] This may be why practice tests are more beneficial for learning than studying or restudying information.[17] Testing helps support learning regardless of whether the testing involves a blocked design (testing one area of knowledge or skill repeatedly) or a mixed design (testing a variety of knowledge and skills).[18] And getting feedback after you take a test can further enhance the beneficial effects.[19]

The act of *pretesting*—taking a test before you begin learning something new—makes learning more effective.[20] It's an even better way to direct your focus than reviewing learning objectives.[21] Pretests can help you direct your focus to what matters most. Sometimes, taking a pretest enables you to identify your misconceptions. Everyone has misconceptions about the world: how it works, how people interact with it, how it changes, and the reasons behind those changes. These misunderstandings are personal notions everyone creates to make meaning of their surroundings. Often, these misunderstandings go unchallenged for a lifetime.[22] By taking a pretest, you can identify the misconceptions and then begin to correct them as you learn more.

Tests needn't always be given by an authority. Self-assessment, which involves taking a test and evaluating your performance, boosts self-regulation (your ability to manage your learning) and self-efficacy (your confidence in your ability).[23] In fact, learners who graded themselves performed better on later tests than those who did not.[24]

Similarly, *peer assessment* is a process whereby learners rely on themselves instead of an expert. In some cases, it may be better than teacher assessment and about as effective as self-assessment.[25] Peer assessment is effective if peers receive training on how to rate or grade assessments[26] and tends to be more effective under certain conditions: in nonmedical/nonclinical subjects; with more self-directed adult learners, such as graduate students; when the work being assessed is individual work as opposed to group work; when learners voluntarily choose to be assessed by peers and know who their assessor is; and when peer evaluators provide both scores and written comments.[27]

Simple Strategy: Test Early and Often

Even if the idea of tests gives you anxiety, you can benefit from taking them. Think of testing as a way to strengthen your memory and learning, just like strengthening a muscle. To get started:

1. **Take a pretest.** If you are about to learn something new, find and take a pretest. If you cannot find a pretest (or a quiz that could function as a pretest), make one of your own by asking yourself three to five questions about what you are going to be studying or doing.

2. **Test yourself.** You can incorporate self-assessment by quizzing yourself after any learning activity. Before you quiz yourself, list the criteria or qualities that you would expect in a good learning performance: accuracy, timeliness, and confidence. Then give yourself points for each of these.

continued

Determine what you could have done more effectively, and make specific notes for your next attempt.

3. **Ask someone to test you.** Find someone to assess you—ideally a fellow learner or someone with knowledge of the subject. Ask this person to consider how they will rate or grade the test. If they are making a rating based on their judgment, work with them to develop criteria for what success looks like. Ask them to provide a score as well as written comments—and then to discuss both the score and the comments with you.

Ask for Feedback

Feedback is at the heart of self-improvement. One of the most important aspects of tests is the feedback that they provide. The feedback you get from tests is far more specific than the more general feedback you may get in other learning contexts. It is feedback that tells you *exactly* what you did right, what you did wrong, and what you need to do better. But does feedback make a difference in your learning performance?

Over the years, numerous researchers have studied feedback. They have found that the focus, specificity, timing, and nature of the feedback all matter.

- **Focus.** Feedback should relate directly to the learning goal and not focus on the "self" but on the process or task.[28] For example, feedback on your running time, not your overall athletic ability, is much more valuable.

- **Specificity.** The feedback given to you should be as specific as possible—clear, meaningful, and actionable—not generic or vague.[29] For example, it's better to hear that you need to lose two minutes on your total running time than simply hearing that you should run faster.

- **Timing.** According to researchers, there are two times to seek feedback: during a process and at the end.[30] For example, imagine that you're trying to improve your running to prepare for a race. You would need feedback on your stride while you were running as well as feedback on your timing when your practice run is over.

- **Nature.** Whether the feedback is positive or negative can make a difference. It all depends on whether you *want* to do something or *must* do something. If you are learning something that you are already motivated to learn, then positive feedback may be rewarding. But if you are learning something that you are unmotivated to learn, then negative feedback may make you avoid the task for fear that you are bad at it.[31] It's important to keep this in mind when you request and receive feedback.

In general, negative feedback does no more damage to your intrinsic motivation than neutral feedback or no feedback at all. However, compared to positive feedback, negative feedback decreases your intrinsic motivation. Negative feedback is more motivating when it includes guidance on how to improve and is delivered in person. Thus, when you do receive negative feedback, seek out details and try to receive it in person.[32]

Simple Strategy: Get Meaningful Feedback

Even if your instructor doesn't provide you with good feedback, you can get enough feedback to help you improve. To get started:

1. **Find an expert.** The more expertise someone has, the better the feedback they will be able to give you.

2. **Request an evaluation.** Ask her or him to evaluate you during and after a task. It's tempting to ask an expert to review just the final product, such as a painting, photograph, or cake, but it's important to ask them to evaluate the process as well as the product.

3. **Request specifics.** If any of the feedback is negative, ask for more specifics about how you might improve.

The Cumulative Effect

Have you ever found yourself learning something new, and it's going okay, but you want to do even better? That's where maximizing your learning through a series of strategic tweaks comes in. Though you can apply each of these techniques separately, the strategies in this chapter can propel your learning forward when combined.

Imagine you've started to pick up something you saw in a spy thriller, like ethical hacking, but you know you can do better. At first, you thought that learning would happen exclusively on your laptop, like searching for worked examples and shortcuts, but then you realize that there are numerous other strategies that happen offline. As you learn new things, you take handwritten notes, produce sketches, and create concept maps to boost your understanding and connect your ideas. You explain ideas to yourself, talking out loud as you work through things, and journal to clarify what you are learning and where you are getting stuck. And you seek feedback from other people—from colleagues and classmates to experienced friends. You find that your abilities improve rapidly and that your well-rounded approach to learning is spilling over into other subjects and accelerating other parts of your career. Eventually, you consider yourself a "learning spy" who is well-equipped to find sneaky ways to maximize learning in every opportunity in your life.

The strategies highlighted in this chapter aren't haphazard—they're part of a measured plan intended to support your learning. This plan includes things like taking notes the right way, mapping out concepts, working through examples, explaining things to yourself, journaling for learning, leaning into testing, and asking for feedback. The effect of using several of these strategies together is often greater than using them alone—and combining them with strategies in other chapters can lead to even better success.

Take Action: Make Your Own Plan

In this chapter, you learned about several strategies that can help amplify learning. These include taking notes, developing concept maps, following worked examples, providing self-explanations, and writing to learn, as well as employing a variety of assessment and feedback techniques. Any one of these can help us learn a little, but combining several of them can help us learn a lot. Just incorporate these tools into your learning toolbox to optimize your learning.

Take a moment to reflect on how you might improve the ways in which you learn. After contemplating the following questions, develop a simple plan to maximize your learning with powerful strategies and consider sharing it with someone who is supporting your learning. If you need more support, be sure to read Chapter 18 on building a robust learning network. For additional resources, visit www.already-smarter.com.

- How might you take notes in ways that support your learning?

- How might producing visual maps help you understand, remember, and learn?

- How might studying an example help you visualize, learn, or remember something?

- Do you ever find yourself trying to explain things to yourself, talking yourself through things, or thinking out loud? How can you make this more effective?

- How might writing or journaling help you sort out your thoughts, remember things, or learn?

- How might you "lean into" different types of testing to learn more and solicit feedback from others?

CHAPTER 18

Build a Robust Learning Network

As you tackle some of your biggest ideas—like summiting some of the world's biggest mountains—you may need one thing: support from others. The bigger the goal, the bigger the network needed to achieve it—and the more important it becomes to participate in new communities. Yet many of us fail to achieve these big dreams because we slog along, underinvested in learning networks or communities that could support us and nurture our growth.

This is a lesson I came to a bit late in life, not realizing the power of building my own learning community made up of a diverse array of helpers. I was surprised to learn how few people regularly established connections to further their learning: only four in one hundred reported doing so.[1] In my experience as a learning and leadership coach, I have worked with people to explore ways to overcome their

"I'm going to do it on my own" mentality and to build their very own learning networks to help them achieve their goals. Building a robust network of people who can help us learn can be one of the most important (and rewarding) ways to go about learning something new.

This chapter can help you identify the types of people who may play a key role in your learning journey—from friends to tutors to mentors. It introduces valuable ways of connecting that may provide significant support for your learning and life goals. With a few strong connections, you might find yourself shifting from learning alone to feeling supported by your learning network.

Before you begin this chapter, think about how your learning network could help you achieve a learning goal and some important career or life goals.

- What types of people might you include in your learning network?

- Why might having a carefully established learning network affect your learning performance?

- How might having a robust learning network help you achieve some of your larger aspirations?

Seek Encouragement

Encouragement can be a very motivating thing to receive. Most people enjoy being told that they are doing good work, making good progress, or otherwise on the right track. Sometimes, a little encouragement can turn an otherwise bad day into a good one. But when it comes to learning, how much of a difference does encouragement actually make?

Around the world, studies have confirmed that encouragement—whether from family or instructors—improves learning performance. Researchers in Thailand examined the relationship between learners' perceived parental encouragement and academic performance, finding that students' perceptions of encouragement were directly related to their academic performance.[2] Researchers in India studied 120 learners and found that encouragement was positively related to academic achievement regardless of what the learners were studying.[3] Researchers in China found that just *believing* you have a supportive family and friends was associated with positive well-being and better academic performance.[4] And researchers in the United States studied engineering learners and found that if learners perceived that their instructors were encouraging them, their performance improved.[5]

However, there's a catch: Not all encouragement is equally effective. Praising learners for their *effort and strategies*—not just their outcomes—leads to higher academic achievement that can persist for as many as seven years later. It may also help instill a growth mindset that fuels motivation.[6] In other words, the praise should be directed at the *process* that led to that final product. And the praise itself must be *accurate*. When parents or children perceive that they are over- or underpraising performance, this predicts poorer performance and higher rates of depression.[7] Thus, praise must be *authentic* to be truly effective.

Simple Strategy: Develop a Support Circle

If you work hard but find encouragement from others to be lacking, don't worry. You can cultivate encouragement in your life. To get started:

continued

1. **Find support.** Surround yourself with family members, friends, and instructors you respect and will give you authentic encouragement.

2. **Ask for feedback.** Solicit feedback from people who tend to praise your effort or your technique, not the outcome itself.

3. **Resist the haters.** Avoid people who tend to criticize your performance or withhold encouragement; they won't help motivate you to do and be your best.

Make Connections

Friendship makes everything in life a bit more enjoyable, whether at work, in your community, or where you play. People are buoyed by friendships under even the most trying of circumstances. But how important is friendship when you are learning? How do friends affect your ability to learn, grow, and change?

Researchers in Israel studied learners who either stayed with their friends when transferring from elementary to middle school or moved without them. They found that the presence of friends had a positive, significant effect on test scores, whereas the absence of reciprocal friendships had a negative effect on learning.[8] Similarly, researchers in Ghana determined that classmate support was critical to student engagement, followed by parental support.[9]

The power of friendship on learning seems to be true across ages, grades, and subjects. Experts have also found that peer support helps children;[10] at-risk and disabled learners;[11] graduate students;[12] adults in the workplace;[13] and even patients managing heart disease, diabetes, and HIV.[14]

Fortunately, quality matters more than quantity. Researchers at UCLA found that learners who had no friends received lower grades and were less engaged than their peers who had as few as one friend.[15] In other words, having a single friend who is involved with your learning can make a world of difference.

Unfortunately, you will not always have access to a circle of friends, especially when you are first learning something new. But there's good news: Researchers found that joining a learning community boosted learners' engagement.[16] If you can't find a formal learning community, look for clubs, meetups, social media groups, and organizations that serve a similar purpose. Or consider creating your own learning community with a few fellow learners who share your interests.

Simple Strategy: Find Friends

Even if you are in a new community and learning something completely foreign, you can find ways to become more connected. You can include friends in your learning process, whether they are your current friends, new classmates, or coworkers. To get started:

1. **Find colearners.** Understand that connection plays a very important role in the success of all kinds of learning experiences. Connection doesn't need to come from close friends; it just needs to be from people who are learning right along with you.

2. **Make one friend.** Try to undertake new learning experiences with a friend or make a point of introducing yourself to at least

continued

one person who's undertaking the same experience. If introducing yourself to a stranger is difficult, use an excuse such as
asking a question, asking for a favor, or asking for help.

3. **Be reciprocal.** As you begin to establish a friendship, make
sure that it is reciprocal, meaning that it goes both ways and
that they consider you a friend, too. This kind of positive
regard not only helps performance but also reduces stress
(an important part of reducing anxiety).

Find a Tutor (or Two)

A tutor is someone who teaches you directly, either one-on-one
or in a very small group. The practice of tutoring has been com-
monplace for centuries, if not longer. Tutoring was, essentially, how
people learned to hunt, farm, and raise children. Today, tutors can
be enlisted to help you learn just about anything. But do tutors
need to be trained teachers, or can they be your friends, peers, or
even robots?

For more than forty years, educational experts have recognized
that tutoring is the gold standard for learning.[17] If you are looking
for a surefire boost for your learning performance, consider engaging
one (or more) of these types of tutors:

- **Academic tutors.** These tutors are employed by educational
  institutions or tutoring services and have experience in
  specific subject areas. You can bring homework, problems,
  or just questions to them, and they can help you work
  through the material.

- **Professional, private tutors**. Private tutors are often self-employed or employed through a tutoring, test-prep, or learning company. They may offer more specialized, personalized support.

- **Peer tutors**. Peer tutors are often fellow learners in your courses or programs. Peer tutoring is among the most widely available and affordable options (often it is free). But does peer tutoring actually work? In short, yes. Peer tutoring has been shown to have a statistically significant effect on academic outcomes.[18] Researchers analyzed the effects of peer tutoring across twenty-six experiments for 938 learners in grades 1–12. They found that tutoring produced moderate to large academic benefits regardless of the amount, grade level, or disability status.[19]

Near-peer teaching—where a more advanced student teaches a less advanced student—is a popular type of tutoring in health-care education and can result in improved overall grades, as well as a significant increase in confidence.[20] Notably, peer education has been effective with public health efforts. For example, peer-to-peer education was associated with a whopping 36 percent reduction in HIV rates.[21] Nurses who finished up their clinical practice paired with a peer, rather than more traditional supervision by a superior, seemed to develop a stronger sense of self-efficacy—that can-do feeling that builds confidence.[22]

Simple Strategy: Find a Tutor

Getting a tutor is easier than it may sound. With a little effort, you may not only find a tutor—you may find a friend. To get started:

continued

1. **Ask your advisor.** If you attend a university or college, ask your advisor or instructor if tutoring is available. Many universities and colleges provide tutoring for free—it's yours to take advantage of.

2. **Search for tutoring companies.** You can hire a tutor through a tutoring company. Tutoring companies typically provide tutors in specific subject areas for a fee or as a service.

3. **Ask a classmate.** If all else fails, you can ask a classmate or friend if they can provide some informal tutoring. Sometimes having this sort of "study buddy" is all you need.

Ask Someone to Coach or Mentor You

Have you ever had a coach or mentor? The word *mentor* typically conjures up the image of someone whose personal experience and hard-won wisdom you would like to learn from. Mentors answer the question: How did you do it? Coaches, on the other hand, play the role of guides and champions, helping you set and accomplish goals, work through challenges, and ultimately achieve your dreams. They ask a different question: Who do you want to become? But how do coaches and mentors help you become a better learner?

Researchers analyzed twenty-five experimental studies and found that mentoring has a positive significant effect on learners sticking with programs and ultimately graduating. Indeed, eight more learners out of one hundred stuck with their programs if they had a mentor.[23] Who benefits from mentors the most? Experts who study mentoring in entrepreneurship found that mentoring is more beneficial for those who don't have a strong goal orientation or clear view of what exactly they want to do or achieve. In these cases, mentors can help establish and foster these goals.[24] What makes a good mentor? Research shows that the best mentor–mentee relationships are based on shared attitudes, values, beliefs, and personalities. They are also strengthened when mentors possess social capital, such as being respected by their mentees, and when the pairs interacted more frequently.[25]

Coaches are fundamentally different from mentors. Unlike mentors, who share their strategies, their experiences, and their advice, coaches tend to focus on you—your dreams, your goals, and your unique strengths. Coaches help their clients get clear on what they value, set goals in alignment with those values, and devise action plans to achieve those goals. A recent meta-analysis found that coaching, including coaching oriented toward goal achievement, improves a variety of outcomes.[26] Similarly, a systematic review published in *Innovations in Education and Teaching International* found that academic coaching significantly enhanced student learning by improving self-regulation, motivation, and academic performance.[27] This success is why coaching is becoming increasingly common in both workplace and academic settings.

Some coaches serve as mentors at times—transparently acknowledging that they are stepping outside of the coaching relationship and offering their personal perspective. However, effective coaches are aware that what worked for them may not work for their clients, so they quickly return to what resonates with their clients. Such client-centered work is the hallmark of coaching—and it's what makes coaching so successful.

Simple Strategy:
Find a Mentor, Coach, or Both

Anyone can find a mentor or coach. Mentors and coaches are pleased to be asked and will willingly offer their support and time. In fact, you may find yourself being mentored, or mentoring someone else, without consciously knowing it. To get started:

1. **To find an effective mentor, look for compatibility and expertise.** Look for a mentor who you are compatible with—someone who shares your attitudes, values, beliefs, and personality traits. If your mentor also has social capital—for instance, holds a role you would like to attain or is respected by others—that may help.

2. **To find an effective coach, look for a coaching certification.** Trained coaches are certified by organizations that enable them to become certified by the International Coaching Federation (ICF) upon completing strict requirements—thereby earning a credential issued by the ICF. You can think of this certification as a testament to their level of professional expertise, experience, and commitment to ethical standards.

3. **To find a coach/mentor, conduct interviews.** Finding someone who functions as both a coach and a mentor means finding a trained coach who also possesses personal expertise aligned with your own goals. When interviewing these types of experts, make sure to ask how they go about shifting between coaching and mentoring—and how they will honor your lived experience, perceptions, and life goals.

Observe as Many Experts as Possible

Who hasn't, at one time or another, emulated an expert? Perhaps you've tried to play an instrument like your favorite musician, or paint like an established artist, or mimic the technique of a professional athlete. Or maybe you've just copied the recipe of an expert chef on YouTube.

The power of learning from watching experts or interacting with experts is a well-known practice for aspiring athletes, and in professional sports more generally.[28] But does this strategy go beyond athletic training? A team of researchers asked forty-five medical students to visualize their problem-solving processes and then reflect on how they differed from an expert's process.[29] They found that the inclusion of the expert improved learners' problem-solving performance, knowledge construction, confidence, and satisfaction.[30]

In some cases, experts don't need to be highly qualified—they just need to be *more* qualified. Researchers who paired expert and novice language learners together found that both partners benefited. With expert guidance, novices are constantly challenged to provide longer and more detailed responses, while the experts benefit from teaching and leadership.[31] Similarly, learners who observed other people modeling behaviors and skills were able to brainstorm more ideas.[32]

It turns out that the more skilled you are at a task, the more you focus on the "task-relevant" regions when watching others.[33] Having a more skilled partner who provides visual cues toward the areas to watch can help you maintain this focus even after the guidance is no longer available and can boost later performance.[34]

When you're looking for an expert, exercise caution. Try to obtain information on the actual *expertise* of the expert and the *quality* of various aspects of the observation in advance. Experts may not have expertise in *every* aspect of something. Being aware of this may help you detect errors in the performance—something novices often have difficulty doing. Error detection, in turn, helps you learn from observations.[35]

Simple Strategy: Learn from Experts

If you do a bit of research, you can find experts—or at least people who are "more expert" than yourself—to support your learning. To get started:

1. **Decide if you should observe.** Decide if what you are trying to learn would benefit from observation. Is it a skill that is observable?

2. **Find your focus.** Find an expert to observe and ask them to indicate where you should focus during the observation.

3. **Consider the quality.** If you can't find an expert, consider viewing a recording or watching a novice, but try to determine the quality of the performance before you begin and any cues for errors you may detect.

Learn to Ask for Help

Regardless of whether you are learning with a friend, tutor, mentor, or expert, there are times when you may find yourself struggling. You may find yourself trying to learn something you lack much prior knowledge about—something completely new. You may find yourself stuck on a concept, process, or procedure that is very technical and difficult, without the right resources. Or maybe you undertake an experience that is poorly designed or poorly taught, making it nearly impossible to follow along and know what is expected. In each of these cases, it's easy to give up. But before you do, there's one important—and difficult—step to take: asking for help. Do you think seeking help aids your learning?

Asking for help is an important, but not always easy, way to foster learning. *Help-seeking theory* suggests that you follow predictable steps when deciding whether and how to seek help. However, that doesn't make the act of seeking help any easier. Researchers found that 72 percent of online actions performed by learners who needed help were unproductive and that learners frequently avoided using help when it was readily available.[36]

Seeking help is a complex decision-making process that starts when you are faced with a problem that challenges your personal abilities.[37] Researchers studied 612 college learners and found that their tendencies to seek help were related to their overall likelihood of engaging in academic activities, their self-esteem, and their perception that asking for help is not threatening.[38] If it's tough for you to ask for help, you're not alone—and fortunately, there are steps you can take to make it easier over time.

Simple Strategy: Ask for Help

Anyone—*anyone*—can ask for help. Once you muster the courage to ask, you'll find it gets easier and easier over time. To get started:

1. **Consider whom to ask.** It might seem like your instructor is the obvious choice, but some questions can also be asked of peers, tutors, or mentors. Consider who is in the best position to quickly answer your questions or provide help.

continued

2. **Consider your request.** Are you asking for help on a specific assignment? Are you in need of general help in a course—perhaps to accommodate a disability? Are you asking a question that can be answered by email, or does it need a discussion? Think carefully about what kind of help you need most.

3. **Ask for what you need directly.** Make your request clear. State the problem, then your request. General questions may be confusing or may result in insufficient help.

The Cumulative Effect

Have you ever contemplated learning something new, but you felt a little isolated, like you lacked the support to even get started? You may have felt alone, even if you knew that you were surrounded by other learners. That's where building a robust learning network comes in. Each of the strategies in this chapter helps you enlist support—but by enlisting complementary types of helpers, you can construct a robust community of practice.

Imagine that you want to learn something simply for fun, like how to be a mountaineer so you can embark on the vacation of a lifetime. You realize that, sure, you could do it alone, but that may not be the wisest (or safest) idea. This skill calls for all the help you can get. You begin by taking a weekend course and making a point of connecting with other learners who you can practice with, knowing that just one supportive peer can improve your motivation and outcomes. You also hire a tutor—no, not the traditional, academic kind of tutor, but a skilled mountaineer who helps you get the right gear, learn navigation skills, and prepare for weather-related emergencies. And you decide you need a mentor, too, who agrees to meet with you every week until your trip to offer advice, guidance, and tips. He's recommended a few expert videos and vlogs, which make you feel connected to knowledgeable influencers. You decide you're not going to be afraid to ask for encouragement and help when you need it, which you've found to be more powerful than you had ever realized. On your trip, after you've summited your first peak, you wonder, *how did I ever think I could learn this—or anything—without a community?*

These aren't lucky choices—they're part of a deliberate plan intended to support your learning. This plan includes things like seeking encouragement, making connections, finding a tutor, asking someone to mentor you, observing as many experts as possible, and learning to ask for help. As you connect these with strategies from other chapters, you may find that your progress accelerates, especially as they become more natural.

Take Action: Make Your Own Plan

In this chapter, you learned about one of the most important aspects of learning: relationships. Connection to other people not only promotes happiness; it also improves our physical and mental health. Human connection is particularly powerful when it comes to learning. Some experts would argue that learning requires other people—even if those people aren't directly with you when you are learning. Receiving encouragement helps you achieve more, and peer support can relieve signs and symptoms of stress. In fact, just one friend can help boost your performance, and a learning community can help even more. Tutors can help you get through some of your most difficult learning challenges, while mentors offer guidance and encouragement. Experts help you learn more, solve problems, build confidence, and feel more satisfied. Don't worry about finding a highly qualified expert; experts just need to be more qualified than you are. And don't be afraid to ask for help. It may be the most important way to enhance your learning.

Take a moment to reflect on your connections and the role they have played in your learning. After contemplating the following questions, develop a simple plan to build a robust learning network with someone who is already supporting your learning (or with someone who you are inviting to join your network). For additional resources, visit www.already-smarter.com.

- When you are learning something new, who in your life offers praise, encouragement, and support?

- How might friends or fellow learners help you learn more or stick with a challenging learning experience?

- Would you benefit from working with a personal tutor—and if so, how might you find one?

- How might a mentor help you learn new things, grow, and change?

- Think back to something you did after closely observing and imitating someone else. How did that help your performance?

- Are you comfortable seeking help from others—and how might you do so effectively?

CHAPTER 19

Become Tech-Enabled for the Future

T oday, there is no goal, big dream, or lofty aspiration—from building a campfire to building a robot—that couldn't benefit from a little technology. Yet many of us learn more slowly because we are simply unaware of how to find and use specific technologies that can help us learn.

This is where I have spent the bulk of my career: helping people acquire educational technologies and helping them adopt other types of technical proficiencies. Given the proliferation of learning technologies, you can imagine my surprise at finding that only a fraction of those surveyed—one in five—regularly use technology to support their learning.[1] Throughout my career, I have worked with people to explore ways to overcome technology trepidation by adopting technologies that can accelerate learning. In working with learners, I often notice how good learning technologies can make a meaningful difference in their performance.

This chapter can help you explore a few simple yet powerful technologies that may amplify your abilities. It introduces five increasingly common types of learning technologies that you can use on your learning journey. Plugged in to the right technologies, you might find yourself moving from feeling stuck to feeling empowered as you become more tech-enabled for the future.

Before you begin this chapter, think about how technology and AI could help you learn faster and better and ultimately contribute to your career and personal goals.

- How have you tried using technology and AI to learn—did they work?

- Why might different types of technology and AI affect your learning performance?

- How might new technologies help you achieve some of your larger aspirations?

Blend Your Learning

Online learning became the new normal during the Covid pandemic. But it may not be the *best* form of online or blended learning that you could have experienced. After all, most of this was "emergency" online learning. How effective, in general, is online or blended learning? According to an extensive review of published research on the effectiveness of online learning, researchers found that online learning can be *at least as* effective as traditional face-to-face learning. And blended learning—combining some online and some traditional methods—was *more effective*.[2] The reason for this is quite simple: Blended learning combines the best of personalized, self-paced learning with interactive, collaborative learning. It's the perfect marriage of past and future.

According to Michael Horn and Heather Staker, authors of *Blended: Using Disruptive Innovation to Improve Schools*, "Blended learning is the engine that can power personalized and competency-based learning. Just as technology enables mass customization in so many sectors to meet the diverse needs of so many people, online learning can allow students to learn any time, in any place, on any path, and at any pace at scale. At its most basic level, it lets learners fast-forward if they have already mastered a concept, pause if they need to digest something, or rewind and slow something down if they need to review. It provides a simple way for learners to take different paths toward a common destination."[3]

Effective blended learning includes additional learning time, instructional resources, and interaction among learners.[4] By this point in this book, it should be clear that these very attributes—time, resources, and interaction—are all important to successful learning. It's no wonder, then, that blended learning provides a strong opportunity to enhance your learning.

Simple Strategy: Learn Online

You can turn nearly any online or in-person learning experience into a blended learning experience. To get started:

1. **Go online.** If you have a learning experience that is entirely in person, do your preparation work online in advance by finding additional resources that will help you get familiar with what you are about to learn.

continued

2. **Make connections.** If you have a learning experience that is entirely online, find ways to safely engage with other learners in person in your community, such as scheduling small study groups.

3. **Prepare yourself.** Try to do your online work ahead of any required or recommended face-to-face work so that you are confident, prepared, and focused.

Augment Your Intelligence with AI

AI is drastically changing many things. Increasingly, we live in a world with AI that sends personalized messages. People can receive personalized advertisements, personalized content, and personalized connections from AI sources. When it comes to learning, AI can provide personalized instruction based on your performance and experiences that adapt to your knowledge, skills, or abilities. And you can use AI tools to answer your questions and generate content.

One of the most long-standing forms of AI for learning is intelligent tutoring systems. These systems respond and adapt to the learner's performance and provide content, assessments, and help at just the right level. According to the research, intelligent tutoring systems can outperform traditional classroom instruction, print and computer materials, and homework.[5] This makes sense because, unlike traditional forms of instruction, AI is focused more on each learner's personalized learning pathway. Some studies have even indicated that intelligent tutoring is about as effective as individualized tutoring and small group learning.[6] These have long been the gold standard of learning, whereby experts work directly with learners and provide feedback, adjustments, and support in direct response to learner performance.

More recently, generative AI tools have gained increasing visibility. Now you can use these tools to generate content based on your own prompts. These prompts might be questions to which you are seeking the answers or commands for AI to produce all types of content—from essays to letters to movie scripts and more. The key to using these tools for learning, of course, is to build your knowledge and skills—and, importantly, to learn how to use these tools ethically, safely, and transparently.

Simple Strategy: Embrace AI

Today, anyone can benefit from intelligent tutoring systems. To get started:

1. **Find intelligent tutors.** Understand that your tutor may not be human—but humanlike gestures or expressions may benefit your learning. If you are considering using an intelligent tutoring system, look for a report on how effective it is.

2. **Safely use AI tools.** Use generative AI tools as a resource for seeking help when you are confused or need more information on a topic, career pathway, or example. But consider verifying the answer you get with an expert, if you can, to ensure it is accurate and up to date.

3. **Be safe.** Be sure to understand the ethical and data privacy aspects of using any AI-based system or tool to ensure you are comfortable sharing your data, avoiding plagiarism, and properly citing the tool.

Take Games Seriously

Playing games is moving from a pastime to an accepted way of learning. Imagine a future where you could play video games to learn. A future in which you could practice skills as complicated as scientific experimentation, health care, emergency management, and military maneuvers with immediate, simulated results. These kinds of games, known as *serious games*, which are any game that supports learning,[7] have been shown to help you learn more when used to supplement learning.[8] The past decade has seen a proliferation of serious games, especially in medical science.[9]

Serious games seem to work. Learning is indeed moderately higher for learners who use serious games—especially if they use them for a shorter duration before the novelty wears off and if they have control over the content, sequence, or pace of the games.[10] Such games can also provide valuable feedback on learning, recognize good performance, and promote goal setting.[11] Combining the fictional world of a game with learning can spark competition and collaboration, and this can improve learning performance.[12] And when people play them, they tend to engage longer and feel more positive.[13]

Simple Strategy: Get Serious with Games

The right serious game can make learning engaging and fun. To get started:

1. **Research games.** Find games that spark competition or collaboration.

2. **Keep it short.** Use serious games for short periods of time— ideally with a partner.

3. **Monitor your mood.** Select games that provide feedback and make you feel competitive, collaborative, or positive.

Reconsider Reality

Augmented, virtual, and mixed realities are making their way into the learning mainstream. Technology is enabling you to go beyond your immediate reality into *mixed reality*—the merging of real and virtual worlds. These allow physical and digital objects to coexist. There are several types of mixed reality. Augmented reality (AR) superimposes a computer-generated visual onto your real world. Virtual reality (VR) enables you to interact with computer-generated or three-dimensional images in ways that seem real. But does mixed reality help you learn?

Augmented reality can effectively boost academic achievement compared to more traditional methods.[14] Researchers analyzed thirty-five research studies and found that immersive virtual reality using head-mounted displays was more effective than non-immersive approaches. This was especially true for younger learners, in the fields of scientific or skill development, and in cases where learners could practice simulations. They found that knowledge and skills were improved and that the effects lasted over time.[15]

Simple Strategy: Use AR and VR Effectively

Adjust your reality to learn things that couldn't happen in your home, school, or workplace. To get started:

continued

1. **Augment your reality.** Understand that augmented and virtual reality can be helpful—even just helping you practice things and spark your motivation and engagement.

2. **Use ahead of actual practice.** Consider using augmented reality before a hands-on practice or hands-on test or in cases where you cannot accomplish a task without some kind of support.

3. **Be careful.** If you get dizzy; have mobility issues; are hearing, vision, or balance impaired; or are managing any other health concerns, exercise caution.

Train Your Brain

Neuroscience—the study of the brain—increasingly allows you to understand how your brain works and how it affects your memory, thinking, and learning. *Neuroenhancement* is the process of augmenting your brain using a variety of means, including "brain training." Brain training may help you build a stronger brain or more cognitive processing power. But how does brain training work?

Advances in neuroscience have enabled researchers to target the parts of the brain that regulate brain plasticity to enhance learning, memory, and recovery from injury or disease. One area of research has been around activities that may train attention, memory, and problem-solving.[16]

An increasing number of apps are available to help you "train your brain." Currently, there is great interest in these apps and a broad perception that they could be beneficial.[17] According to experts, there is optimism that brain-training tools may help you improve your mind, brain, and memory.[18] Although early, some research has indicated that cognitive training may benefit your brain and mind and that programs that work on visuospatial working memory seem to be most promising.[19]

Simple Strategy: Train Your Brain

Today, brain-training apps are becoming increasingly available and showing promise. To get started:

1. **Research effectiveness.** When selecting brain-training apps, look for research on their effectiveness (and for whom and under what circumstances they are effective).

2. **Monitor your confidence.** Consider using them if they spark your confidence and motivation.

3. **Take a break.** Consider using them for a cognitive microbreak or as a wake-up for your brain.

The Cumulative Effect

Have you ever needed to learn something new—and fast? Did you wonder, *is there a technology that can help me learn this?* The good news is this: There is no shortage of educational technologies today. You know that educational technology can help you learn, but there is an overwhelming number of products. What should you choose, and why? That's where becoming tech-enabled comes in. Each technique in this chapter can provide a bit of a tech-enabled boost, but by combining several of them, you may experience an even bigger benefit.

Imagine you want a job that will propel society into the future, like developing health-care robotics, and you need to get there fast. You start by registering for a blended learning course, taking portions on your own time and joining remote lectures and discussions on certain days, creating a structure that fits your schedule. From there, you find an intelligent tutoring system that quizzes you and some serious games that actually make it fun to learn real-world skills. Augmented reality brings you into a simulated environment, helping you practice skills before applying them in real life. And to give yourself an edge, you try brain-training apps, hoping that regular practice can improve your overall cognitive function. Before you know it, your interest shifts from designing health-care robotics to robotics-for-learning, hoping to help others to learn more effectively, too. In fact, you begin to consider yourself a learning mentor—which is what the next chapter is all about.

These choices aren't accidental—they're part of a thoughtful plan intended to support your learning. This plan includes things like blending your learning, augmenting your intelligence with AI, taking games seriously, reconsidering reality, and training your brain. Each chapter offers something meaningful, but the real power can come when they are thoughtfully and consistently combined with other strategies in this book.

Take Action: Make Your Own Plan

This chapter focused on the types of technology that may affect your learning. Today, we are experiencing a boom in educational technology. We have access to blended learning, which can be more effective than traditional or online learning. AI is powering intelligent and adaptive tutoring systems, which may be as effective as human tutoring. Serious games simulate real-world environments and help us set goals, monitor our performance, and adapt to feedback, all while lifting our moods. Augmented reality brings computer-generated visuals into our real worlds and helps us understand how to perform a procedure or hands-on activities before doing so in real life. And some brain-training apps purport to improve our cognitive functions, with emerging evidence that they can work. Leveraging these technologies can complement our other learning behaviors and compound our learning performance.

Take a moment to reflect on your use of technology and the role it might play in your learning. After contemplating the following questions, develop a simple plan to leverage technology to accelerate your learning and consider sharing it with someone who is supporting your learning. If you need more support, be sure to read Chapter 18 on building a robust learning network. For additional resources, visit www.already-smarter.com.

- How might online or blended learning be effective for you?
- How could an AI or a personalized learning system help you learn something?
- What would you prefer to learn using games?
- How might virtual or augmented reality allow you to experience something unusual?
- Have you tried strengthening your brain using games, puzzles, or other techniques?

CHAPTER 20

Champion Others—Lead, Mentor, and Inspire

C ongratulations—you've almost made it to the end of this book. Now that you know how to use learning to achieve everything from a small task to a big dream, what else could be left? Something big: helping others follow in your footsteps. Many of us want to help others, but we forget that the ultimate gift is helping them to help themselves. The beauty of giving the gift of learning is that it truly does keep on giving.

In my experience as a leader, I have seen the power of learning firsthand, when people realize their potential and begin to pursue their goals. Yet so few leaders—instructors, managers, coaches, mentors, friends, and parents—actually leverage learning science to help others learn. In fact, a third of those surveyed were completely unfamiliar with this body of research, and only 4 percent actually use this research to help others learn.[1] In my experience as a leadership coach, I have worked with people to explore ways to become learning leaders by using learning science techniques to benefit their families, friends, and colleagues. In my experience, championing others as they learn is one of the most powerful ways to demonstrate leadership, show genuine positive regard, and unlock lifelong opportunities.

This chapter can help you explore how to support others in their learning journeys—and why doing so can mark a milestone in your growth. It introduces five strategies that may help you guide and support those around you, which may enhance their growth and your own. By sharing what you have learned, you might find yourself evolving from learner to leader as you champion others through mentoring, coaching, and inspiration.

Before you begin this chapter, think about how leading others in their learning could contribute to their growth and enhance your life.

- What are some of the ways you have tried helping others learn—personally or professionally?

- Why might leading others in their learning affect their learning performance?

- How might leading others in their learning support your values and purpose?

Be Transformative

No matter what roles you assume in your life, you will undoubtedly find that one of them is the role of a learning leader. You may be a learning leader by profession, such as a teacher, instructor, or coach, in which case understanding learning will be invaluable. You may also become a learning leader quite by accident—you may find that a friend, partner, or child needs someone to help them conquer the anxieties and uncertainties of learning. Or you may become a learning leader by necessity—helping others solve problems and make changes under urgent, challenging circumstances. What leadership qualities best foster learning?

Learning leaders do many things well—some are clear communicators, others are good at applying learning theories, and yet others masterfully design learning experiences. More often than not, learning leaders share one common trait: They embrace change and growth. According to researchers, the most effective learning leaders are transformational.[2] Transformational leadership inspires people to make significant positive changes, in part because transformational leaders are motivational, inspiring, and supportive. This isn't surprising, given that learning is itself transformational.

What, then, do transformational leaders do? To learn from the most prominent learning leaders, just look to school principals. Researchers evaluated forty years of school leadership research and found a few common themes among the best leaders, including using leadership to build the capacity for improvement.[3] Improvement happens at both the individual level and the organizational level. That is, individual growth contributes to systemic changes in institutions, organizations, and communities. Transformative leadership has the power to change everything.

Simple Strategy: Embrace Transformation

If you lead an organization—a business, school, community-based organization, or even just a family unit—leading learning puts you in the position to provide systemic organizational change. To get started:

continued

1. **Envision the future.** Help learners in your life see what the world can be—and how they can contribute to it—when they embrace the difficult, messy work of learning.

2. **Cultivate enthusiasm.** Bring optimism, hope, confidence, creativity, experimentation, and celebration to the learning environment. Begin to associate learning with what *can be* and celebrate even the smallest successes.

3. **Enable change.** Provide the resources to enable learners to make the most of their learning. This may include support, opportunities, and connections depending upon what each individual learner, or type of learner, needs.

Codesign Experiences

Engage with learners to creatively codesign experiences. All too often, learners get focused on *what* to learn, and not on the best strategies, processes, or journeys for learning. As leaders, coaches, and instructors, part of your work is to help learners unpack those processes and develop ways of learning that make them successful and help them reach their goals. How can you begin to help learners evolve their approach to learning?

Codesign is a cooperative creative process that prompts inquiry into a subject and creative collaboration around the design process.[4] It's a common process in user experience design for technology and services and has become increasingly popular for learning designers, who are keen to make sure that their experiences are meeting the needs of their learners.

In learning codesign, it's important to prime the learner to have the right mindset and motivation around the experience—making it both desirable and challenging. How they currently feel about the learning topic—enthusiastic, apprehensive, downright anxious—can also provide valuable insight into the elements you should codesign with learners.[5]

It's also important to include the principles provided in this book to ensure that the experience is based on learning science. By undertaking codesign with learners, you begin to help them formulate their own self-regulated learning techniques. In particular, they should be contemplating their goals and planning to engage in activities that achieve those goals.

For example, suppose one of your colleagues wants to learn how to become a better communicator. You might work with them to identify what kinds of contexts they would like to communicate in better and what their ultimate learning goal is, such as facilitating a workshop or delivering a knockout presentation. From there, the two of you could layer in a full journey of learning activities, mentorship, and practices that would help them achieve even their loftiest communication goal.

Simple Strategy: Codesign with Learners

Codesigning with learners means being the guide on the side and letting learners take the lead in terms of what they want to learn and how they ultimately want to go about learning it. As a learning leader, however, you can play a unique role in informing that learning journey. To get started:

1. **Narrow the learning topic.** What, specifically, does your learner want to learn, and what is their attitude toward this topic? How might their attitude shape how you construct the learning experience?

continued

2. **Establish the ultimate goal.** What does the endgame look like for your learner? What do they want to be able to think, feel, know, or do? What outcome do they ultimately want to achieve?

3. **Devise a learning journey.** Using tips in this book, co-construct a learning experience that is engaging, challenging, and well-supported by learning strategies. This should include addressing any limiting factors that may inhibit their success.

Point Out Problems

In life, learning isn't always related to big dreams and personal aspirations. In fact, it can simply be necessary to solve problems and complete projects. Learning how to correct mistakes in computer code or undertake a long-delayed plumbing project is every bit as valid as learning how to ski or become a doctor. And those everyday learnings may open up new pathways for future learning. How can projects and problems help you become a better learner?

Everyday problems are rich opportunities for learning projects. In all aspects of life, you are surrounded by problems. In the workplace, in your community, and in your home, problems often go unchecked because you lack the time, resources, or know-how to address them. These problems, then, become fertile ground for learning. By keeping a list of problems—a list that you revisit and prioritize over time—you can begin to take action through learning. This action often results in projects that require learning how to do things in certain ways or how to show up in certain situations. Such projects are valuable opportunities for learning.

Indeed, there's an approach to learning called *problem-based learning* (PBL). Not surprisingly, it is particularly good for developing problem-solving skills, such as those used in many fields, especially those related to science, technology, and engineering. Problem-based learning simply means solving real-world problems—often with other learners or with the support of an expert. By solving authentic problems, you become more fluent at problem-solving when problems arise organically. Better yet, problem-based learning has been demonstrated to improve learners' attitudes, critical thinking skills, motivation, and satisfaction.[6]

In organizations, including educational institutions, businesses, and even family systems, problems abound. Many of these—how to operate, how to produce stellar products and services, how to cooperate to complete tasks—are handled in the standard course of business. Nevertheless, numerous "fringe cases" never get prioritized but represent not only rich veins for learning but also exceptional opportunities for innovation. Having a backlog of problems that need to be solved, both large and small, provides microlearning and macrolearning opportunities that enable people to grow and expand their range.

Simple Strategy:
Create a Backlog of Problems to Solve

As you encounter problems—be it in your community, workplace, or home—begin to compile these into problems that can morph into learning projects. To get started:

1. **Select juicy problems to solve.** Identify problems that are ambiguous, complex, and require new levels of skill or

continued

knowledge. In the workplace, you might consider them "stretch goals" that go beyond day-to-day business and begin to resemble innovation.

2. **Identify what types of learning may be needed.** Determine which tools, techniques, and knowledge will be needed to be able to solve the problem or complete the project.

3. **Determine who can provide support.** Consider the kind of individuals—known experts, specialized mentors, or industry leaders—who may be able to help provide guidance, support, and insight.

Cultivate a Growth Culture

Learning is more than an isolated activity. It can become a culture—not dissimilar to the campus culture that exists in many schools, colleges, or universities or the corporate innovation labs that promote experimentation and discovery. In nontraditional settings—from homes to businesses—a learning culture may be a bit more elusive. How can you build learning cultures that promote and sustain learning and systematically embed it in everything from daily activities to annual events?

Learning cultures encourage and sustain growth. Today, many organizations believe that they are building a learning culture by providing employee training, tuition reimbursement, and access to e-learning products. While these things do support learning, they only scratch the surface of what organizations can do to truly support learning and growth. Similarly, parents may encourage their children to go to school, or even college, without setting them up for success. A learning culture does just this: It establishes learning as a part of the fabric of organizational or family life, on par with other workplace or home activities.

If developing a learning culture sounds frivolous, think again. Learning cultures improve job satisfaction, which also leads to staff hanging in there when things get tough.[7] It's an investment in the future—and one that amplifies the effectiveness of the team. Even tasks like manager coaching are more effective in a learning culture.[8]

Building a learning culture means rethinking the aspects of an institution, organization, or even a family system that you have influence over. In the workplace, for example, this may mean reconsidering the proportion of time that employees spend learning each week or each year, flexing employee hours and locations, and building the infrastructure to support and maintain learning interactions. Importantly, learning cultures also support career pathways and promotions. While these reforms may sound daunting, any learning leader—operating in both formal and informal contexts—can take small but important steps toward developing a bootstrapped learning culture. The good news is that, with a few seeds planted, learning cultures begin to take root and grow on their own.

Simple Strategy: Begin Culture Building

There are three simple steps any leader can take to build a learning culture. To get started:

1. **Encourage knowledge sharing.** Connecting learners with experts, mentors, and coaches is a simple way of enabling the sharing of knowledge, practices, and procedures throughout

continued

an organization, system, or community. This can be further enhanced through information systems and platforms that make knowledge-sharing easy and transparent.

2. **Build communities of practice.** Communities of practice are dynamic networks of individuals who are connected by a common interest, such as learning. Such groups enable peer-to-peer learning, information sharing, and networking in ways that advance the collective knowledge of the community. Robust communities of practice may morph into knowledge networks or learning labs.

3. **Enable advancement.** True learning cultures create, illuminate, and honor career pathways. Pathways help individuals get into new careers or advance within a career domain. Learning cultures provide the guidance to help learners gain the skills to advance along these pathways.

Believe in the Power of Learning

Sharing successes amplifies the effect. When I work with learners as a leader, coach, or instructor, I never tire of witnessing the impact it has on that individual. This is true regardless of how the learning actually propels them forward; that is, whether it's toward a degree, toward a new job, or just toward a personal interest. However, the very process of learning can have huge benefits for your career and workplace. How does the process of learning affect broader institutions and organizations?

As a leader who champions learning, it serves you well to be able to recognize, articulate, and support the benefits that come with devoting time each day, week, month, or year to learning. A champion supports learning even when learners are uncertain about undertaking it and when executives are reluctant to invest in it. You remain a steadfast supporter, always believing that people can grow. This faith in the power of learning becomes the true hallmark of a learning leader.

Over the past few years, research has borne out the impact of quality learning programs. In fact, researchers have found that it is the secret ingredient for success. Learning improves not only employee performance but also employee satisfaction, retention, and innovation.[9] This means that organizations that prioritize learning have happier employees who stay longer and drive new and improved products, services, and ways of working. In other words, learning directly contributes to the bottom line.

Simple Strategy: Share the Value

Sharing success stories is an important part of learning leadership that amplifies the impact (and, if necessary, justifies the investment). To get started:

1. **Describe the impact on performance.** Use your platform as a learning leader to share stories of how learning enhances performance for both individuals and groups, including how learning makes them more effective at problem-solving, business practices, and interpersonal relationships.

2. **Evaluate satisfaction and stick-to-itiveness.** Consider the effect of learning on both your satisfaction and persistence, especially in the workplace and amid challenging circumstances. The growth and accomplishment that come from learning are both motivational and empowering and can keep people going when other perks fall short.

continued

3. **Celebrate creativity and innovation.** Share results of learning activities that improved creativity and innovation, resulting in new ways of thinking, behaving, relating, and operating. This is the ultimate result of learning, and it is well worth celebrating.

The Cumulative Effect

Have you ever imagined yourself as a learning leader? After putting some of the strategies in this book into practice, you may just qualify as one! This could be at home, at work, or in any number of organizational or community settings. It stems from your interest in helping others to learn, change, and grow. But how can you become the champion they need? That's where championing others by leading, mentoring, and inspiring comes in. The strategies in this chapter each help you lead through learning, and when used together, they can build a powerful approach to fostering growth.

Imagine that you want to help people transform their lives by supporting them as they build a new vision for how learning can enable them to achieve just about anything. As a learning leader, you begin to codesign powerful experiences focused on each learner's goals, interests, and mindsets. You facilitate problem-based learning to help learners tackle real-life challenges and apply their knowledge and skills in practical ways. You build a learning culture everywhere in your life, supporting small efforts, peer learning, and career pathways. What you find most enjoyable is celebrating the impact that may follow: improved performance, satisfaction, and advancement. The success stories you help nurture reinforce the value of learning as an amazing opportunity for personal and professional transformation—which all started with your own learning journey.

These aren't scattershot choices—they're part of an intentional plan to support learning. This plan includes things like being transformative, codesigning experiences, pointing out problems, cultivating a growth culture, and believing in the power of learning. Building your own learning leadership strategy builds a stronger foundation for you and those you are supporting.

Take Action: Make Your Own Plan

The final chapter in this book focused on your next step: moving from learner to learning leader. As learners, we may start off by thinking about how learning can help us improve in any number of ways. Only later do we begin to understand the value that we can bring to others through learning leadership. We may start simply by becoming learning champions, then advance to learning codesigners or problem curators, helping to actively facilitate learning experiences. Later, still, we may build learning cultures and begin to lead programs with significant results. Regardless of where you are as a learning leader, you are now equipped to lead your own learning and that of others.

Take a moment to reflect on how you might help those around you become better learners and achieve their goals. After contemplating the following questions, develop a simple plan to help others find their inner learner with someone who has supported you. For additional resources, visit www.already-smarter.com.

- What are the unique qualities that might make you an outstanding learning leader?

- How might you work with learners to codesign learning experiences?
- How can everyday problems become rich learning projects?
- What might you do to build a learning culture that promotes and supports learning?
- How can you share the results of successful learning stories—including your own?

Conclusion

B y now, I hope you have come to realize that learning has many benefits. These range from personal growth to professional advancement and everything in between. Learning has been a survival tactic since the dawn of humanity and has aided humans in every innovation. Few can argue with the psychological benefits of learning—the boost of confidence and agency that comes from accomplishing something new. Learning is a cornerstone of our uniquely human condition and one that we share with many other creatures across the planet.

When I set out to write this book, I wanted to write it for the inner learner in each of us. I especially wanted to write it for those of you who have felt, as I have, like maybe there's something you couldn't quite learn to do or could never accomplish. If that describes you—or someone on your team, in your care, or in your life—I hope this book has served its purpose. And if there is someone in your life who would benefit from being a better learner, I would encourage you to pass this book along to them. This small act of kindness could forever change their life.

My sincere hope is that this book has helped you set your own learning intention, establish a solid learning foundation, engage actively with the process of learning, leverage your body and senses to help you, and resolve to evolve into the human you want to be. Mostly, I hope that this book has helped you see that you have unlimited potential to learn, change, and grow and that all of your dreams are within reach.

Acknowledgments

T he purpose of this book is to translate evidence-based topics into plain language and simple actions that anyone can use—easily and quickly. I have taken great care in selecting sources written by esteemed authors and published in peer-reviewed journals or in evidence-based books, the lion's share produced in the past decade. In addition, the whole of the text has been peer-reviewed by a cognitive psychologist, influenced by an advisory team composed of experts in elementary education, higher education, and workforce development, and validated by a team of fact-checkers. In particular, I would like to thank Dr. Matthew Ventura for his painstaking fact-checking; Dr. Shawn Mahoney, Dr. PJ Henry, and Dr. Holly Custard for their thoughtful guidance; and Dr. Duane Roen, Dr. Jan Jones-Shenk, Dr. Chris Dede, and Dr. Mark McDaniel for their timely support and encouragement. Most importantly, I would like to thank the researchers whose work has informed this book. They do a great service to society by enabling each of us to learn and grow. Finally, I would like to thank the team at Fast Company Press for their sage guidance and precise editorial work.

Such an effort comes with several risks that I would like to acknowledge. First, I have referenced several hundred books and scholarly articles—many of which are dense, nuanced, and limited in their applicability to other contexts. Second, research in all of the various branches that inform learning science can be contradictory, deeply contextual, and subject to rapid change. Third, scholars have different points of view on many of these concepts and, like all of science, these points of view change based on new findings. For all of these reasons, in the chance this work may come off—to academics, scientists, and scholars—as an oversimplification, may I gently remind the reader that my purpose here is to make complex, evidence-based material accessible and actionable and to help readers take more control over their learning and, at their readiness, help them begin to implement more successful learning practices.

I would encourage readers to use the information in this book that appeals to them and read the original research more deeply for those aspects they have questions about. Similarly, I would encourage the authors of original work to reach out to me directly if there are any unintentional misrepresentations of their work or if their research no longer aligns with my interpretation. I will do my best to address these in future editions. Your work is of great regard to me, and I extend my gratitude for your efforts to make the invisible visible when it comes to learning effectively.

Notes

Introduction

1. Survey conducted by Jeffrey Bergin. 2025.

2. Winerman, Lea. "By the Numbers: Lifelong Learning." *Monitor on Psychology*, vol. 48, no. 2, Feb. 2017, www.apa.org/monitor/2017/ 02/numbers.

3. Weise, Michelle R. *Long Life Learning: Preparing for Jobs That Don't Even Exist Yet.* Wiley, 2020, p. 5.

4. Weise. *Long Life Learning*, p. 5.

5. Rainie, Lee, and Janna Anderson. "The Future of Jobs and Jobs Training." *Pew Research Center*, 3 May 2017, www.pewresearch.org/ internet/2017/05/03/the-future-of-jobs-and-jobs-training/.

6. "Unemployment Rates and Earnings by Educational Attainment: U.S. Bureau of Labor Statistics." *Bureau of Labor Statistics*, 8 Jan. 2019, www.bls.gov/emp/chart-unemployment-earnings-education.htm.

7. Barnes, Deborah E., and Kristine Yaffe. "The Projected Effect of Risk Factor Reduction on Alzheimer's Disease Prevalence." *The Lancet Neurology*, vol. 10, no. 9, Sept. 2011, pp. 819–28, https://doi. org/10.1016/s1474-4422(11)70072-2.

8. Dekhtyar, Serhiy, et al. "Genetic Risk of Dementia Mitigated by Cognitive Reserve: A Cohort Study." *Annals of Neurology*, vol. 86, no. 1, 22 May 2019, pp. 68–78, https://doi.org/10.1002/ana.25501. Accessed 25 Oct. 2020.

9. Vemuri, Prashanthi, et al. "Association of Lifetime Intellectual Enrichment with Cognitive Decline in the Older Population." *JAMA Neurology*, vol. 71, no. 8, 1 Aug. 2014, pp. 1017–24, pubmed.ncbi.nlm. nih.gov/25054282/.

10. Geda, Yonas E., et al. "Engaging in Cognitive Activities, Aging, and Mild Cognitive Impairment: A Population-Based Study." *The Journal of Neuropsychiatry and Clinical Neurosciences*, vol. 23, no. 2, Jan. 2011, pp. 149–54, https://doi.org/10.1176/jnp.23.2.jnp149.

11. Winerman. "By the Numbers."

12. Illeris, Knud, editor. *Contemporary Theories of Learning: Learning Theorists . . . In Their Own Words*. Routledge, 2018.; Torre, Dario M., et al. "Overview of Current Learning Theories for Medical Educators." *The American Journal of Medicine*, vol. 119, no. 10, Oct. 2006, pp. 903–7, https://doi.org/10.1016/j.amjmed.2006.06.037.

13. Bergin. Survey. 2025.

Chapter 1

1. Survey conducted by Jeffrey Bergin. 2025.

2. Elango, Munusamy, and Ganesan Manimozhi. "Meta Analysis of Study Habits and Academic Achievement." *Shanlax International Journal of Arts, Science and Humanities*, vol. 8, no. 4, 1 Apr. 2021, pp. 139–45, https://doi.org/10.34293/sijash.v8i4.3722.

3. Norris, Catherine J. "The Negativity Bias, Revisited: Evidence from Neuroscience Measures and an Individual Differences Approach." *Social Neuroscience*, vol. 16, no. 1, 12 Dec. 2019, pp. 1–15, https://doi.org/10.1080/17470919.2019.1696225.

4. Peters, Uwe. "What Is the Function of Confirmation Bias?" *Erkenntnis*, vol. 87, 20 Apr. 2020, pp. 1351–76, https://link.springer.com/article/10.1007/s10670-020-00252-1.

5. Learning Disabilities Association of America. "Types of Learning Disabilities." *Learning Disabilities Association of America*, 2013, ldaamerica.org/types-of-learning-disabilities/.

6. Learning Disabilities Association of America. "Types of Learning Disabilities."

7. Learning Disabilities Association of America. "Types of Learning Disabilities."

8. "The State of LD: Understanding the 1 in 5—NCLD." *NCLD*, 2 May 2017, https://assets.ctfassets.net/p0qf7j048i0q/2Q2TsAzUSM9TX-q22LPxQwY/658d54ed0529acddf70f89d367db7915/2017_State_of_LD_-_Executive_Summary_Final_Accessible.pdf.

9. Learning Disabilities Association of America. "Types of Learning Disabilities."

10. Taylor, H., and Martin Vestergaard. "Developmental Dyslexia: Disorder or Specialization in Exploration?" *Frontiers in Psychology*, vol. 13, 23 June 2022, https://doi.org/10.3389/fpsyg.2022.889245.

11. Goto, Stanford T., and Connie Martin. "Psychology of Success: Overcoming Barriers to Pursuing Further Education." *The Journal of Continuing Higher Education*, vol. 57, no. 1, 17 Apr. 2009, pp. 10–21, https://doi.org/10.1080/07377360902810744. Accessed 20 Aug. 2019.

12. Goto and Martin. "Psychology of Success."

13. Goto and Martin. "Psychology of Success."

14. Burke, Kathryn M., et al. "A Meta-Analysis of Interventions to Promote Self-Determination for Students with Disabilities." *Remedial and Special Education*, vol. 41, no. 3, 4 Oct. 2018, https://doi.org/10.1177/0741932518802274.

15. Ryan, Richard M., and Edward L. Deci. "Self-Determination Theory and the Facilitation of Intrinsic Motivation, Social Development, and Well-Being." *American Psychologist*, vol. 55, no. 1, 2000, pp. 68–78, https://doi.org/10.1037/0003-066X.55.1.68.

16. Ryan, Richard M., and Edward L. Deci. *Self-Determination Theory: Basic Psychological Needs in Motivation, Development, and Wellness.* Guilford Press, 2017.

17. Duckworth, Angela. *Grit: The Power of Passion and Perseverance.* Scribner, 2016, p. 8.

18. Duckworth. *Grit.*

19. Jachimowicz, Jon M., et al. "Why Grit Requires Perseverance and Passion to Positively Predict Performance." *Proceedings of the National Academy of Sciences*, vol. 115, no. 40, 2 Oct. 2018, pp. 9980–85, www.pnas.org/content/115/40/9980.short.

20. Crane, M. F., et al. "How Resilience Is Strengthened by Exposure to Stressors: The Systematic Self-Reflection Model of Resilience Strengthening." *Anxiety, Stress, & Coping*, vol. 32, no. 1, Aug. 2018, pp. 1–17, https://doi.org/10.1080/10615806.2018.1506640.

Chapter 2

1. Survey conducted by Jeffrey Bergin. 2025.

2. Dweck, Carol S. *Mindset: The New Psychology of Success*. Random House, 2016, p. 12.

3. Dweck. *Mindset*.

4. Zhang, Junfeng, et al. "How Teachers' and Students' Mindsets in Learning Have Been Studied: Research Findings on Mindset and Academic Achievement." *Psychology*, vol. 8, no. 9, 2017, pp. 1363–77, https://doi.org/10.4236/psych.2017.89089. Accessed 9 Apr. 2019.

5. Zhang et al. "How Teachers' and Students'."

6. Bandura, Albert. "Self-Efficacy." *Encyclopedia of Human Behavior*, edited by Vilayanur Ramachandran, vol. 4, Academic Press, 1998, pp. 71–81.

7. Richardson, Michelle, et al. "Psychological Correlates of University Students' Academic Performance: A Systematic Review and Meta-Analysis." *Psychological Bulletin*, vol. 138, no. 2, Mar. 2012, psycnet. apa.org/buy/2012-04281-001.; Stajkovic, Alexander D., and Fred Luthans. "Self-Efficacy and Work-Related Performance: A Meta-Analysis." *Psychological Bulletin*, vol. 124, no. 2, 1998, psycnet.apa.org/ doiLanding?doi=10.1037%2F0033-2909.124.2.240.

8. Talsma, Kate, et al. "I Believe, Therefore I Achieve (and Vice Versa): A Meta-Analytic Cross-Lagged Panel Analysis of Self-Efficacy and Academic Performance." *Learning and Individual Differences*, vol. 61, Jan. 2018, pp. 136–50, https://doi.org/10.1016/j.lindif.2017.11.015. Accessed 27 Apr. 2020.

9. Jackson, Jay. "Enhancing Self-Efficacy and Learning Performance." *The Journal of Experimental Education*, vol. 70, no. 3, 2002, pp. 243–54, https://doi.org/10.1080/00220970209599508.

10. Hsu, Hsien-Yuan, et al. "Exploring the Relationship between Student-Perceived Faculty Encouragement, Self-Efficacy, and Intent to Persist in Engineering Programs." *European Journal of Engineering Education*, vol. 46, 1 Mar. 2021, pp. 1–17, https://doi.org/10.1080/03043797.2021.1889469. Accessed 21 Sept. 2021.

11. Cascio, Christopher N., et al. "Self-Affirmation Activates Brain Systems Associated with Self-Related Processing and Reward and Is Reinforced by Future Orientation." *Social Cognitive and Affective Neuroscience*, vol. 11, no. 4, 5 Nov. 2015, pp. 621–29, https://doi.org/10.1093/scan/nsv136.

12. Albalooshi, Sumaya, et al. "Reinstating the Resourceful Self: When and How Self-Affirmations Improve Executive Performance of the Powerless." *Personality and Social Psychology Bulletin*, vol. 46, no. 2, 11 June 2019, pp. 189–203, https://doi.org/10.1177/0146167219853840.

13. Sherman, David K. "Self-Affirmation: Understanding the Effects." *Social and Personality Psychology Compass*, vol. 7, no. 11, Nov. 2013, pp. 834–45, https://doi.org/10.1111/spc3.12072.; Layous, Kristin, et al. "Feeling Left Out, but Affirmed: Protecting against the Negative Effects of Low Belonging in College." *Journal of Experimental Social Psychology*, vol. 69, Mar. 2017, pp. 227–31, https://doi.org/10.1016/j.jesp.2016.09.008. Accessed 7 May 2020.

14. Barroso, C., et al. "A Meta-Analysis of the Relation between Math Anxiety and Math Achievement." *Psychological Bulletin*, vol. 147, no. 2, 2021, pp. 134–68, https://doi.org/10.1037/bul0000307.

15. Chou, Shih-Chi, and Chi-Cheng Chang. "The Relationship between Academic Stress and Health Status—the Moderating Role of Social Support." *Lecture Notes in Computer Science*, vol. 11937, 2019, pp. 685–694, 10.1007/978-3-030-35343-8_72. Accessed 16 Feb. 2022.

16. Misra, Ranjita, and Michelle McKean. "College Students' Academic Stress and Its Relation to Their Anxiety, Time Management, and Leisure Satisfaction." *American Journal of Health Studies*, vol. 16, no. 1, 2000. *ProQuest*, search.proquest.com/openview/c2c1309ac42c1cc4b74e146f6b0e260c/1?pq-origsite=gscholar&cbl=30166.

17. Eisenbeck, Nikolett, et al. "Effects of a Focused Breathing Mindfulness Exercise on Attention, Memory, and Mood: The Importance of Task Characteristics." *Behaviour Change*, vol. 35, no. 1, Apr. 2018, pp. 54–70, https://doi.org/10.1017/bec.2018.9. Accessed 4 Mar. 2020.

18. Ma, Xiao, et al. "The Effect of Diaphragmatic Breathing on Attention, Negative Affect and Stress in Healthy Adults." *Frontiers in Psychology*, vol. 8, no. 874, 6 June 2017, https://doi.org/10.3389/fpsyg.2017.00874.

19. De Couck, Marijke, et al. "How Breathing Can Help You Make Better Decisions: Two Studies on the Effects of Breathing Patterns on Heart Rate Variability and Decision-Making in Business Cases." *International Journal of Psychophysiology*, vol. 139, May 2019, pp. 1–9, https://doi.org/10.1016/j.ijpsycho.2019.02.011.

20. Ching, Ho-Hoi, et al. "Effects of a Mindfulness Meditation Course on Learning and Cognitive Performance among University Students in Taiwan." *Evidence-Based Complementary and Alternative Medicine*, 10 Nov. 2015, www.hindawi.com/journals/ecam/2015/254358/.

21. Jha, Amishi P., et al. "Examining the Protective Effects of Mindfulness Training on Working Memory Capacity and Affective Experience." *Emotion*, vol. 10, no. 1, 2010, pp. 54–64, https://doi.org/10.1037/a0018438.

22. Gabriely, Ranit, et al. "The Influence of Mindfulness Meditation on Inattention and Physiological Markers of Stress on Students with Learning Disabilities and/or Attention Deficit Hyperactivity Disorder." *Research in Developmental Disabilities*, vol. 100, May 2020, p. 103630, https://doi.org/10.1016/j.ridd.2020.103630.

23. Hassirim, Zuriel, et al. "Pre-Sleep Cognitive Arousal Decreases Following a 4-Week Introductory Mindfulness Course." *Mindfulness*, vol. 10, no. 11, 20 Aug. 2019, pp. 2429–38, https://doi.org/10.1007/s12671-019-01217-4. Accessed 16 Feb. 2022.

24. Malinowski, Peter, and Liliana Shalamanova. "Meditation and Cognitive Ageing: The Role of Mindfulness Meditation in Building Cognitive Reserve." *Journal of Cognitive Enhancement*, vol. 1, no. 2, 12 Apr. 2017, pp. 96–106, https://doi.org/10.1007/s41465-017-0022-7.

25. Jha. "Examining the Protective Effects."

26. Beauchemin, James, et al. "Mindfulness Meditation May Lessen Anxiety, Promote Social Skills, and Improve Academic Performance among Adolescents with Learning Disabilities." *Complementary Health Practice Review*, vol. 13, no. 1, Jan. 2008, pp. 34–45, https://doi.org/10.1177/1533210107311624.

27. Zeidan, Fadel, et al. "Mindfulness Meditation Improves Cognition: Evidence of Brief Mental Training." *Consciousness and Cognition*, vol. 19, no. 2, June 2010, pp. 597–605, https://doi.org/10.1016/j.concog.2010.03.014.

28. Burgstahler, Matthew S., and Mary C. Stenson. "Effects of Guided Mindfulness Meditation on Anxiety and Stress in a Pre-Healthcare College Student Population: A Pilot Study." *Journal of American College Health*, vol. 68, no. 6, 2 Apr. 2019, pp. 1–7, https://doi.org/10.1080/07448481.2019.1590371.

Chapter 3

1. Survey conducted by Jeffrey Bergin. 2025.

2. Renninger, Ann, et al. "Motivation, Engagement, and Interest: In the End, It Came Down to You and How You Think of the Problem." *International Handbook of the Learning Sciences*, edited by Frank Fischer, et al., Routledge, 2018.

3. Orhan Özen, Sevil. "The Effect of Motivation on Student Achievement." *The Factors Effecting Student Achievement*, edited by Engin Karadag, Springer, 2017, pp. 35–56, https://doi.org/10.1007/978-3-319-56083-0_3.

4. Panksepp, Jaak, et al. *The Archaeology of Mind: Neuroevolutionary Origins of Human Emotions*. W. W. Norton & Co., 2012.; Panksepp, Jaak, and Oxford University Press. *Affective Neuroscience: The Foundations of Human and Animal Emotions*. Oxford University Press, 2014.

5. Duan, Hongxia, et al. "The Effect of Intrinsic and Extrinsic Motivation on Memory Formation: Insight from Behavioral and Imaging Study." *Brain Structure and Function*, vol. 225, 29 Apr. 2020, pp. 1561–74, https://doi.org/10.1007/s00429-020-02074-x.

6. Liu, Yuan, and Shumeng Hou. "Potential Reciprocal Relationship between Motivation and Achievement: A Longitudinal Study." *School Psychology International*, vol. 39, no. 1, 14 June 2017, https://doi.org/10.1177/0143034317710574. Accessed 20 June 2019.

7. Kuvaas, Bård, et al. "Do Intrinsic and Extrinsic Motivation Relate Differently to Employee Outcomes?" *Journal of Economic Psychology*, vol. 61, Aug. 2017, pp. 244–58, https://doi.org/10.1016/j.joep.2017.05.004.

8. Ryan, Richard M., and Edward L. Deci. *Self-Determination Theory: Basic Psychological Needs in Motivation, Development, and Wellness.* Guilford Press, 2017.

9. Fong, Carlton J., et al. "A Meta-Analysis of Negative Feedback on Intrinsic Motivation." *Educational Psychology Review*, vol. 31, no. 1, 15 Aug. 2018, pp. 121–62, https://doi.org/10.1007/s10648-018-9446-6.

10. Nerstad, Christina G. L., et al. "Who Are the High Achievers at Work? Perceived Motivational Climate, Goal Orientation Profiles, and Work Performance." *Scandinavian Journal of Psychology*, vol. 59, no. 6, 28 Sept. 2018, pp. 661–77, https://doi.org/10.1111/sjop.12490. Accessed 11 Dec. 2021.

11. Nerstad et al. "Who Are the High Achievers at Work?"

12. Fong, Carlton J., et al. "A Person-Centered Investigation of Achievement Motivation Goals and Correlates of Community College Student Achievement and Persistence." *Journal of College Student Retention: Research, Theory & Practice*, vol. 20, no. 3, 18 Oct. 2016, pp. 369–87, https://doi.org/10.1177/1521025116673374. Accessed 13 Nov. 2019.

13. Deci, Edward L., et al. "A Meta-Analytic Review of Experiments Examining the Effects of Extrinsic Rewards on Intrinsic Motivation." *Psychological Bulletin*, vol. 125, no. 6, 1999, pp. 627–68, https://doi.org/10.1037/0033-2909.125.6.627. Accessed 15 Feb. 2019.

14. Fischer, Carmen, et al. "The Influence of Intrinsic Motivation and Synergistic Extrinsic Motivators on Creativity and Innovation." *Frontiers in Psychology*, vol. 10, 4 Feb. 2019, https://doi.org/10.3389/fpsyg.2019.00137.

15. Deci et al. "A Meta-Analytic Review."

16. Gneezy, Uri, et al. "When and Why Incentives (Don't) Work to Modify Behavior." *Journal of Economic Perspectives*, vol. 25, no. 4, Nov. 2011, pp. 191–210, https://doi.org/10.1257/jep.25.4.191.

17. Kurtovic, Ana, et al. "Contribution to Family, Friends, School, and Community Is Associated with Fewer Depression Symptoms in Adolescents—Mediated by Self-Regulation and Academic Performance." *Frontiers in Psychology*, vol. 11, 20 Jan. 2021, https://doi.org/10.3389/fpsyg.2020.615249. Accessed 26 Nov. 2021.

18. Yeager, David S., et al. "Boring but Important: A Self-Transcendent Purpose for Learning Fosters Academic Self-Regulation." *Journal of Personality and Social Psychology*, vol. 107, no. 4, 2014, pp. 559–80, https://doi.org/10.1037/a0037637.

19. Lewis, Nathan A., et al. "Purpose in Life and Cognitive Functioning in Adulthood." *Aging, Neuropsychology, and Cognition*, vol. 24, no. 6, 7 Nov. 2016, pp. 662–71, https://doi.org/10.1080/13825585.2016.1251549. Accessed 14 Apr. 2020.

Chapter 4

1. Survey conducted by Jeffrey Bergin. 2025.

2. National Academies of Sciences, Engineering, and Medicine. *Supporting Students' College Success: The Role of Assessment of Intrapersonal and Interpersonal Competencies*, edited by Joan Herman and Margaret Hilton. The National Academies Press, 2017, www.nap.edu/catalog/24697/supporting-students-college-success-the-role-of-assessment-of-intrapersonal. Accessed 22 Feb. 2022.

3. Hamm, Jeremy M., et al. "A Motivation Treatment to Enhance Goal Engagement in Online Learning Environments: Assisting Failure-Prone College Students with Low Optimism." *Motivation Science*, vol. 5, no. 2, June 2019, pp. 116–34, https://doi.org/10.1037/mot0000107. Accessed 19 Jan. 2020.

4. Handoko, Erwin, et al. "Goal Setting and MOOC Completion." *The International Review of Research in Open and Distributed Learning*, vol. 20, no. 3, 5 Feb. 2019, https://doi.org/10.19173/irrodl.v20i4.4270. Accessed 14 Sept. 2019.

5. National Academies of Sciences, Engineering, and Medicine. *Supporting Students' College Success.*

6. Höchli, Bettina, et al. "Making New Year's Resolutions That Stick: Exploring How Superordinate and Subordinate Goals Motivate Goal Pursuit." *Applied Psychology: Health and Well-Being*, vol. 12, no. 1, 24 June 2019, https://doi.org/10.1111/aphw.12172. Accessed 23 Oct. 2019.

7. Schippers, Michaéla C., et al. "Writing about Personal Goals and Plans Regardless of Goal Type Boosts Academic Performance." *Contemporary Educational Psychology*, vol. 60, 1 Jan. 2020, p. 101823, https://doi.org/10.1016/j.cedpsych.2019.101823.

8. Epton, Tracy, et al. "Unique Effects of Setting Goals on Behavior Change: Systematic Review and Meta-Analysis." *Journal of Consulting and Clinical Psychology*, vol. 85, no. 12, 2017, pp. 1182–98, https://doi.org/10.1037/ccp0000260.

9. Robison, Matthew K., et al. "Examining the Effects of Goal-Setting, Feedback, and Incentives on Sustained Attention." *Journal of Experimental Psychology: Human Perception and Performance*, vol. 47, no. 6, June 2021, pp. 869–91, https://doi.org/10.1037/xhp0000926.

10. Park, Jooyoung, et al. "Relative Effects of Forward and Backward Planning on Goal Pursuit." *Psychological Science*, vol. 28, no. 11, 14 Sept. 2017, pp. 1620–30, https://doi.org/10.1177/0956797617715510. Accessed 25 Oct. 2020.

11. Takarada, Yudai, and Daichi Nozaki. "Motivational Goal-Priming with or without Awareness Produces Faster and Stronger Force Exertion." *Scientific Reports*, vol. 8, no. 1, 4 July 2018, https://doi.org/10.1038/s41598-018-28410-0. Accessed 20 May 2020.; Itzchakov, Guy, and Gary P. Latham. "The Moderating Effect of Performance Feedback and the Mediating Effect of Self-Set Goals on the Primed Goal Performance Relationship." *Applied Psychology*, vol. 69, no. 2, 12 Dec. 2018, https://doi.org/10.1111/apps.12176. Accessed 17 Dec. 2019.

12. Stroebe, Wolfgang, et al. "Why Most Dieters Fail but Some Succeed: A Goal Conflict Model of Eating Behavior." *Psychological Review*, vol. 120, no. 1, 2013, pp. 110–38, https://doi.org/10.1037/a0030849.

13. Latham, Gary P. "Toward an Integration of Goal Setting Theory and the Automaticity Model." *Applied Psychology*, vol. 66, no. 1, 18 Oct. 2016, pp. 25–48, https://doi.org/10.1111/apps.12087. Accessed 18 Mar. 2019.

Chapter 5

1. Survey conducted by Jeffrey Bergin. 2025.

2. Hilton, John. "Open Educational Resources, Student Efficacy, and User Perceptions: A Synthesis of Research Published between 2015 and 2018." *Educational Technology Research and Development*, vol. 68, 6 Aug. 2019, pp. 853-76, https://doi.org/10.1007/s11423-019-09700-4. Accessed 25 Nov. 2019.

3. Cerasoli, Christopher P., et al. "Antecedents and Outcomes of Informal Learning Behaviors: A Meta-Analysis." *Journal of Business and Psychology*, vol. 33, no. 2, 26 Apr. 2017, pp. 203–30, https://doi.org/10.1007/s10869-017-9492-y. Accessed 14 Apr. 2020.

4. Fahrenkopf, Erin, et al. "Personnel Mobility and Organizational Performance: The Effects of Specialist vs. Generalist Experience and Organizational Work Structure." *Organization Science*, vol. 31, no. 6, 7 Oct. 2020, https://doi.org/10.1287/orsc.2020.1373. Accessed 3 Nov. 2020.

5. Bijjahalli, Manav Chethan. "Implementing Real World Learning Experiences—a Comparative Study of Competency Levels between Students Going through Current Curriculum and Having Real World Learning Experiences." *Advances in Intelligent Systems and Computing*, vol. 1135, 2020, pp. 409–19, https://doi.org/10.1007/978-3-030-40271-6_41. Accessed 23 Feb. 2022.

6. Gauthier, Thomas. "The Value of Microcredentials: The Employer's Perspective." *The Journal of Competency-Based Education*, vol. 5, no. 2, 4 May 2020, https://doi.org/10.1002/cbe2.1209.

7. Wyness, Gillian, and Richard Murphy. "What Is the Nature and Extent of Student–University Mismatch?" *IZA World of Labor*, 2020, https://doi.org/10.15185/izawol.477.; Kang, Chungseo, and Darlene García Torres. "College Undermatching, Bachelor's Degree Attainment, and Minority Students." *Journal of Diversity in Higher Education*, vol. 14, no. 2, 26 Sept. 2019, https://doi.org/10.1037/dhe0000145.

8. Sladek, Michael R., et al. "Latino Adolescents' Cultural Values Associated with Diurnal Cortisol Activity." *Psychoneuroendocrinology*, vol. 109, Nov. 2019, p. 104403, https://doi.org/10.1016/j.psyneuen.2019.104403. Accessed 4 July 2020.

9. Phillips, L. Taylor, et al. "Access Is Not Enough: Cultural Mismatch Persists to Limit First-Generation Students' Opportunities for Achievement throughout College." *Journal of Personality and Social Psychology*, vol. 119, no. 5, 27 Feb. 2020, https://doi.org/10.1037/pspi0000234. Accessed 29 Feb. 2020.

10. Wurster, Kristin G., et al. "Does Person-Group Fit Matter? A Further Examination of Hope and Belongingness in Academic Enhancement Groups." *Journal of Counseling Psychology*, vol. 68, no. 1, Jan. 2021, pp. 67–76, https://doi.org/10.1037/cou0000437. Accessed 19 Feb. 2021.

11. Kivlighan, D. Martin, et al. "Are Belongingness and Hope Essential Features of Academic Enhancement Groups? A Psychosociocultural Perspective." *Journal of Counseling Psychology*, vol. 65, no. 2, Mar. 2018, pp. 204–13, https://doi.org/10.1037/cou0000266. Accessed 23 Feb. 2022.

12. Korpershoek, H., et al. "The Relationships between School Belonging and Students' Motivational, Social-Emotional, Behavioural, and Academic Outcomes in Secondary Education: A Meta-Analytic Review." *Research Papers in Education*, vol. 35, no. 6, 27 May 2019, pp. 1–40, https://doi.org/10.1080/02671522.2019.1615116.

Chapter 6

1. Survey conducted by Jeffrey Bergin. 2025.

2. Neroni, Joyce, et al. "Learning Strategies and Academic Performance in Distance Education." *Learning and Individual Differences*, vol. 73, July 2019, pp. 1–7, https://doi.org/10.1016/j.lindif.2019.04.007.

3. Trentepohl, Sebastian, et al. "How Did It Get So Late So Soon? The Effects of Time Management Knowledge and Practice on Students' Time Management Skills and Academic Performance." *Sustainability*, vol. 14, no. 9, 2022, article 5097. https://doi.org/10.3390/su1409509.

4. Macan, Therese H., et al. "College Students' Time Management: Correlations with Academic Performance and Stress." *Journal of Educational Psychology*, vol. 82, no. 4, 1990, pp. 760–68, https://doi.org/10.1037/0022-0663.82.4.760.

5. Claessens, Brigitte J. C., et al. "A Review of the Time Management Literature." *Personnel Review*, vol. 36, no. 2, 13 Feb. 2007, pp. 255–76, https://doi.org/10.1108/00483480710726136. Accessed 27 Nov. 2019.

6. Rawashdeh, Oliver, et al. "Clocking in Time to Gate Memory Processes: The Circadian Clock Is Part of the Ins and Outs of Memory." *Neural Plasticity*, vol. 2018, 2018, pp. 1–11, https://doi.org/10.1155/2018/6238989.

7. Baddeley, A. D., et al. "Memory and Time of Day." *Quarterly Journal of Experimental Psychology*, vol. 22, no. 4, Nov. 1970, pp. 605–09, https://doi.org/10.1080/14640747008401939.

8. Trockel, Mickey T., et al. "Health-Related Variables and Academic Performance among First-Year College Students: Implications for Sleep and Other Behaviors." *Journal of American College Health*, vol. 49, no. 3, Nov. 2000, pp. 125–31, https://doi.org/10.1080/07448480009596294.

9. Massing, Till, et al. "When Is the Best Time to Learn?—Evidence from an Introductory Statistics Course." *Open Education Studies*, vol. 3, no. 1, 1 Jan. 2021, pp. 84–95, https://doi.org/10.1515/edu-2020-0144.

10. Mei, Jianyang. "Learning Management System Calendar Reminders and Effects on Time Management and Academic Performance." *International Research and Review*, vol. 6, no. 1, 2016, pp. 29–45, https://eric.ed.gov/?id=EJ1148410. Accessed 23 Feb. 2022.

11. Goldhammer, Frank, et al. "The Time on Task Effect in Reading and Problem Solving Is Moderated by Task Difficulty and Skill: Insights from a Computer-Based Large-Scale Assessment." *Journal of Educational Psychology*, vol. 106, no. 3, 2014, pp. 608–26, https://doi.org/10.1037/a0034716. Accessed 4 May 2019.

12. Blunt, Allan K., and Timothy A. Pychyl. "Task Aversiveness and Procrastination: A Multi-Dimensional Approach to Task Aversiveness across Stages of Personal Projects." *Personality and Individual Differences*, vol. 28, no. 1, Jan. 2000, pp. 153–67, https://doi.org/10.1016/s0191-8869(99)00091-4. Accessed 30 July 2019.

13. Eckert, Marcus, et al. "Overcome Procrastination: Enhancing Emotion Regulation Skills Reduce Procrastination." *Learning and Individual Differences*, vol. 52, Dec. 2016, pp. 10–18, https://doi.org/10.1016/j.lindif.2016.10.001.

14.　Eckert et al. "Overcome Procrastination."

15.　Gurumoorthy, Raghul, and Nikhilesh S. Kumar. "Study of Impactful Motivational Factors to Overcome Procrastination among Engineering Students." *Procedia Computer Science*, vol. 172, 2020, pp. 709–17, https://doi.org/10.1016/j.procs.2020.05.101.; Eerde, Wendelien van, and Katrin B. Klingsieck. "Overcoming Procrastination? A Meta-Analysis of Intervention Studies." *Educational Research Review*, vol. 25, Nov. 2018, pp. 73–85, https://doi.org/10.1016/j.edurev.2018.09.002. Accessed 7 May 2019.

16.　Otermin-Cristeta, Solange, and Martin Hautzinger. "Developing an Intervention to Overcome Procrastination." *Journal of Prevention & Intervention in the Community*, vol. 46, no. 2, 27 Feb. 2018, pp. 171–83, https://doi.org/10.1080/10852352.2016.1198169. Accessed 27 July 2019.

17.　Sirwan Mohammed, Gona, et al. "The Effectiveness of Microlearning to Improve Students' Learning Ability." *International Journal of Educational Research Review*, vol. 3, no. 3, 16 Apr. 2018, pp. 32–38, https://doi.org/10.24331/ijere.415824. Accessed 23 Sept. 2019.

18.　Nikou, S. A., and A. A. Economides. "Mobile-Based Micro-Learning and Assessment: Impact on Learning Performance and Motivation of High School Students." *Journal of Computer Assisted Learning*, vol. 34, no. 3, 13 Feb. 2018, pp. 269–78, https://doi.org/10.1111/jcal.12240.

19.　Rahmatika, Rahmatika, et al. "The Effectiveness of Youtube as an Online Learning Media." *Journal of Education Technology*, vol. 5, no. 1, 8 Apr. 2021, p. 152, https://doi.org/10.23887/jet.v5i1.33628.

20.　Romero-Hall, Enilda. "Posting, Sharing, Networking, and Connecting: Use of Social Media Content by Graduate Students." *TechTrends*, vol. 61, no. 6, 22 Mar. 2017, pp. 580–88, https://doi.org/10.1007/s11528-017-0173-5. Accessed 10 Oct. 2019.

21.　Liu, Dong, et al. "A Meta-Analysis of the Relationship of Academic Performance and Social Network Site Use among Adolescents and Young Adults." *Computers in Human Behavior*, vol. 77, Dec. 2017, pp. 148–57, https://doi.org/10.1016/j.chb.2017.08.039. Accessed 16 Apr. 2019.

Chapter 7

1. Survey conducted by Jeffrey Bergin. 2025.

2. Abdous, M'hammed. "Well Begun Is Half Done: Using Online Orientation to Foster Online Students' Academic Self-Efficacy." *Online Learning*, vol. 23, no. 3, 1 Sept. 2019, https://doi.org/10.24059/olj. v23i3.1437. Accessed 8 Sept. 2019.

3. Lerner Colucci, Rachel. "The Impact of an Online Orientation Program on Student Success at a Community College." *Journal of College Orientation, Transition, and Retention*, vol. 27, no. 1, 11 May 2020, https://doi.org/10.24926/jcotr.v27i1.2251. Accessed 27 July 2020.

4. Raymark, Patrick H., and Patricia A. Connor-Greene. "The Syllabus Quiz." *Teaching of Psychology*, vol. 29, no. 4, Oct. 2002, pp. 286–88, https://doi.org/10.1207/s15328023top2904_05. Accessed 8 Apr. 2020.

5. Osueke, Bethany, et al. "How Undergraduate Science Students Use Learning Objectives to Study." *Journal of Microbiology & Biology Education*, vol. 19, no. 2, 25 May 2018, https://doi.org/10.1128/jmbe. v19i2.1510.

6. Schneider, Sascha, et al. "A Meta-Analysis of How Signaling Affects Learning with Media." *Educational Research Review*, vol. 23, Feb. 2018, pp. 1–24, https://doi.org/10.1016/j.edurev.2017.11.001. Accessed 11 Dec. 2019.

7. Bogaerds Hazenberg, Suzanne T. M., et al. "A Meta-Analysis on the Effects of Text Structure Instruction on Reading Comprehension in the Upper Elementary Grades." *Reading Research Quarterly*, vol. 56, no. 3, 17 Apr. 2020, https://doi.org/10.1002/rrq.311.

8. Dirksen, Julie. *Design for How People Learn*. New Riders, 2015, p. 2.

9. Dirksen. *Design for How People Learn*, p. 43.

10. Witherby, Amber E., and Shana K. Carpenter. "The Rich-Get-Richer Effect: Prior Knowledge Predicts New Learning of Domain-Relevant Information." *Journal of Experimental Psychology: Learning, Memory, and Cognition*, 4 Feb. 2021, https://doi.org/10.1037/xlm0000996. Accessed 26 Apr. 2021.

11. Liu, Zhong-Xu, et al. "The Effect of Prior Knowledge on Post-Encoding Brain Connectivity and Its Relation to Subsequent Memory." *NeuroImage*, vol. 167, Feb. 2018, pp. 211–23, https://doi. org/10.1016/j.neuroimage.2017.11.032. Accessed 29 July 2020.

12. Witherby and Carpenter. "The Rich-Get-Richer Effect."

13. Wade, Shirlene, and Celeste Kidd. "The Role of Prior Knowledge and Curiosity in Learning." *Psychonomic Bulletin & Review*, vol. 26, no. 4, 11 May 2019, pp. 1377–87, https://doi.org/10.3758/s13423-019-01598-6.

14. Brooks, D. Christopher. "Space Matters: The Impact of Formal Learning Environments on Student Learning." *British Journal of Educational Technology*, vol. 42, no. 5, 7 June 2010, pp. 719–26, https://doi.org/10.1111/j.1467-8535.2010.01098.x.

15. Loderer, Kristina, et al. "Beyond Cold Technology: A Systematic Review and Meta-Analysis on Emotions in Technology-Based Learning Environments." *Learning and Instruction*, vol. 70, Nov. 2018, p. 101162, https://doi.org/10.1016/j.learninstruc.2018.08.002. Accessed 22 Feb. 2020.

16. Sage, Kara, et al. "Reading from Print, Laptop Computer, and E-Reader: Differences and Similarities for College Students' Learning." *Journal of Research on Technology in Education*, vol. 52, no. 4, 7 May 2020, pp. 441–60, https://doi.org/10.1080/15391523.2020.1713264.

Chapter 8

1. Survey conducted by Jeffrey Bergin. 2025.

2. Donker, A. S., et al. "Effectiveness of Learning Strategy Instruction on Academic Performance: A Meta-Analysis." *Educational Research Review*, vol. 11, Jan. 2014, pp. 1–26, https://doi.org/10.1016/j.edurev.2013.11.002. Accessed 29 July 2019.

3. Boer, Hester de, et al. "Long-Term Effects of Metacognitive Strategy Instruction on Student Academic Performance: A Meta-Analysis." *Educational Research Review*, vol. 24, June 2018, pp. 98–115, https://doi.org/10.1016/j.edurev.2018.03.002. Accessed 24 Apr. 2020.

4. Ergen, Binnur, and Sedat Kanadli. "The Effect of Self-Regulated Learning Strategies on Academic Achievement: A Meta-Analysis Study." *Eurasian Journal of Educational Research*, vol. 69, 2017, https://eric.ed.gov/?id=EJ1148778. Accessed 25 Feb. 2022.

5. Panadero, Ernesto. "A Review of Self-Regulated Learning: Six Models and Four Directions for Research." *Frontiers in Psychology*, vol. 8, no. 422, 28 Apr. 2017, https://doi.org/10.3389/fpsyg.2017.00422.

6. Panadero. "A Review of Self-Regulated Learning."

7. Schunk, Dale, and Barry Zimmerman. *Self-Regulated Learning: From Teaching to Self-Reflective Practice.* The Guilford Press, 1998, p. 2.

8. Zimmerman, Barry J. "Attaining Self-Regulation: A Social Cognitive Perspective." *Handbook of Self-Regulation*, edited by M. Boekaerts, et al., Academic Press, 2000, pp. 13–40.

9. Zimmerman. "Attaining Self-Regulation."

10. Zimmerman. "Attaining Self-Regulation."

11. Ellis, Shmuel, et al. "Systematic Reflection: Implications for Learning from Failures and Successes." *Current Directions in Psychological Science*, vol. 23, no. 1, Feb. 2014, pp. 67–72, https://doi.org/10.1177/0963721413504106. Accessed 7 July 2019.

12. Anseel, Frederik, et al. "Reflection as a Strategy to Enhance Task Performance after Feedback." *Organizational Behavior and Human Decision Processes*, vol. 110, no. 1, Sept. 2009, pp. 23–35, https://doi.org/10.1016/j.obhdp.2009.05.003.

13. Darabi, Aubteen, et al. "Learning from Failure: A Meta-Analysis of the Empirical Studies." *Educational Technology Research and Development*, vol. 66, no. 5, 2018, pp. 1101–18, https://doi.org/10.1007/s11423-018-9579-9.

14. DeRue, D. Scott, et al. "A Quasi-Experimental Study of After-Event Reviews and Leadership Development." *Journal of Applied Psychology*, vol. 97, no. 5, 2012, pp. 997–1015, https://doi.org/10.1037/a0028244. Accessed 6 May 2020.

15. Zimmerman. "Attaining Self-Regulation."

16. Seufert, Tina. "The Interplay between Self-Regulation in Learning and Cognitive Load." *Educational Research Review*, vol. 24, June 2018, pp. 116–29, https://doi.org/10.1016/j.edurev.2018.03.004. Accessed 11 Nov. 2019.

Chapter 9

1. Survey conducted by Jeffrey Bergin. 2025.

2. Choi, Hwan-Hee, et al. "Effects of the Physical Environment on Cognitive Load and Learning: Towards a New Model of Cognitive Load." *Educational Psychology Review*, vol. 26, no. 2, 3 Apr. 2014, pp. 225–44, https://doi.org/10.1007/s10648-014-9262-6.

3. Knight, Craig, and S. Alexander Haslam. "The Relative Merits of Lean, Enriched, and Empowered Offices: An Experimental Examination of the Impact of Workspace Management Strategies on Well-Being and Productivity." *Journal of Experimental Psychology: Applied*, vol. 16, no. 2, 2010, pp. 158–72, https://doi.org/10.1037/a0019292.

4. Knight and Haslam. "The Relative Merits."

5. Nieuwenhuis, Marlon, et al. "The Relative Benefits of Green versus Lean Office Space: Three Field Experiments." *Journal of Experimental Psychology: Applied*, vol. 20, no. 3, 2014, pp. 199–214, https://doi.org/10.1037/xap0000024.

6. Rau, Martina, et al. "Do Affordances of Classroom Furniture Affect Learning in Undergraduate Active-Learning Courses?" *ISLS Repository*, June 2020, https://repository.isls.org/handle/1/6841.

7. Angwin, Anthony J., et al. "White Noise Enhances New-Word Learning in Healthy Adults." *Scientific Reports*, vol. 7, no. 1, 12 Oct. 2017, https://doi.org/10.1038/s41598-017-13383-3.; Angwin, Anthony J., et al. "White Noise Facilitates New-Word Learning from Context." *Brain and Language*, vol. 199, 1 Dec. 2019, p. 104699, https://doi.org/10.1016/j.bandl.2019.104699.

8. Rausch, Vanessa H., et al. "White Noise Improves Learning by Modulating Activity in Dopaminergic Midbrain Regions and Right Superior Temporal Sulcus." *Journal of Cognitive Neuroscience*, vol. 26, no. 7, July 2014, pp. 1469–80, https://doi.org/10.1162/jocn_a_00537.

9. DeLoach, Alana G., et al. "Tuning the Cognitive Environment: Sound Masking with 'Natural' Sounds in Open-Plan Offices." *The Journal of the Acoustical Society of America*, vol. 137, no. 4, Apr. 2015, p. 2291, https://doi.org/10.1121/1.4920363.

10. Fernandez, Diego Carlos, et al. "Light Affects Mood and Learning through Distinct Retina-Brain Pathways." *Cell*, vol. 175, no. 1, 20 Sept. 2018, pp. 71–84.e18, https://doi.org/10.1016/j.cell.2018.08.004.

11. Gilavand, Abdolreza, et al. "Investigating the Impact of Lighting Educational Spaces on Learning and Academic Achievement of Elementary Students." *International Journal of Pediatrics*, vol. 4, no. 5, 2016, pp. 1819–28, https://doi.org/10.22038/ijp.2016.6768. Accessed 16 Feb. 2022.; Pettersen, Jacqueline A., et al. "The Effects of Vitamin D Insufficiency and Seasonal Decrease on Cognition." *Canadian Journal of Neurological Sciences*, vol. 41, no. 4, 1 July 2014, pp. 459–65, https://doi.org/10.1017/S0317167100018497. Accessed 16 Feb. 2022.

12. Zhu, Yingying, et al. "Effects of Illuminance and Correlated Color Temperature on Daytime Cognitive Performance, Subjective Mood, and Alertness in Healthy Adults." *Environment and Behavior*, vol. 51, no. 2, 28 Oct. 2017, pp. 199–230, https://doi.org/10.1177/0013916517738077.

13. Barkmann, Claus, et al. "Applicability and Efficacy of Variable Light in Schools." *Physiology & Behavior*, vol. 105, no. 3, Feb. 2012, pp. 621–27, https://doi.org/10.1016/j.physbeh.2011.09.020.

14. Goodman, Joshua, et al. "Heat and Learning." *National Bureau of Economic Research Working Paper Series*, 24 May 2018, www.nber.org/papers/w24639.

15. Seppänen, O, et al. *Room Temperature and Productivity in Office Work.* Conference proceedings, Indoor Environment Berkeley Lab, University of California, 2006, https://indoor.lbl.gov/publications/room-temperature-and-productivity.

16. Amani, Hamed, et al. "Color and Its Impact on People in the Workplace: A Systematic Review Article." *Iranian Journal of Ergonomics*, vol. 8, no. 1, 10 May 2020, pp. 1–11, https://doi.org/10.30699/jergon.8.1.8.

17. Skaugset, L. Melissa, et al. "Can You Multitask? Evidence and Limitations of Task Switching and Multitasking in Emergency Medicine." *Annals of Emergency Medicine*, vol. 68, no. 2, Aug. 2016, pp. 189–95, https://doi.org/10.1016/j.annemergmed.2015.10.003. Accessed 7 Jan. 2021.

18. Fernandes, Myra A., and Morris Moscovitch. "Divided Attention and Memory: Evidence of Substantial Interference Effects at Retrieval and Encoding." *Journal of Experimental Psychology: General*, vol. 129, no. 2, 2000, pp. 155–76, https://doi.org/10.1037/0096-3445.129.2.155.

19. Junco, Reynol. "In-Class Multitasking and Academic Performance." *Computers in Human Behavior*, vol. 28, no. 6, Nov. 2012, pp. 2236–43, https://doi.org/10.1016/j.chb.2012.06.031.

20. Pijeira-Díaz, H. J., et al. "Profiling Sympathetic Arousal in a Physics Course: How Active Are Students?" *Journal of Computer Assisted Learning*, vol. 34, no. 4, 8 May 2018, pp. 397–408, https://doi.org/10.1111/jcal.12271.

21. Raichle, M. E., and D. A. Gusnard. "Appraising the Brain's Energy Budget." *Proceedings of the National Academy of Sciences*, vol. 99, no. 16, 29 July 2002, pp. 10237–39, https://doi.org/10.1073/pnas.172399499.

22. Ko, Li-Wei, et al. "Sustained Attention in Real Classroom Settings: An EEG Study." *Frontiers in Human Neuroscience*, vol. 11, 31 July 2017, https://doi.org/10.3389/fnhum.2017.00388.

23. Lovato, Nicole, and Leon Lack. "The Effects of Napping on Cognitive Functioning." *Progress in Brain Research*, vol. 185, 2010, pp. 155–66, https://doi.org/10.1016/B978-0-444-53702-7.00009-9.

24. Basu, Avik, et al. "Attention Restoration Theory: Exploring the Role of Soft Fascination and Mental Bandwidth." *Environment and Behavior*, vol. 51, no. 9–10, 16 May 2018, https://doi.org/10.1177/0013916518774400.

25. Geraerts, Elke, et al. "Suppression of Intrusive Thoughts and Working Memory Capacity in Repressive Coping." *The American Journal of Psychology*, vol. 120, no. 2, 1 July 2007, p. 205, https://doi.org/10.2307/20445395. Accessed 27 Mar. 2020.

26. Kim, Hyojeong, et al. "Changes to Information in Working Memory Depend on Distinct Removal Operations." *Nature Communications*, vol. 11, no. 1, 7 Dec. 2020, p. 6239, https://doi.org/10.1038/s41467-020-20085-4. Accessed 18 Jan. 2021.

27. Stramaccia, Davide F., et al. "Memory Suppression and Its Deficiency in Psychological Disorders: A Focused Meta-Analysis." *Journal of Experimental Psychology: General*, vol. 150, no. 5, May 2021, pp. 828–50, https://doi.org/10.1037/xge0000971. Accessed 8 Nov. 2021.

28. Morris, Jenny, et al. "A High Perceptual Load Task Reduces Thoughts about Chocolate, Even While Hungry." *Appetite*, vol. 151, Aug. 2020, p. 104694, https://doi.org/10.1016/j.appet.2020.104694. Accessed 14 Feb. 2021.

29. Kim, Sooyeol, et al. "Daily Micro-Breaks and Job Performance: General Work Engagement as a Cross-Level Moderator." *Journal of Applied Psychology*, vol. 103, no. 7, July 2018, pp. 772–86, https://doi.org/10.1037/apl0000308.

30. Fenesi, Barbara, et al. "Sweat So You Don't Forget: Exercise Breaks during a University Lecture Increase On-Task Attention and Learning." *Journal of Applied Research in Memory and Cognition*, vol. 7, no. 2, June 2018, pp. 261–69, https://doi.org/10.1016/j.jarmac.2018.01.012. Accessed 20 Nov. 2019.

31. Mullins, Nicole M., et al. "Elementary School Classroom Physical Activity Breaks: Student, Teacher, and Facilitator Perspectives." *Advances in Physiology Education*, vol. 43, no. 2, 1 June 2019, pp. 140–48, https://doi.org/10.1152/advan.00002.2019.

32. Inchara, Naidu, et al. "The Hidden Benefits of Daydreaming." *Drug Invention Today*, vol. 10, no. 11, Nov. 2018, pp. 2127–29, https://openurl.ebsco.com/EPDB%3Agcd%3A2%3A11694066/detailv2?sid=ebsco%3Aplink%3Ascholar&id=ebsco%3Agc-d%3A132173452&crl=c&link_origin=www.google.com. Accessed 23 Feb. 2022.

33. Golchert, Johannes, et al. "Individual Variation in Intentionality in the Mind-Wandering State Is Reflected in the Integration of the Default-Mode, Fronto-Parietal, and Limbic Networks." *NeuroImage*, vol. 146, Feb. 2017, pp. 226–35, https://doi.org/10.1016/j.neuroimage.2016.11.025. Accessed 16 Jan. 2021.

34. Seli, Paul, et al. "Mind-Wandering with and without Intention." *Trends in Cognitive Sciences*, vol. 20, no. 8, Aug. 2016, pp. 605–17, https://doi.org/10.1016/j.tics.2016.05.010.

35. Baer, Markus, et al. "Zoning Out or Breaking Through? Linking Daydreaming to Creativity in the Workplace." *Academy of Management Journal*, vol. 64, no. 5, 1 July 2020, https://doi.org/10.5465/amj.2017.1283.

36. Zedelius, Claire, and Jonathan Schooler, "The Richness of Inner Experience: Relating Styles of Daydreaming to Creative Process." *Frontiers in Psychology*, vol. 6, 1 Feb. 2016, https://doi.org/10.3389/fpsyg.2015.02063.

Chapter 10

1. Survey conducted by Jeffrey Bergin. 2025.

2. Nadel, L., et al. "Memory Formation, Consolidation and Transformation." *Neuroscience & Biobehavioral Reviews*, vol. 36, no. 7, Aug. 2012, pp. 1640–45, https://doi.org/10.1016/j.neubiorev.2012.03.001.

3. Shipstead, Zach, et al. "Is Working Memory Training Effective?" *Psychological Bulletin*, vol. 138, no. 4, 2012, pp. 628–54. https://doi.org/10.1037/a0027473. Accessed 23 Feb. 2022.

4. Pappa, Katerina, et al. "Working Memory Updating Training Promotes Plasticity & Behavioural Gains: A Systematic Review & Meta-Analysis." *Neuroscience & Biobehavioral Reviews*, vol. 118, Nov. 2020, pp. 209–35, https://doi.org/10.1016/j.neubiorev.2020.07.027. Accessed 13 Apr. 2021.

5. Autin, Frédérique, and Jean-Claude Croizet. "Improving Working Memory Efficiency by Reframing Metacognitive Interpretation of Task Difficulty." *Journal of Experimental Psychology: General*, vol. 141, no. 4, 2012, pp. 610–18, https://doi.org/10.1037/a0027478. Accessed 2 Apr. 2020.

6. Reichardt, Robert M., et al. "Novelty Manipulations, Memory Performance, and Predictive Coding: The Role of Unexpectedness." *Frontiers in Human Neuroscience*, vol. 14, 2020, article 152, https://doi.org/10.3389/fnhum.2020.00152.

7. Kafkas, Alex, and Daniela Montaldi. "How Do Memory Systems Detect and Respond to Novelty?" *Neuroscience Letters*, vol. 680, July 2018, pp. 60–68, https://doi.org/10.1016/j.neulet.2018.01.053.

8. Reichardt, Richárd, et al. "Novelty Manipulations, Memory Performance, and Predictive Coding: The Role of Unexpectedness." *Frontiers in Human Neuroscience*, vol. 14, 29 Apr. 2020, https://doi.org/10.3389/fnhum.2020.00152. Accessed 25 Feb. 2022.

9. Boeve-de Pauw, Jelle, et al. "Effective Field Trips in Nature: The Interplay between Novelty and Learning." *Journal of Biological Education*, vol. 53, no. 1, 22 Jan. 2018, pp. 21–33, https://doi.org/10.108 0/00219266.2017.1418760.

10. Oltmanns, Jan, et al. "Don't Lose Your Brain at Work—the Role of Recurrent Novelty at Work in Cognitive and Brain Aging." *Frontiers in Psychology*, vol. 8, 6 Feb. 2017, https://doi.org/10.3389/ fpsyg.2017.00117. Accessed 15 Dec. 2019.

11. Bakken, Jeffrey P. "Mnemonic Strategies: Helping Students with Intellectual and Developmental Disabilities Remember Important Information." *Global Journal of Intellectual & Developmental Disabilities*, vol. 2, no. 3, 28 July 2017, https://doi.org/10.19080/ gjidd.2017.02.555587. Accessed 11 Dec. 2018.

12. Laing, G. "An Empirical Test of Mnemonic Devices to Improve Learning in Elementary Accounting." *Journal of Education for Business*, vol. 85, no. 6, 2010, pp. 349–358.

13. Dresler, Martin, et al. "Mnemonic Training Reshapes Brain Networks to Support Superior Memory." *Neuron*, vol. 93, no. 5, Mar. 2017, pp. 1227–35.e6, https://doi.org/10.1016/j.neuron.2017.02.003.

14. Bakken. "Mnemonic Strategies."

15. Bakken. "Mnemonic Strategies."

16. Tullis, Jonathan G., and Jason R. Finley. "Self-Generated Memory Cues: Effective Tools for Learning, Training, and Remembering." *Policy Insights from the Behavioral and Brain Sciences*, vol. 5, no. 2, 21 Aug. 2018, pp. 179–86, https://doi.org/10.1177/2372732218788092. Accessed 29 Sept. 2020.

17. Ericsson, K. A., and W. Kintsch. "Long-Term Working Memory." *Psychological Review*, vol. 102, no. 2, 1995, pp. 211–45, https://doi. org/10.1037/0033-295x.102.2.211.

18. Fernandes, Myra A., et al. "The Surprisingly Powerful Influence of Drawing on Memory." *Current Directions in Psychological Science*, vol. 27, no. 5, 30 Aug. 2018, pp. 302–08, https://doi. org/10.1177/0963721418755385.

19. Wammes, Jeffrey D, et al. "Creating a Recollection-Based Memory through Drawing." *Journal of Experimental Psychology: Learning, Memory, and Cognition*, vol. 44, no. 5, 2018, pp. 734–51, https://doi. org/10.1037/xlm0000445. Accessed 3 Oct. 2019.

20. Meade, Melissa E., et al. "Drawing as an Encoding Tool: Memorial Benefits in Younger and Older Adults." *Experimental Aging Research*, vol. 44, no. 5, 9 Oct. 2018, pp. 369–96, https://doi.org/10.1080/03610 73x.2018.1521432. Accessed 19 Apr. 2020.

21. Swallow, Khena M., and Yuhong V. Jiang. "The Attentional Boost Effect Really Is a Boost: Evidence from a New Baseline." *Attention, Perception, & Psychophysics*, vol. 76, no. 5, 8 May 2014, pp. 1298–1307, https://doi.org/10.3758/s13414-014-0677-4. Accessed 16 Apr. 2021.

22. Swallow, Khena M., and Yuhong V. Jiang. "The Attentional Boost Effect: Transient Increases in Attention to One Task Enhance Performance in a Second Task." *Cognition*, vol. 115, no. 1, Apr. 2010, pp. 118–32, https:// doi.org/10.1016/j.cognition.2009.12.003. Accessed 4 Mar. 2020.

23. Bartsch, Lea M., et al. "Dissociating Refreshing and Elaboration and Their Impacts on Memory." *NeuroImage*, vol. 199, Oct. 2019, pp. 585–97, https://doi.org/10.1016/j.neuroimage.2019.06.028. Accessed 18 July 2021.

24. Amaral, Juliana. "Note Taking, Highlighting, Rereading: Comparing the Effectiveness of Study Strategies on Comprehension, Retention, and Learning from EFL Texts." *UFSC Institutional Repository*, 2019, https://repositorio.ufsc.br/handle/123456789/211518. Accessed 25 Feb. 2022.

25. Bartsch et al. "The Effects of Refreshing."

26. Oberauer, Klaus. "Is Rehearsal an Effective Maintenance Strategy for Working Memory?" *Trends in Cognitive Sciences*, vol. 23, no. 9, Sept. 2019, pp. 798–809, https://doi.org/10.1016/j.tics.2019.06.002.

27. Himmer, L., et al. "Rehearsal Initiates Systems Memory Consolidation, Sleep Makes It Last." *Science Advances*, vol. 5, no. 4, Apr. 2019, p. eaav1695, https://doi.org/10.1126/sciadv.aav1695. Accessed 4 Aug. 2019.

28. Hostetter, Autumn B., et al. "The Role of Retrieval Practice in Memory and Analogical Problem-Solving." *Quarterly Journal of Experimental Psychology*, vol. 72, no. 4, 7 May 2018, pp. 858–71, https://doi. org/10.1177/1747021818771928.

Chapter 11

1. Survey conducted by Jeffrey Bergin. 2025.

2. Freeman, S., et al. "Active Learning Increases Student Performance in Science, Engineering, and Mathematics." *Proceedings of the National Academy of Sciences*, vol. 111, no. 23, 12 May 2014, pp. 8410–15, https://doi.org/10.1073/pnas.1319030111.

3. Nokes-Malach, Timothy J., et al. "When Is It Better to Learn Together? Insights from Research on Collaborative Learning." *Educational Psychology Review*, vol. 27, no. 4, 6 June 2015, pp. 645–56, https://doi.org/10.1007/s10648-015-9312-8. Accessed 26 Mar. 2019.

4. Nokes-Malach et al. "When Is It Better?"

5. Apugliese, Andrew, and Scott E. Lewis. "Impact of Instructional Decisions on the Effectiveness of Cooperative Learning in Chemistry through Meta-Analysis." *Chemistry Education Research and Practice*, vol. 18, no. 1, 2017, pp. 271–78, https://doi.org/10.1039/c6rp00195e. Accessed 5 Apr. 2021.

6. Nokes-Malach et al. "When Is It Better?"

7. Chen, Juanjuan, et al. "The Role of Collaboration, Computer Use, Learning Environments, and Supporting Strategies in CSCL: A Meta-Analysis." *Review of Educational Research*, vol. 88, no. 6, Dec. 2018, pp. 799–843, https://doi.org/10.3102/0034654318791584.

8. Jeong, Heisawn, et al. "Ten Years of Computer-Supported Collaborative Learning: A Meta-Analysis of CSCL in STEM Education During 2005–2014." *Educational Research Review*, vol. 28, Nov. 2019, p. 100284, https://doi.org/10.1016/j.edurev.2019.100284.

9. Sung, Yao-Ting, et al. "The Effects of Mobile-Computer-Supported Collaborative Learning: Meta-Analysis and Critical Synthesis." *Review of Educational Research*, vol. 87, no. 4, 27 Apr. 2017, pp. 768–805, https://doi.org/10.3102/0034654317704307.

10. Madland, Colin, and Griff Richards. "Enhancing Student-Student Online Interaction: Exploring the Study Buddy Peer Review Activity." *The International Review of Research in Open and Distributed Learning*, vol. 17, no. 3, 16 May 2016, https://doi.org/10.19173/irrodl.v17i3.2179. Accessed 21 Nov. 2019.

11. Tenenbaum, Harriet R., et al. "How Effective Is Peer Interaction in Facilitating Learning? A Meta-Analysis." *Journal of Educational Psychology*, vol. 112, no. 7, 12 Dec. 2019, https://doi.org/10.1037/edu0000436.

12. Bredow, Carrie A., et al. "To Flip or Not to Flip? A Meta-Analysis of the Efficacy of Flipped Learning in Higher Education." *Review of Educational Research*, vol. 91, no. 6, 28 June 2021, p. 003465432110191, https://doi.org/10.3102/00346543211019122.

13. Kim, Shin Hyang, and Jong Mi Lim. "A Systematic Review and Meta-Analysis of Flipped Learning among University Students in Korea: Self-Directed Learning, Learning Motivation, Efficacy, and Learning Achievement." *The Journal of Korean Academic Society of Nursing Education*, vol. 27, no. 1, 28 Feb. 2021, pp. 5–15, https://doi:10.5977/jkasne.2021.27.1.5.

14. Kozikoglu, Ishak. "Analysis of the Studies Concerning Flipped Learning Model: A Comparative Meta-Synthesis Study." *International Journal of Instruction*, vol. 12, no. 1, 1 Jan. 2019, pp. 851–68, https://eric.ed.gov/?id=EJ1201225. Accessed 26 Feb. 2022.

15. Låg, Torstein, and Rannveig Grøm Sæle. "Does the Flipped Classroom Improve Student Learning and Satisfaction? A Systematic Review and Meta-Analysis." *AERA Open*, vol. 5, no. 3, July 2019, p. 233285841987048, https://doi.org/10.1177/2332858419870489.

16. Karagöl, İbrahim, and Emrullah Esen. "The Effect of Flipped Learning Approach on Academic Achievement: A Meta-Analysis Study." *Hacettepe Üniversitesi Eğitim Fakültesi Dergisi*, vol. 34, no. 3, 31 July 2019, pp. 708–27, https://doi.org/10.16986/HUJE.2018046755. Accessed 26 Feb. 2022.

17. Kolb, David. *Experiential Learning: Experience as the Source of Learning and Development*. Pearson FT Press, 2014, p. 2.

18. Kolb. *Experiential Learning*, p. 6.

19. Burch, Gerald F., et al. "A Meta-Analysis of the Relationship between Experiential Learning and Learning Outcomes." *Decision Sciences Journal of Innovative Education*, vol. 17, no. 3, July 2019, pp. 239–73, https://doi.org/10.1111/dsji.12188.

20. Morris, Thomas Howard. "Experiential Learning—A Systematic Review and Revision of Kolb's Model." *Interactive Learning Environments*, vol. 28, no. 6, 2020, pp. 1–14, https://doi.org/10.1080/10 494820.2019.1570279.

21. Alibali, Martha W., and Mitchell J. Nathan. "Embodied Cognition in Learning and Teaching." *International Handbook of the Learning Sciences*, edited by Frank Fischer et al., Routledge, 2018.

22. Fugate, Jennifer M. B., et al. "The Role of Embodied Cognition for Transforming Learning." *International Journal of School & Educational Psychology*, vol. 7, no. 4, 1 Aug. 2018, pp. 274–88, https://doi.org/10.10 80/21683603.2018.1443856.; Kosmas, Panagiotis, et al. "Implementing Embodied Learning in the Classroom: Effects on Children's Memory and Language Skills." *Educational Media International*, vol. 56, no. 1, 20 Nov. 2018, pp. 59–74, https://doi.org/10.1080/09523987.2 018.1547948.

23. Hattie, John, et al. "Effects of Learning Skills Interventions on Student Learning: A Meta-Analysis." *Review of Educational Research*, vol. 66, no. 2, June 1996, pp. 99–136, https://doi. org/10.3102/00346543066002099.

24. Voyer, Daniel, and Petra Jansen. "Motor Expertise and Performance in Spatial Tasks: A Meta-Analysis." *Human Movement Science*, vol. 54, Aug. 2017, pp. 110–24, https://doi.org/10.1016/j.humov.2017.04.004. Accessed 26 Sept. 2020.; O'Brien, Bridget C., and Alexis Battista. "Situated Learning Theory in Health Professions Education Research: A Scoping Review." *Advances in Health Sciences Education*, vol. 25, 22 June 2019, https://doi.org/10.1007/s10459-019-09900-w.

Chapter 12

1. Survey conducted by Jeffrey Bergin. 2025.

2. Ericsson, K. Anders, and Kyle W. Harwell. "Deliberate Practice and Proposed Limits on the Effects of Practice on the Acquisition of Expert Performance: Why the Original Definition Matters and Recommendations for Future Research." *Frontiers in Psychology*, vol. 10, 25 Oct. 2019, https://doi.org/10.3389/fpsyg.2019.02396.

3. Bested, Stephen R., et al. "Combining Unassisted and Robot-Guided Practice Benefits Motor Learning for a Golf Putting Task." *Journal of Motor Learning and Development*, vol. 7, no. 3, 1 Dec. 2019, pp. 408–25, https://doi.org/10.1123/jmld.2018-0040. Accessed 17 Apr. 2020.

4. Macnamara, Brooke N., et al. "Deliberate Practice and Performance in Music, Games, Sports, Education, and Professions: A Meta-Analysis." *Psychological Science*, vol. 25, no. 8, July 2014, pp. 1608–18, https://doi.org/10.1177/0956797614535810.

5. Ragazou, Vasiliki, and Ilias Karasavvidis. "The Effects of Blocked and Massed Practice Opportunities on Learning Software Applications with Video Tutorials." *Journal of Computers in Education*, vol. 9, pp. 173–93, 10 Aug. 2021, https://doi.org/10.1007/s40692-021-00198-5. Accessed 13 Nov. 2021.; Richter, Juliane, et al. "How Massed Practice Improves Visual Expertise in Reading Panoramic Radiographs in Dental Students: An Eye Tracking Study." *PLOS ONE*, vol. 15, no. 12, 3 Dec. 2020, p. e0243060, https://doi.org/10.1371/journal.pone.0243060. Accessed 20 Apr. 2021.; Mustofa, Fuad, et al. "Differences in the Effect of Learning Methods Massed Practice Throwing and Distributed Practice on Learning Outcomes Skills for the Accuracy of Top Softball." *Spor Bilimleri Araştırmaları Dergisi*, vol. 4, no. 2, 31 Dec. 2019, pp. 213–22, https://doi.org/10.25307/jssr.571793. Accessed 27 Jan. 2020.

6. Barzagar Nazari, Katharina, and Mirjam Ebersbach. "Distributed Practice: Rarely Realized in Self-Regulated Mathematical Learning." *Frontiers in Psychology*, vol. 9, 20 Nov. 2018, https://doi.org/10.3389/fpsyg.2018.02170.; Suzuki, Yuichi. "Optimizing Fluency Training for Speaking Skills Transfer: Comparing the Effects of Blocked and Interleaved Task Repetition." *Language Learning*, vol. 71, no. 2, 24 Sept. 2020, https://doi.org/10.1111/lang.12433. Accessed 31 Dec. 2020.

7. Chen, O., et al. "Spacing and Interleaving Effects Require Distinct Theoretical Bases: A Systematic Review Testing the Cognitive Load and Discriminative-Contrast Hypotheses." *Educational Psychology Review*, vol. 3, 2021, pp. 1499–1522, https://doi.org/10.1007/s10648-021-09613-w.

8. Carvalho, Paulo F., et al. "Self-Regulated Spacing in a Massive Open Online Course Is Related to Better Learning." *npj Science of Learning*, vol. 5, no. 1, 16 Mar. 2020, pp. 1–7, https://doi.org/10.1038/s41539-020-0061-1. Accessed 25 May 2020.

9. Johanson, Colby, et al. "Press Pause When You Play: Comparing Spaced Practice Intervals for Skill Development in Games." *Proceedings of the Annual Symposium on Computer-Human Interaction in Play*, 17 Oct. 2019, https://doi.org/10.1145/3311350.3347195. Accessed 30 Aug. 2020.

10. Kaipa, Ramesh, et al. "Role of Massed versus Distributed Practice in Learning Novel Foreign Language Utterances." *Motor Control*, vol. 24, no. 1, 27 June 2019, pp. 1–22, https://doi.org/10.1123/mc.2018-0007.

11. Foster, Nathaniel L., et al. "Why Does Interleaving Improve Math Learning? The Contributions of Discriminative Contrast and Distributed Practice." *Memory & Cognition*, vol. 47, 15 Mar. 2019, https://doi.org/10.3758/s13421-019-00918-4. Accessed 9 Apr. 2019.

12. Foster, Nathaniel L. "Why Does Interleaving Improve Math Learning?"

13. Brunmair, Matthias, and Tobias Richter. "Supplemental Material for Similarity Matters: A Meta-Analysis of Interleaved Learning and Its Moderators." *Psychological Bulletin*, vol. 145, no. 11, 2019, https://doi.org/10.1037/bul0000209.supp. Accessed 14 Nov. 2019.

14. Apolinário-Souza, Tércio, et al. "Molecular Mechanisms Associated with the Benefits of Variable Practice in Motor Learning." *Journal of Motor Behavior*, vol. 52, no. 5, 7 Aug. 2019, pp. 515–26, https://doi.org/10.1080/00222895.2019.1649997. Accessed 21 June 2021.

15. Stambaugh, Laura A. "When Repetition Isn't the Best Practice Strategy: Effects of Blocked and Random Practice Schedules." *Journal of Research in Music Education*, vol. 58, no. 4, 2 Nov. 2010, pp. 368–83, https://doi.org/10.1177/0022429410385945. Accessed 19 Oct. 2020.

16. Sharp, Matthew, et al. "The Effect of Blocked versus Random Practice on Dominant and Non-Dominant Baseball Swing." *Journal of Sports and Human Performance*, vol. 8, no. 1, 2020, pp. 1–8. https://doi.org/10.12922/jshp.v8i1.163. Accessed 25 Feb. 2022.

17. Merbah, Sarah, and Thierry Meulemans. "Learning a Motor Skill: Effects of Blocked versus Random Practice a Review." *Psychologica Belgica*, vol. 51, no. 1, 1 Feb. 2011, p. 15, https://doi.org/10.5334/pb-51-1-15.

18. Cruz, Madson Pereira, et al. "Constant and Random Practice on Learning of Volleyball Serve." *Brazilian Journal of Kinanthropometry and Human Performance*, vol. 20, no. 6, 19 Feb. 2019, pp. 598–606, https://doi.org/10.5007/1980-0037.2018v20n6p598. Accessed 15 Nov. 2019.

19. Getchell, Nancy, et al. "Chapter 86—a Random Practice Schedule Provides Better Retention and Transfer than Blocked When Learning Computer Mazes: Preliminary Results." *ScienceDirect*, Academic Press, 1 Jan. 2018, www.sciencedirect.com/science/article/pii/B9780128119266000865.

Chapter 13

1. Survey conducted by Jeffrey Bergin. 2025.

2. Merhej, Rita. "Dehydration and Cognition: An Understated Relation." *International Journal of Health Governance*, vol. 24, no. 1, 22 Feb. 2019, pp. 19–30, https://doi.org/10.1108/ijhg-10-2018-0056. Accessed 9 Apr. 2020.

3. Zhang Na, et al. "Effects of Dehydration and Rehydration on Cognitive Performance and Mood among Male College Students in Cangzhou, China: A Self-Controlled Trial." *International Journal of Environmental Research and Public Health*, vol. 16, no. 11, 29 May 2019, p. 1891, https://doi.org/10.3390/ijerph16111891.

4. En Hui Tung, Serene, et al. "Fluid Intake, Hydration Status, and Its Association with Cognitive Function among Adolescents in Petaling Perdana, Selangor, Malaysia." *Nutrition Research and Practice*, vol. 14, no. 5, 24 June 2020, pp. 490–500, https://doi.org/10.4162/nrp.2020.14.5.490.

5. Masento, Natalie, et al. "Effects of Hydration Status on Cognitive Performance and Mood." *British Journal of Nutrition*, vol. 111, no. 10, 28 May 2014, pp. 1841–52, https://doi.org/10.1017/S0007114513004455.

6. En Hui Tung et al. "Fluid Intake."

7. Bookheimer, Susan Y., et al. "Pomegranate Juice Augments Memory and FMRI Activity in Middle-Aged and Older Adults with Mild Memory Complaints." *Evidence-Based Complementary and Alternative Medicine*, vol. 2013, 2013, pp. 1–14, https://doi.org/10.1155/2013/946298. Accessed 24 Nov. 2020.

8. Haskell-Ramsay, C. F., et al. "Cognitive and Mood Improvements Following Acute Supplementation with Purple Grape Juice in Healthy Young Adults." *European Journal of Nutrition*, vol. 56, no. 8, 20 Apr. 2017, pp. 2621–31, https://doi.org/10.1007/s00394-017-1454-7. Accessed 26 Nov. 2019.

9. Lamport, Daniel J., et al. "Concord Grape Juice, Cognitive Function, and Driving Performance: A 12-Wk, Placebo-Controlled, Randomized Crossover Trial in Mothers of Preteen Children." *The American Journal of Clinical Nutrition*, vol. 103, no. 3, 10 Feb. 2016, pp. 775–83, https://doi.org/10.3945/ajcn.115.114553. Accessed 9 Sept. 2020.

10. Alharbi, Mudi H., et al. "Flavonoid-Rich Orange Juice Is Associated with Acute Improvements in Cognitive Function in Healthy Middle-Aged Males." *European Journal of Nutrition*, vol. 55, no. 6, 18 Aug. 2015, pp. 2021–29, https://doi.org/10.1007/s00394-015-1016-9. Accessed 17 Feb. 2022.

11. Lamport, Daniel J., et al. "The Effects of Flavanone-Rich Citrus Juice on Cognitive Function and Cerebral Blood Flow: An Acute, Randomised, Placebo-Controlled Cross-over Trial in Healthy, Young Adults." *British Journal of Nutrition*, vol. 116, no. 12, 28 Dec. 2016, pp. 2160–68, https://doi.org/10.1017/s000711451600430x. Accessed 18 Mar. 2021.

12. Kean, Rebecca J., et al. "Chronic Consumption of Flavanone-Rich Orange Juice Is Associated with Cognitive Benefits: An 8-Wk, Randomized, Double-Blind, Placebo-Controlled Trial in Healthy Older Adults." *The American Journal of Clinical Nutrition*, vol. 101, no. 3, 14 Jan. 2015, pp. 506–14, https://doi.org/10.3945/ajcn.114.088518. Accessed 6 Oct. 2020.

13. Grgic, Jozo, et al. "Wake up and Smell the Coffee: Caffeine Supplementation and Exercise Performance—an Umbrella Review of 21 Published Meta-Analyses." *British Journal of Sports Medicine*, vol. 54, no. 11, 29 Mar. 2019, p. bjsports-2018-100278, https://doi.org/10.1136/bjsports-2018-100278.

14. McLellan, Tom M., et al. "A Review of Caffeine's Effects on Cognitive, Physical and Occupational Performance." *Neuroscience & Biobehavioral Reviews*, vol. 71, Dec. 2016, pp. 294–312, https://doi.org/10.1016/j.neubiorev.2016.09.001.

15. Almosawi, Sayed, et al. "Acute Administration of Caffeine: The Effect on Motor Coordination, Higher Brain Cognitive Functions, and the Social Behavior of BLC57 Mice." *Behavioral Sciences*, vol. 8, no. 8, 25 July 2018, p. 65, https://doi.org/10.3390/bs8080065. Accessed 25 Feb. 2019.

16. Dong, X., et al. "Association of Coffee, Decaffeinated Coffee and Caffeine Intake from Coffee with Cognitive Performance in Older Adults: National Health and Nutrition Examination Survey (NHANES) 2011–2014." *Nutrients*, vol. 12, no. 3, 2020, p. 840, https://doi.org/10.3390/nu12030840.

17. Panza, Francesco, et al. "Coffee, Tea, and Caffeine Consumption and Prevention of Late-Life Cognitive Decline and Dementia: A Systematic Review." *The Journal of Nutrition, Health & Aging*, vol. 19, no. 3, 5 Dec. 2014, pp. 313–28, https://doi.org/10.1007/s12603-014-0563-8. Accessed 19 Oct. 2019.

18. Kim, Hayom, et al. "Drinking Coffee Enhances Neurocognitive Function by Reorganizing Brain Functional Connectivity." *Scientific Reports*, vol. 11, no. 1, 13 July 2021, p. 14381, https://doi.org/10.1038/s41598-021-93849-7.

19. Palmer, Matthew A., et al. "Caffeine Cravings Impair Memory and Metacognition." *Memory* (Hove, England), vol. 25, no. 9, 2017, pp. 1225–34, https://doi.org/10.1080/09658211.2017.1282968.

20. Dietz, Christina, and Matthijs Dekker. "Effect of Green Tea Phytochemicals on Mood and Cognition." *Current Pharmaceutical Design*, vol. 23, no. 19, 2017, pp. 2876–2905, https://doi.org/10.2174/1381612823666170105151800.

21. Farkhondeh, Tahereh, et al. "The Protective Effects of Green Tea Catechins in the Management of Neurodegenerative Diseases: A Review." *Current Drug Discovery Technologies*, vol. 16, no. 1, 10 Apr. 2019, pp. 57–65, https://doi.org/10.2174/1570163815666180219115453. Accessed 9 Mar. 2020.

22. Kochman, Joanna, et al. "Health Benefits and Chemical Composition of Matcha Green Tea: A Review." *Molecules*, vol. 26, no. 1, 27 Dec. 2020, p. 85, https://doi.org/10.3390/molecules26010085.

23. Pervin, Monira, et al. "Beneficial Effects of Green Tea Catechins on Neurodegenerative Diseases." *Molecules*, vol. 23, no. 6, 29 May 2018, https://doi.org/10.3390/molecules23061297. Accessed 17 Feb. 2020.

24. Boolani, Ali, et al. "Acute Effects of Brewed Cocoa Consumption on Attention, Motivation to Perform Cognitive Work and Feelings of Anxiety, Energy and Fatigue: A Randomized, Placebo-Controlled Crossover Experiment." *BMC Nutrition*, vol. 3, no. 1, 13 Jan. 2017, https://doi.org/10.1186/s40795-016-0117-z.

25. Martín, María Angeles, et al. "Effect of Cocoa and Cocoa Products on Cognitive Performance in Young Adults." *Nutrients*, vol. 12, no. 12, 30 Nov. 2020, p. 3691, https://doi.org/10.3390/nu12123691. Accessed 7 Dec. 2020.

26. Socci, Valentina, et al. "Enhancing Human Cognition with Cocoa Flavonoids." *Frontiers in Nutrition*, vol. 4, 16 May 2017, https://doi.org/10.3389/fnut.2017.00019.

27. Calabrò, Rocco Salvatore, et al. "The Efficacy of Cocoa Polyphenols in the Treatment of Mild Cognitive Impairment: A Retrospective Study." *Medicina*, vol. 55, no. 5, 17 May 2019, p. 156, https://doi.org/10.3390/medicina55050156. Accessed 19 Mar. 2020.; Martín, María Ángeles, and Sonia Ramos. "Health Beneficial Effects of Cocoa Phenolic Compounds: A Mini-Review." *Current Opinion in Food Science*, vol. 14, Apr. 2017, pp. 20–25, https://doi.org/10.1016/j.cofs.2016.12.002. Accessed 20 Feb. 2020.

28. Loprinzi, Paul D., et al. "The Effects of Exercise on Memory Function among Young to Middle-Aged Adults: Systematic Review and Recommendations for Future Research." *American Journal of Health Promotion*, vol. 32, no. 3, 2018, pp. 691–704, https://doi.org/10.1177/0890117117737409.

29. Audiffren, Michel, and Nathalie André. "The Exercise–Cognition Relationship: A Virtuous Circle." *Journal of Sport and Health Science*, vol. 8, no. 4, July 2019, pp. 339–47, https://doi.org/10.1016/j.jshs.2019.03.001.

30. Chapman, Sandra B., et al. "Shorter Term Aerobic Exercise Improves Brain, Cognition, and Cardiovascular Fitness in Aging." *Frontiers in Aging Neuroscience*, vol. 5, 2013, https://doi.org/10.3389/fnagi.2013.00075.

31. Moreau, David, and Edward Chou. "The Acute Effect of High-Intensity Exercise on Executive Function: A Meta-Analysis." *Perspectives on Psychological Science*, vol. 14, no. 5, 31 July 2019, p. 174569161985056, https://doi.org/10.1177/1745691619850568.

32. Jeon, Yong Kyun, and Chang Ho Ha. "The Effect of Exercise Intensity on Brain Derived Neurotrophic Factor and Memory in Adolescents." *Environmental Health and Preventive Medicine*, vol. 22, no. 1, 2017, p. 27, https://doi.org/10.1186/s12199-017-0643-6.

33. Wheeler, Michael J., et al. "Distinct Effects of Acute Exercise and Breaks in Sitting on Working Memory and Executive Function in Older Adults: A Three-Arm, Randomised Cross-over Trial to Evaluate the Effects of Exercise with and without Breaks in Sitting on Cognition." *British Journal of Sports Medicine*, vol. 54, 29 Apr. 2019, p. bjsports-2018-100168, https://doi.org/10.1136/bjsports-2018-100168.

34. Ludyga, Sebastian, et al. "Systematic Review and Meta-Analysis Investigating Moderators of Long-Term Effects of Exercise on Cognition in Healthy Individuals." *Nature Human Behaviour*, vol. 4, 30 Mar. 2020, https://doi.org/10.1038/s41562-020-0851-8. Accessed 2 Apr. 2020.

35. Pinho, Ricardo A., et al. "Effects of Resistance Exercise on Cerebral Redox Regulation and Cognition: An Interplay between Muscle and Brain." *Antioxidants*, vol. 8, no. 11, 6 Nov. 2019, p. 529, https://doi.org/10.3390/antiox8110529. Accessed 6 Apr. 2021.

36. Landrigan, Jon-Frederick, et al. "Lifting Cognition: A Meta-Analysis of Effects of Resistance Exercise on Cognition." *Psychological Research*, vol. 84, no. 5, 9 Jan. 2019, pp. 1167–83, https://doi.org/10.1007/s00426-019-01145-x. Accessed 15 Jan. 2021.; Chang, Yu-Kai, et al. "Effects of Acute Resistance Exercise on Cognition in Late Middle-Aged Adults: General or Specific Cognitive Improvement?" *Journal of Science and Medicine in Sport*, vol. 17, no. 1, Jan. 2014, pp. 51–55, https://doi.org/10.1016/j.jsams.2013.02.007. Accessed 26 Oct. 2019.

37. Best, John R., et al. "Long-Term Effects of Resistance Exercise Training on Cognition and Brain Volume in Older Women: Results from a Randomized Controlled Trial." *Journal of the International Neuropsychological Society*, vol. 21, no. 10, Nov. 2015, pp. 745–56, https://doi.org/10.1017/s1355617715000673. Accessed 21 Oct. 2020.

38. Loprinzi, Paul D., et al. "The Temporal Effects of Acute Exercise on Episodic Memory Function: Systematic Review with Meta-Analysis." *Brain Sciences*, vol. 9, no. 4, 18 Apr. 2019, p. 87, https://doi.org/10.3390/brainsci9040087. Accessed 14 Aug. 2019.

39. Gothe, Neha P., and Edward McAuley. "Yoga and Cognition." *Psychosomatic Medicine*, vol. 77, no. 7, Sept. 2015, pp. 784–97, https://doi.org/10.1097/psy.0000000000000218. Accessed 22 Apr. 2019.

40. Brunner, Devon, et al. "A Yoga Program for Cognitive Enhancement." *PLOS ONE*, vol. 12, no. 8, 4 Aug. 2017, p. e0182366, https://doi.org/10.1371/journal.pone.0182366. Accessed 7 Jan. 2020.

41. Ji, Zhiguang, et al. "The Benefits of Tai Chi and Brisk Walking for Cognitive Function and Fitness in Older Adults." *PeerJ*, vol. 5, 20 Oct. 2017, p. e3943, https://doi.org/10.7717/peerj.3943. Accessed 15 Apr. 2020.; Zhang, Yanjie, et al. "The Effects of Mind-Body Exercise on Cognitive Performance in Elderly: A Systematic Review and Meta-Analysis." *International Journal of Environmental Research and Public Health*, vol. 15, no. 12, 9 Dec. 2018, p. 2791, https://doi.org/10.3390/ijerph15122791. Accessed 2 Apr. 2020.

42. Pritchard, Alison, et al. "The Relationship Between Nature Connectedness and Eudaimonic Well-Being: A Meta-Analysis." *Journal of Happiness Studies*, vol. 21, 30 Apr. 2019, https://doi.org/10.1007/s10902-019-00118-6.

43. Zijlema, Wilma L., et al. "The Relationship Between Natural Outdoor Environments and Cognitive Functioning and Its Mediators." *Environmental Research*, vol. 155, May 2017, pp. 268–75, https://doi.org/10.1016/j.envres.2017.02.017. Accessed 28 Jan. 2020.

44. Meredith, Genevive R., et al. "Minimum Time Dose in Nature to Positively Impact the Mental Health of College-Aged Students, and How to Measure It: A Scoping Review." *Frontiers in Psychology*, vol. 10, 14 Jan. 2020, https://doi.org/10.3389/fpsyg.2019.02942.

45. Gale, Catharine R., et al. "The Dynamic Relationship Between Cognitive Function and Walking Speed: The English Longitudinal Study of Ageing." *AGE*, vol. 36, no. 4, 5 July 2014, https://doi.org/10.1007/s11357-014-9682-8. Accessed 4 Nov. 2019.

46. Ji et al. "The Benefits of Tai Chi."

47. Simons, Leon A., et al. "Lifestyle Factors and Risk of Dementia: Dubbo Study of the Elderly." *Medical Journal of Australia*, vol. 184, no. 2, Jan. 2006, pp. 68–70, https://doi.org/10.5694/j.1326-5377.2006.tb00120.x.

48. Park, Sin-Ae, et al. "Benefits of Gardening Activities for Cognitive Function According to Measurement of Brain Nerve Growth Factor Levels." *International Journal of Environmental Research and Public Health*, vol. 16, no. 5, 2 Mar. 2019, p. 760, https://doi.org/10.3390/ijerph16050760. Accessed 31 July 2020.

Chapter 14

1. Survey conducted by Jeffrey Bergin. 2025.

2. Kühnel, Jana, et al. "Take a Break! Benefits of Sleep and Short Breaks for Daily Work Engagement." *European Journal of Work and Organizational Psychology*, vol. 26, no. 4, 26 Dec. 2016, pp. 481–91, https://doi.org/10.1080/1359432x.2016.1269750.

3. Stee, Whitney, and Philippe Peigneux. "Post-Learning Micro- and Macro-Structural Neuroplasticity Changes with Time and Sleep." *Biochemical Pharmacology*, vol. 191, Dec. 2020, p. 114369, https://doi.org/10.1016/j.bcp.2020.114369. Accessed 28 Mar. 2021.

4. Hobson, J. Allan, and Edward F. Pace-Schott. "The Cognitive Neuroscience of Sleep: Neuronal Systems, Consciousness and Learning." *Nature Reviews Neuroscience*, vol. 3, no. 9, Sept. 2002, pp. 679–93, https://doi.org/10.1038/nrn915. Accessed 24 May 2019.

5. Kurdziel, Laura B. F., et al. "Novel Word Learning in Older Adults: A Role for Sleep?" *Brain and Language*, vol. 167, Apr. 2017, pp. 106–13, https://doi.org/10.1016/j.bandl.2016.05.010. Accessed 31 Mar. 2020.; Rasch, Björn, and Jan Born. "About Sleep's Role in Memory." *Physiological Reviews*, vol. 93, no. 2, Apr. 2013, pp. 681–766, https://doi.org/10.1152/physrev.00032.2012.

6. Acosta, María Teresa. "[Sleep, Memory and Learning]." *Medicina*, vol. 79, suppl. 3, 1 Jan. 2019, pp. 29–32, https://europepmc.org/article/med/31603840. Accessed 18 Feb. 2022.; Backhaus, Jutta, et al. "Immediate as well as Delayed Post Learning Sleep but Not Wakefulness Enhances Declarative Memory Consolidation in Children." *Neurobiology of Learning and Memory*, vol. 89, no. 1, Jan. 2008, pp. 76–80, https://doi.org/10.1016/j.nlm.2007.08.010.

7. Lim, Julian, and David F. Dinges. "A Meta-Analysis of the Impact of Short-Term Sleep Deprivation on Cognitive Variables." *Psychological Bulletin*, vol. 136, no. 3, 2010, pp. 375–89, https://doi.org/10.1037/a0018883.

8. National Institutes of Health. "Brain Basics: Understanding Sleep." https://www.ninds.nih.gov/health-information/public-education/brain-basics.

9. Alhola, Paula, and Päivi Polo-Kantola. "Sleep Deprivation: Impact on Cognitive Performance." *Neuropsychiatric Disease and Treatment*, vol. 3, no. 5, Oct. 2007, pp. 553–67, www.ncbi.nlm.nih.gov/pmc/articles/PMC2656292/.

10. Mantua, Janna, and Guido Simonelli. "Sleep Duration and Cognition: Is There an Ideal Amount?" *Sleep*, vol. 42, no. 3, 12 Jan. 2019, https://doi.org/10.1093/sleep/zsz010.

11. Santisteban, Jose Arturo, et al. "Cumulative Mild Partial Sleep Deprivation Negatively Impacts Working Memory Capacity but Not Sustained Attention, Response Inhibition, or Decision Making: A Randomized Controlled Trial." *Sleep Health*, vol. 5, no. 1, Feb. 2019, pp. 101–18, https://doi.org/10.1016/j.sleh.2018.09.007.

12. Lovato, Nicole, and Leon Lack. "The Effects of Napping on Cognitive Functioning." *Progress in Brain Research*, vol. 185, 2010, pp. 155–66, https://doi.org/10.1016/B978-0-444-53702-7.00009-9.

13. Lim, Julian, et al. "Assessing the Benefits of Napping and Short Rest Breaks on Processing Speed in Sleep-Restricted Adolescents." *Journal of Sleep Research*, vol. 26, no. 2, 24 Jan. 2017, pp. 219–26, https://doi.org/10.1111/jsr.12497.

14. Robertson, Edwin M., et al. "Awareness Modifies the Skill-Learning Benefits of Sleep." *Current Biology*, vol. 14, no. 3, Feb. 2004, pp. 208–12, https://doi.org/10.1016/j.cub.2004.01.027. Accessed 11 Mar. 2020.

15. Mednick, Sara, et al. "Sleep-Dependent Learning: A Nap Is as Good as a Night." *Nature Neuroscience*, vol. 6, 22 June 2003, https://doi.org/10.1038/nn1078.

16. Diekelmann, Susanne. "Sleep for Cognitive Enhancement." *Frontiers in Systems Neuroscience*, vol. 8, 2 Apr. 2014, https://doi.org/10.3389/fnsys.2014.00046.

17. Reinoso Suárez, F. "[The Neurobiology of Slow-Wave Sleep]." *Anales de la Real Academia Nacional de Medicina*, vol. 116, no. 1, 1999, pp. 209–24, https://pubmed.ncbi.nlm.nih.gov/10554397/. Accessed 18 Feb. 2022.

18. Tulving, Endel, and Donald M. Thomson. "Encoding Specificity and Retrieval Processes in Episodic Memory." *Psychological Review*, vol. 80, no. 5, 1973, pp. 352–73, https://doi.org/10.1037/h0020071.

Chapter 15

1. Survey conducted by Jeffrey Bergin. 2025.

2. Adler, Melissa. "The Effect of Emotion on Associative Memory: Anger versus Fear." *Oregon Undergraduate Research Journal*, vol. 17, no. 1, Aug. 2020, pp. 1–18, https://doi.org/10.5399/uo/ourj/17.1.2. Accessed 16 Dec. 2020.

3. Fredrickson, Barbara L. "The Role of Positive Emotions in Positive Psychology: The Broaden-and-Build Theory of Positive Emotions." *American Psychologist*, vol. 56, no. 3, 2001, pp. 218–26, https://doi.org/10.1037//0003-066x.56.3.218.

4. Clore, Gerald L., et al. "Affect and Cognition: Three Principles." *Current Opinion in Behavioral Sciences*, vol. 19, Feb. 2018, pp. 78–82, https://doi.org/10.1016/j.cobeha.2017.11.010. Accessed 16 July 2020.

5. Taruffi, Liila, et al. "Effects of Sad and Happy Music on Mind-Wandering and the Default Mode Network." *Scientific Reports*, vol. 7, no. 1, 31 Oct. 2017, https://doi.org/10.1038/s41598-017-14849-0.

6. Culot, Catherine, et al. "The Influence of Sad Mood Induction on Task Performance and Metacognition." *Quarterly Journal of Experimental Psychology*, vol. 74, no. 9, 27 Mar. 2021, pp. 1605–14, https://doi.org/10.1177/17470218211004205. Accessed 1 Oct. 2021.

7. Forgas, Joseph P. "Happy Believers and Sad Skeptics? Affective Influences on Gullibility." *Current Directions in Psychological Science*, vol. 28, no. 3, 5 Apr. 2019, pp. 306–13, https://doi.org/10.1177/0963721419834543.

8. Savage, Brandon M., et al. "Humor, Laughter, Learning, and Health! A Brief Review." *Advances in Physiology Education*, vol. 41, no. 3, Sept. 2017, pp. 341–47, https://doi.org/10.1152/advan.00030.2017.

9. Maric, Vojislav, et al. "Respiratory Regulation & Interactions with Neuro-Cognitive Circuitry." *Neuroscience & Biobehavioral Reviews*, vol. 112, 1 May 2020, pp. 95–106, https://doi.org/10.1016/j.neubiorev.2020.02.001.

10. Perl, Ofer, et al. "Human Non-Olfactory Cognition Phase-Locked with Inhalation." *Nature Human Behaviour*, vol. 3, no. 5, 1 May 2019, pp. 501–12, https://doi.org/10.1038/s41562-019-0556-z. Accessed 18 Feb. 2022.

11. Olofsson, Jonas K., et al. "Smell-Based Memory Training: Evidence of Olfactory Learning and Transfer to the Visual Domain." *Chemical Senses*, vol. 45, no. 7, 9 July 2020, pp. 593–600, https://doi.org/10.1093/chemse/bjaa049.

12. Dahmani, Louisa, et al. "An Intrinsic Association between Olfactory Identification and Spatial Memory in Humans." *Nature Communications*, vol. 9, no. 1, 16 Oct. 2018, https://doi.org/10.1038/s41467-018-06569-4.

13. Hawiset, Thaneeya. "Effect of One Time Coffee Fragrance Inhalation on Working Memory, Mood, and Salivary Cortisol Level in Healthy Young Volunteers: A Randomized Placebo Controlled Trial." *Integrative Medicine Research*, vol. 8, no. 4, 1 Dec. 2019, pp. 273–78, https://doi.org/10.1016/j.imr.2019.11.007. Accessed 27 Sept. 2020.

14. Woo, Cynthia, et al. "Overnight Olfactory Enrichment Using an Odorant Diffuser Improves Memory and Modifies the Uncinate Fasciculus in Older Adults." *Frontiers in Neuroscience*, vol. 17, 23 July 2023, https://doi.org/10.3389/fnins.2023.1200448.

15. Liaw, Hongming, et al. "Relationships Between Facial Expressions, Prior Knowledge, and Multiple Representations: A Case of Conceptual Change for Kinematics Instruction." *Journal of Science Education and Technology*, vol. 30, no. 2, 12 Sept. 2020, pp. 227–38, https://doi.org/10.1007/s10956-020-09863-3. Accessed 20 Feb. 2022.

16. Gagnon, Marie-Ève, et al. "Exploring the Mechanisms Responsible for the Modulating Role of Frowning in Emotional Reasoning: An ERP Study." *Brain and Cognition*, vol. 152, 1 Aug. 2021, p. 105750, https://doi.org/10.1016/j.bandc.2021.105750. Accessed 20 Feb. 2022.

17. Sharma, Kshitij, et al. "Assessing Cognitive Performance Using Physiological and Facial Features." *Proceedings of the ACM on Interactive, Mobile, Wearable and Ubiquitous Technologies*, vol. 4, no. 3, 4 Sept. 2020, pp. 1–41, https://doi.org/10.1145/3411811. Accessed 10 Jan. 2022.

18. Mudrick, Nicholas V., et al. "Toward Affect-Sensitive Virtual Human Tutors: The Influence of Facial Expressions on Learning and Emotion." *IEEE Xplore*, 1 Oct. 2017, ieeexplore.ieee.org/abstract/document/8273598. Accessed 20 Feb. 2022.

19. Lin, Yen-Liang. "Gestures as Scaffolding for L2 Narrative Recall: The Role of Gesture Type, Task Complexity, and Working Memory." *Language Teaching Research*, 8 Oct. 2021, p. 136216882110445, https://doi.org/10.1177/13621688211044584. Accessed 4 Jan. 2022.

20. Schneider, Sascha, et al. "The Impact of Video Lecturers' Nonverbal Communication on Learning—an Experiment on Gestures and Facial Expressions of Pedagogical Agents." *Computers & Education*, vol. 176, Jan. 2022, p. 104350, https://doi.org/10.1016/j.compedu.2021.104350. Accessed 21 Nov. 2021.

21. Pi, Zhongling, et al. "Effects of the Instructor's Pointing Gestures on Learning Performance in Video Lectures." *British Journal of Educational Technology*, vol. 48, no. 4, 6 May 2016, pp. 1020–29, https://doi.org/10.1111/bjet.12471. Accessed 28 Oct. 2019.

22. Cherdieu, Mélaine, et al. "Make Gestures to Learn: Reproducing Gestures Improves the Learning of Anatomical Knowledge More than Just Seeing Gestures." *Frontiers in Psychology*, vol. 8, 5 Oct. 2017, https://doi.org/10.3389/fpsyg.2017.01689.

23. Hietanen, Jari K. "Affective Eye Contact: An Integrative Review." *Frontiers in Psychology*, vol. 9, 28 Aug. 2018, https://doi.org/10.3389/fpsyg.2018.01587.

24. Lanthier, Sophie N., et al. "The Costs and Benefits to Memory When Observing and Experiencing Live Eye Contact." *Visual Cognition*, 21 May 2021, pp. 1–15, https://doi.org/10.1080/13506285.2021.1926381.

25. Fiorella, Logan, et al. "Instructor Presence in Video Lectures: The Role of Dynamic Drawings, Eye Contact, and Instructor Visibility." *Journal of Educational Psychology*, vol. 111, no. 7, Oct. 2019, pp. 1162–71, https://doi.org/10.1037/edu0000325. Accessed 19 Mar. 2020.

26. Pi, Zhongling, et al. "Instructor Presence in Video Lectures: Eye Gaze Matters, but Not Body Orientation." *Computers & Education*, vol. 144, Jan. 2020, p. 103713, https://doi.org/10.1016/j.compedu.2019.103713. Accessed 29 Apr. 2020.

Chapter 16

1. Survey conducted by Jeffrey Bergin. 2025.

2. Harvey, Allison G., et al. "Applying the Science of Habit Formation to Evidence-Based Psychological Treatments for Mental Illness." *Perspectives on Psychological Science*, 8 Sept. 2021, p. 174569162199575, https://doi.org/10.1177/1745691621995752. Accessed 23 Jan. 2022.

3. Harvey et al. "Applying the Science."

4. Gardner, Benjamin, and Phillippa Lally. "Modelling Habit Formation and Its Determinants." *The Psychology of Habit*, 2018, pp. 207–29, https://doi.org/10.1007/978-3-319-97529-0_12. Accessed 15 June 2019.; Gardner, Benjamin, and Amanda L. Rebar. "Habit Formation and Behavior Change." *Oxford Research Encyclopedia of Psychology*, Oxford University Press, https://doi.org/10.1093/acrefore/9780190236557.013.129. Accessed 1 Mar. 2022.

5. Carden, Lucas, and Wendy Wood. "Habit Formation and Change." *Current Opinion in Behavioral Sciences*, vol. 20, Apr. 2018, pp. 117–22, https://doi.org/10.1016/j.cobeha.2017.12.009.

6. Harvey et al. "Applying the Science."

7. Lally, Phillippa, et al. "How Are Habits Formed: Modelling Habit Formation in the Real World." *European Journal of Social Psychology*, vol. 40, no. 6, 16 July 2009, pp. 998–1009, https://doi.org/10.1002/ejsp.674.

Chapter 17

1. Ose Askvik, Eva, et al. "The Importance of Cursive Handwriting over Typewriting for Learning in the Classroom: A High-Density EEG Study of 12-Year-Old Children and Young Adults." *Frontiers in Psychology*, vol. 11, 28 July 2020, https://doi.org/10.3389/fpsyg.2020.01810.

2. Allen, Mike, et al. "Is the Pencil Mightier than the Keyboard? A Meta-Analysis Comparing the Method of Notetaking Outcomes." *Southern Communication Journal*, vol. 85, no. 3, 20 May 2020, pp. 143–54, https://doi.org/10.1080/1041794x.2020.1764613.

3. Widjaja, Caroline, and Stefanus Satria Sumali. "Short-Term Memory Comparison of Students of Faculty of Medicine Pelita Harapan University Batch 2015 between the Handwriting and Typing Method." *Medicinus*, vol. 7, no. 4, 3 Apr. 2020, p. 108, https://doi.org/10.19166/med.v7i4.2385. Accessed 28 Oct. 2020.

4. Meer, Audrey L. H. van der, and F. R. (Rudd) van der Weel. "Only Three Fingers Write, but the Whole Brain Works: A High-Density EEG Study Showing Advantages of Drawing over Typing for Learning." *Frontiers in Psychology*, 9 May 2017, https://doi.org/10.3389/fpsyg.2017.00706. Accessed 28 Feb. 2022.

5. Schroeder, Noah L., et al. "Studying and Constructing Concept Maps: A Meta-Analysis." *Educational Psychology Review*, vol. 30, no. 2, 21 Mar. 2017, pp. 431–55, https://doi.org/10.1007/s10648-017-9403-9.

6. Schroeder et al. "Studying and Constructing Concept Maps."

7. Barbieri, Christina Areizaga, et al. "The Effect of Worked Examples on Student Learning and Error Anticipation in Algebra." *Instructional Science*, vol. 49, 16 June 2021, https://doi.org/10.1007/s11251-021-09545-6. Accessed 11 July 2021.

8. Chen, Ouhao, et al. "Effects of Worked Examples on Step Performance in Solving Complex Problems." *Educational Psychology*, vol. 39, no. 2, 13 Oct. 2018, pp. 188–202, https://doi.org/10.1080/01443410.2018.1515891. Accessed 9 Jan. 2020.

9. Bisra, Kiran, et al. "Inducing Self-Explanation: A Meta-Analysis." *Educational Psychology Review*, vol. 30, no. 3, 29 Mar. 2018, pp. 703–25, https://doi.org/10.1007/s10648-018-9434-x. Accessed 15 Apr. 2019.

10. Bisra et al. "Inducing Self-Explanation."

11. Hebert, Michael, et al. "Comparing Effects of Different Writing Activities on Reading Comprehension: A Meta-Analysis." *Reading and Writing*, vol. 26, no. 1, 6 June 2012, pp. 111–38, https://doi.org/10.1007/s11145-012-9386-3. Accessed 11 Dec. 2019.

12. Graham, Steve, et al. "The Effects of Writing on Learning in Science, Social Studies, and Mathematics: A Meta-Analysis." *Review of Educational Research*, vol. 90, no. 2, 19 Mar. 2020, pp. 179–226, https://doi.org/10.3102/0034654320914744.

13. Brown, Peter, et al. *Make It Stick: The Science of Successful Learning.* Belknap Press, 2014, p. 19.

14. Brown et al. *Make It Stick*, p. 20.

15. Eisenkraemer, Raquel Eloisa, et al. "A Systematic Review of the Testing Effect in Learning." *Paidéia (Ribeirão Preto)*, vol. 23, no. 56, Sept. 2013, pp. 397–406, https://doi.org/10.1590/1982-43272356201314. Accessed 3 Nov. 2020.

16. Richland, Lindsey E., et al. "The Pretesting Effect: Do Unsuccessful Retrieval Attempts Enhance Learning?" *Journal of Experimental Psychology: Applied*, vol. 15, no. 3, 2009, pp. 243–57, https://doi.org/10.1037/a0016496.

17. Richland et al. "The Pretesting Effect."; Adesope, Olusola O., et al. "Rethinking the Use of Tests: A Meta-Analysis of Practice Testing." *Review of Educational Research*, vol. 87, no. 3, Feb. 2017, pp. 659–701, https://doi.org/10.3102/0034654316689306.

18. Abel, Magdalena, and Henry L. Roediger. "Comparing the Testing Effect under Blocked and Mixed Practice: The Mnemonic Benefits of Retrieval Practice Are Not Affected by Practice Format." *Memory & Cognition*, vol. 45, no. 1, 27 July 2016, pp. 81–92, https://doi.org/10.3758/s13421-016-0641-8. Accessed 17 Apr. 2020.

19. Schwieren, Juliane, et al. "The Testing Effect in the Psychology Classroom: A Meta-Analytic Perspective." *Psychology Learning & Teaching*, vol. 16, no. 2, 17 Mar. 2017, https://doi.org/10.1177/1475725717695149.

20. Little, Jeri, and Elizabeth Bjork. "Pretesting with Multiple-Choice Questions Facilitates Learning." *UC Merced Proceedings of the Annual Meeting of the Cognitive Science Society*, 2011, https://escholarship.org/uc/item/9xn3f39q.

21. Sana, Faria, et al. "Optimizing the Efficacy of Learning Objectives through Pretests." *CBE—Life Sciences Education*, vol. 19, no. 3, 1 Sep. 2020, https://doi.org/10.1187/cbe.19-11-0257.

22. Gooding, Julia, and Bill Metz. "From Misconceptions to Conceptual Change: Tips for Identifying and Overcoming Students' Misconceptions." *The Science Teacher*, Apr. 2011, https://teaching.fsu.edu/wp-content/uploads/2018/01/tst1104_34.pdf.

23. Panadero, Ernesto. "A Review of Self-Regulated Learning: Six Models and Four Directions for Research." *Frontiers in Psychology*, vol. 8, no. 422, 28 Apr. 2017, https://doi.org/10.3389/fpsyg.2017.00422.

24. Sanchez, Carmen E., et al. "Self-Grading and Peer-Grading for Formative and Summative Assessments in 3rd through 12th Grade Classrooms: A Meta-Analysis." *Journal of Educational Psychology*, vol. 109, no. 8, Nov. 2017, pp. 1049–66, https://doi.org/10.1037/edu0000190. Accessed 26 Aug. 2020.

25. Double, Kit S., et al. "The Impact of Peer Assessment on Academic Performance: A Meta-Analysis of Control Group Studies." *Educational Psychology Review*, vol. 32, 10 Dec. 2019, https://doi.org/10.1007/s10648-019-09510-3.

26. Li, Hongli, et al. "Does Peer Assessment Promote Student Learning? A Meta-Analysis." *Assessment & Evaluation in Higher Education*, vol. 45, 2 June 2019, pp. 1–19, https://doi.org/10.1080/02602938.2019.162 0679. Accessed 29 Dec. 2019.

27. Li, Hongli, et al. "Peer Assessment in the Digital Age: A Meta-Analysis Comparing Peer and Teacher Ratings." *Assessment & Evaluation in Higher Education*, vol. 41, no. 2, 3 Feb. 2015, pp. 245–64, https://doi.org/10.1080/02602938.2014.999746. Accessed 13 Feb. 2020.

28. Hattie, John, and Helen Timperley. "The Power of Feedback." *Review of Educational Research*, vol. 77, no. 1, 1 Mar. 2007, pp. 81–112, https://doi.org/10.3102/003465430298487.

29. Hattie and Timperley. "The Power of Feedback."

30. Hattie and Timperley. "The Power of Feedback."

31. Hattie and Timperley. "The Power of Feedback."

32. Fong, Carlton J., et al. "A Meta-Analysis of Negative Feedback on Intrinsic Motivation." *Educational Psychology Review*, vol. 31, no. 1, 15 Aug. 2018, pp. 121–62, https://doi.org/10.1007/s10648-018-9446-6.

Chapter 18

1. Survey conducted by Jeffrey Bergin. 2025.

2. Zhang, Jingji, and Richard Lynch. "The Relationship between Primary 5 and 6 Students' Perceptions of Parental Encouragement and Their Academic Achievement in Mandarin Learning at an International School, Bangkok." *Scholar: Human Sciences*, vol. 9, no. 2, 2017, p. 243, www.assumptionjournal.au.edu/index.php/Scholar/article/view/3000. Accessed 16 Feb. 2022.

3. Sudarshan, M. "Academic Achievement of Pre-University Students in Relation to Parental Encouragement." *Indian Journals*, vol. 13, no. 1, 2019, www.indianjournals.com/ijor.aspx?target=ijor:ajdm&volume=13&issue=1&article=018. Accessed 16 Feb. 2022.

4. Ma, Cecilia M. S., and Catie C. W. Lai. "Contextual Influence of Risk and Protective Factors on Chinese Adolescent Psychological Well-Being, Delinquent Behavior and Academic Performance: The Role of Family and Friends." *Applied Research in Quality of Life*, vol. 16, 21 Jan. 2021, https://doi.org/10.1007/s11482-021-09909-7. Accessed 23 Sept. 2021.

5. Hsu, Hsien-Yuan, et al. "Exploring the Relationship Between Student-Perceived Faculty Encouragement, Self-Efficacy, and Intent to Persist in Engineering Programs." *European Journal of Engineering Education*, vol. 46, 1 Mar. 2021, pp. 1–17, https://doi.org/10.1080/03043797.2021.1889469. Accessed 21 Sept. 2021.

6. Gunderson, Elizabeth A., et al. "Parent Praise to Toddlers Predicts Fourth Grade Academic Achievement via Children's Incremental Mindsets." *Developmental Psychology*, vol. 54, no. 3, Mar. 2018, pp. 397–409, https://doi.org/10.1037/dev0000444.

7. Lee, Hae In, et al. "Understanding When Parental Praise Leads to Optimal Child Outcomes." *Social Psychological and Personality Science*, vol. 8, no. 6, 22 Dec. 2016, pp. 679–88, https://doi.org/10.1177/1948550616683020. Accessed 23 Mar. 2021.

8. Lavy, Victor, and Edith Sand. "The Friends Factor: How Students' Social Networks Affect Their Academic Achievement and Well-Being?" *National Bureau of Economic Research*, 1 Oct. 2012, www.nber.org/papers/w18430.

9. Ansong, David, et al. "The Role of Parent, Classmate, and Teacher Support in Student Engagement: Evidence from Ghana." *International Journal of Educational Development*, vol. 54, May 2017, pp. 51–58, https://doi.org/10.1016/j.ijedudev.2017.03.010.

10. Tenenbaum, Harriet R., et al. "How Effective Is Peer Interaction in Facilitating Learning? A Meta-Analysis." *Journal of Educational Psychology*, vol. 112, no. 7, 12 Dec. 2019, https://doi.org/10.1037/edu0000436.

11. Moeyaert, Mariola, et al. "Three-Level Meta-Analysis of Single-Case Data Regarding the Effects of Peer Tutoring on Academic and Social-Behavioral Outcomes for At-Risk Students and Students with Disabilities." *Remedial and Special Education*, vol. 42, no. 2, 13 July 2019, p. 074193251985507, https://doi.org/10.1177/0741932519855079.

12. Madland, Colin, and Griff Richards. "Enhancing Student-Student Online Interaction: Exploring the Study Buddy Peer Review Activity." *The International Review of Research in Open and Distributed Learning*, vol. 17, no. 3, 16 May 2016, https://doi.org/10.19173/irrodl.v17i3.2179. Accessed 21 Nov. 2019.

13. Pålsson, Ylva, et al. "A Peer Learning Intervention for Nursing Students in Clinical Practice Education: A Quasi-Experimental Study." *Nurse Education Today*, vol. 51, Apr. 2017, pp. 81–87, https://doi.org/10.1016/j.nedt.2017.01.011.

14. Ebrahimi, Hossein, et al. "The Role of Peer Support Education Model on the Quality of Life and Self-Care Behaviors of Patients with Myocardial Infarction." *Patient Education and Counseling*, vol. 104, no. 1, Jan. 2021, pp. 130–35, https://doi.org/10.1016/j.pec.2020.08.002. Accessed 1 Apr. 2021.; Castillo-Hernandez, Karen G., et al. "Peer Support Added to Diabetes Education Improves Metabolic Control and Quality of Life in Mayan Adults Living with Type 2 Diabetes: A Randomized Controlled Trial." *Canadian Journal of Diabetes*, vol. 45, no. 3, Sept. 2020, https://doi.org/10.1016/j.jcjd.2020.08.107. Accessed 8 Sept. 2020.; He, Jiayu, et al. "Peer Education for HIV Prevention among High-Risk Groups: A Systematic Review and Meta-Analysis." *BMC Infectious Diseases*, vol. 20, no. 1, 12 May 2020, https://doi.org/10.1186/s12879-020-05003-9. Accessed 18 Sept. 2020.

15. Juvonen, Jaana, et al. "Promoting Social Inclusion in Educational Settings: Challenges and Opportunities." *Educational Psychologist*, vol. 54, no. 4, 2 Oct. 2019, pp. 250–70, https://doi.org/10.1080/00461520.2019.1655645.

16. Timms, Carolyn, et al. "Psychological Engagement of University Students." *Journal of Applied Research in Higher Education*, vol. 10, no. 3, 5 June 2018, pp. 243–55, https://doi.org/10.1108/jarhe-09-2017-0107. Accessed 16 Feb. 2022.

17. Bloom, Benjamin. "The 2 Sigma Problem: The Search for Methods of Group Instruction as Effective as One-to-One Tutoring." *Educational Researcher*, vol. 13, no. 6, June–July 1984, pp. 4–16, https://web.mit.edu/5.95/www/readings/bloom-two-sigma.pdf.

18. Moeyaert et al. "Three-Level Meta-Analysis."

19. Bowman-Perrott, Lisa, et al. "Academic Benefits of Peer Tutoring: A Meta-Analytic Review of Single-Case Research." *School Psychology Review*, vol. 42, no. 1, 1 Mar. 2013, pp. 39–55, https://doi.org/10.1080/02796015.2013.12087490.

20. Williams, Brett, and James Fowler. "Can Near-Peer Teaching Improve Academic Performance?" *International Journal of Higher Education*, vol. 3, no. 4, 11 Nov. 2014, https://doi.org/10.5430/ijhe.v3n4p142. Accessed 16 Dec. 2019.; Iqbal, Fatima, et al. "The Use of Near-Peer Tutors to Improve Level of Learning & Confidence in Areas of Human Physiology." *Journal of Biological Education*, 25 Apr. 2020, pp. 1–10, https://doi.org/10.1080/00219266.2020.1756898.

21. He, Jiayu, et al. "Peer Education for HIV Prevention among High-Risk Groups: A Systematic Review and Meta-Analysis." *BMC Infectious Diseases*, vol. 20, no. 1, 12 May 2020, https://doi.org/10.1186/s12879-020-05003-9. Accessed 18 Sept. 2020.

22. Pålsson et al. "A Peer Learning Intervention."

23. Sneyers, Eline, and Kristof De Witte. "Interventions in Higher Education and Their Effect on Student Success: A Meta-Analysis." *Educational Review*, vol. 70, no. 2, 31 Mar. 2017, pp. 208–28, https://doi.org/10.1080/00131911.2017.1300874.

24. St-Jean, Etienne, et al. "Can Less Be More? Mentoring Functions, Learning Goal Orientation, and Novice Entrepreneurs' Self-Efficacy." *International Journal of Entrepreneurial Behavior & Research*, vol. 24, no. 1, 8 Jan. 2018, pp. 2–21, https://doi.org/10.1108/ijebr-09-2016-0299. Accessed 29 Sept. 2019.

25. Eby, Lillian Turner de Tormes, et al. "An Interdisciplinary Meta-Analysis of the Potential Antecedents, Correlates, and Consequences of Protégé Perceptions of Mentoring." *Psychological Bulletin*, vol. 139, no. 2, Mar. 2013, pp. 441–76, https://doi.org/10.1037/a0029279.

26. Cannon-Bowers, Janis A., et al. "Workplace Coaching: A Meta-Analysis and Recommendations for Advancing the Science of Coaching." *Frontiers in Psychology*, vol. 14, 2023, https://doi.org/10.3389/fpsyg.2023.1204166.

27. Campbell, Anita L., and D. Mogashana. "Assessing the Effectiveness of Academic Coaching Interventions for Student Success in Higher Education: A Systematic Review." *Innovations in Education and Teaching International*, 2024, pp. 1–23, https://doi.org/10.1080/14703297.2024.2417173.

28. Williams and Fowler. "Near-Peer Teaching."

29. Wang, Minhong, et al. "Reflective Learning with Complex Problems in a Visualization-Based Learning Environment with Expert Support." *Computers in Human Behavior*, vol. 87, Oct. 2018, pp. 406–15, https://doi.org/10.1016/j.chb.2018.01.025.

30. Wang et al. "Reflective Learning."

31. Stilp, Lance, and Malcolm Larking. "Learning Opportunities among Expert–Novice Pairs in the L2 Classroom." *Language Teaching in a Global Age: Shaping the Classroom, Shaping the World*, edited by P. Clements, et al., JALT, 2018, https://jalt-publications.org/sites/default/files/pdf-article/jalt2017-pcp-015.pdf.

32. Groenendijk, Talita, et al. "Learning to Be Creative. The Effects of Observational Learning on Students' Design Products and Processes." *Learning and Instruction*, vol. 28, Dec. 2013, pp. 35–47, https://doi.org/10.1016/j.learninstruc.2013.05.001. Accessed 21 Apr. 2019.

33. D'Innocenzo, Giorgia, et al. "Looking to Learn: The Effects of Visual Guidance on Observational Learning of the Golf Swing." *PLOS ONE*, vol. 11, no. 5, 25 May 2016, p. e0155442, https://doi.org/10.1371/journal.pone.0155442.

34. D'Innocenzo et al. "Looking to Learn."

35. Andrieux, Mathieu, and Luc Proteau. "Observational Learning: Tell Beginners What They Are About to Watch and They Will Learn Better." *Frontiers in Psychology*, vol. 7, 29 Jan. 2016, https://doi.org/10.3389/fpsyg.2016.00051.

36. Aleven, V., et al. "Toward Tutoring Help Seeking." *Intelligent Tutoring Systems*, Springer, 2004, pp. 227–39, https://doi.org/10.1007/978-3-540-30139-4_22.

37. Cornally, Nicola, and Geraldine McCarthy. "Help-Seeking Behaviour: A Concept Analysis." *International Journal of Nursing Practice*, vol. 17, no. 3, 24 May 2011, pp. 280–88, https://doi.org/10.1111/j.1440-172x.2011.01936.x.

38. Karabenick, Stuart A., and John R. Knapp. "Relationship of Academic Help Seeking to the Use of Learning Strategies and Other Instrumental Achievement Behavior in College Students." *Journal of Educational Psychology*, vol. 83, no. 2, 1991, pp. 221–30, https://doi.org/10.1037/0022-0663.83.2.221. Accessed 1 Nov. 2020.

Chapter 19

1. Survey conducted by Jeffrey Bergin. 2025.

2. Means, Barbara, et al. "The Effectiveness of Online and Blended Learning: A Meta-Analysis of the Empirical Literature." *Teachers College Record*, vol. 115, no. 3, 1 Mar. 2013, pp. 1–47, https://www.sri.com/wp-content/uploads/2021/12/effectiveness_of_online_and_blended_learning.pdf.

3. Horn, Michael, and Heather Staker. *Blended: Using Disruptive Innovation to Improve Schools.* Jossey-Bass, 2014, p. 10.

4. Means et al. "The Effectiveness of Online and Blended Learning."

5. Steenbergen-Hu, Saiying, and Harris Cooper. "A Meta-Analysis of the Effectiveness of Intelligent Tutoring Systems on College Students' Academic Learning." *Journal of Educational Psychology*, vol. 106, no. 2, 2014, pp. 331–47, https://doi.org/10.1037/a0034752. Accessed 28 Aug. 2018.

6. Ma, Wenting, et al. "Intelligent Tutoring Systems and Learning Outcomes: A Meta-Analysis." *Journal of Educational Psychology*, vol. 106, no. 4, 2014, pp. 901–18, https://doi.org/10.1037/a0037123. Accessed 14 Dec. 2019.

7. Girard, C., et al. "Serious Games as New Educational Tools: How Effective Are They? A Meta-Analysis of Recent Studies." *Journal of Computer Assisted Learning*, vol. 29, no. 3, 13 June 2012, pp. 207–19, https://doi.org/10.1111/j.1365-2729.2012.00489.x.

8. Wouters, Pieter, et al. "A Meta-Analysis of the Cognitive and Motivational Effects of Serious Games." *Journal of Educational Psychology*, vol. 105, no. 2, 2013, pp. 249–65, https://doi.org/10.1037/a0031311. Accessed 14 Feb. 2020.

9. Zhonggen, Yu. "A Meta-Analysis of Use of Serious Games in Education over a Decade." *International Journal of Computer Games Technology*, vol. 2019, 3 Feb. 2019, pp. 1–8, https://doi.org/10.1155/2019/4797032.

10. Riopel, Martin, et al. "Impact of Serious Games on Science Learning Achievement Compared with More Conventional Instruction: An Overview and a Meta-Analysis." *Studies in Science Education*, vol. 55, no. 2, 3 July 2019, pp. 169–214, https://doi.org/10.1080/03057267.2019.1722420. Accessed 1 Mar. 2022.

11. Bai, Shurui, et al. "Does Gamification Improve Student Learning Outcome? Evidence from a Meta-Analysis and Synthesis of Qualitative Data in Educational Contexts." *Educational Research Review*, vol. 30, June 2020, p. 100322, https://doi.org/10.1016/j.edurev.2020.100322.

12. Sailer, Michael, and Lisa Homner. "The Gamification of Learning: A Meta-Analysis." *Educational Psychology Review*, vol. 32, 15 Aug. 2019, https://doi.org/10.1007/s10648-019-09498-w.

13. Zhonggen. "A Meta-Analysis of Use."

14. Ozdemir, Muzaffer, et al. "The Effect of Augmented Reality Applications in the Learning Process: A Meta-Analysis Study." *Eurasian Journal of Educational Research*, vol. 18, no. 74, 20 Mar. 2018, pp. 165–86, https://dergipark.org.tr/en/pub/ejer/issue/42528/512469. Accessed 1 Mar. 2022.

15. Wu, Bian, et al. "Effectiveness of Immersive Virtual Reality Using Head Mounted Displays on Learning Performance: A Meta-Analysis." *British Journal of Educational Technology*, vol. 51, no. 6, 8 Sept. 2020, pp. 1991–2005, https://doi.org/10.1111/bjet.13023.

16. Voss, Patrice, et al. "Dynamic Brains and the Changing Rules of Neuroplasticity: Implications for Learning and Recovery." *Frontiers in Psychology*, vol. 8, 4 Oct. 2017, https://doi.org/10.3389/fpsyg.2017.01657.

17. Torous, John, et al. "Barriers, Benefits, and Beliefs of Brain Training Smartphone Apps: An Internet Survey of Younger US Consumers." *Frontiers in Human Neuroscience*, vol. 10, 20 Apr. 2016, https://doi.org/10.3389/fnhum.2016.00180.

18. Morrison, Alexandra B., and Jason M. Chein. "Does Working Memory Training Work? The Promise and Challenges of Enhancing Cognition by Training Working Memory." *Psychonomic Bulletin & Review*, vol. 18, no. 1, 17 Nov. 2010, pp. 46–60, https://doi.org/10.3758/s13423-010-0034-0.

19. Au, Jacky, et al. "Improving Fluid Intelligence with Training on Working Memory: A Meta-Analysis." *Psychonomic Bulletin & Review*, vol. 22, no. 2, 8 Aug. 2014, pp. 366–77, https://doi.org/10.3758/s13423-014-0699-x.; Melby-Lervåg, Monica, and Charles Hulme. "Is Working Memory Training Effective? A Meta-Analytic Review." *Developmental Psychology*, vol. 49, no. 2, 2013, pp. 270–91, https://doi.org/10.1037/a0028228.

Chapter 20

1. Survey conducted by Jeffrey Bergin. 2025.

2. Alanoğlu, M., and S. Karabatak. "The Relationship between School Administrators' Leadership Traits and Learning Schools: A Meta-Analysis Study." *Participatory Educational Research*, vol. 9, no. 3, 2022, pp. 403–27, https://eric.ed.gov/?id=EJ1324996.; Xie, Lei. "The Impact of Servant Leadership and Transformational Leadership on Learning Organization: A Comparative Analysis." *Leadership & Organization Development Journal*, vol. 41, no. 2, 2020, pp. 220–36, https://doi.org/10.1108/LODJ-04-2019-0148.

3. Hallinger, Philip. "Leadership for Learning: Lessons from 40 Years of Empirical Research." *Journal of Educational Administration*, vol. 49, no. 2, 2011, pp. 125–42, https://doi.org/10.1108/09578231111116699.

4.   Sanders, Elizabeth B.-N., and Pieter Jan Stappers. "Co-Design as a Process of Joint Inquiry and Imagination." *Design Issues*, vol. 29, no. 2, 2013, pp. 16–28, https://www.jstor.org/stable/24266991.

5.   Örnekoğlu-Selçuk, M., et al. "A Systematic Literature Review on Co-Design Education and Preparing Future Designers for Their Role in Co-Design." *CoDesign*, 2023, pp. 1–16, https://doi.org/10.1080/157 10882.2023.2242840.

6.   Demirel, Melek, and Miray Dağyar. "Effects of Problem-Based Learning on Attitude: A Meta-Analysis Study." *EURASIA Journal of Mathematics, Science and Technology Education*, vol. 12, no. 8, Aug. 2016, pp. 2115–37, https://doi.org/10.12973/eurasia.2016.1293a.; Anggraeni, Desak Made, et al. "Systematic Review of Problem-Based Learning Research in Fostering Critical Thinking Skills." *Thinking Skills and Creativity*, vol. 49, 2023, https://doi.org/10.1016/j.tsc.2023.101334.; Liu, Yong, and Attila Pásztor. "Effects of Problem-Based Learning Instructional Intervention on Critical Thinking in Higher Education: A Meta-Analysis." *Thinking Skills and Creativity*, vol. 45, 2022, https://doi.org/10.1016/j.tsc.2022.101069.; Wijnia, Lisette, et al. "The Effects of Problem-Based, Project-Based, and Case-Based Learning on Students' Motivation: A Meta-Analysis." *Educational Psychology Review*, vol. 36, no. 1, 2024, p. 29, https://link.springer.com/article/10.1007/s10648-024-09864-3.; Shin, In-Sook, and Joon-Ho Kim. "The Effect of Problem-Based Learning in Nursing Education: A Meta-Analysis." *Advances in Health Sciences Education*, vol. 18, 2013, pp. 1103–20, https://doi.org/10.1007/s10459-012-9436-2.

7.   Lin, Chun-Yu, and Chung-Kai Huang. "Employee Turnover Intentions and Job Performance from a Planned Change: The Effects of an Organizational Learning Culture and Job Satisfaction." *International Journal of Manpower*, vol. 42, no. 4, 2021, https://doi.org/10.1108/IJM-08-2018-0281.

8.   Ladyshewsky, R. K., and R. Taplin. "The Interplay Between Organisational Learning Culture, the Manager as Coach, Self-Efficacy and Workload on Employee Work Engagement." *International Journal of Evidence Based Coaching and Mentoring*, vol. 16, no. 2, 2018, pp. 3–19, https://psycnet.apa.org/record/2018-57314-001.

9. Nguyen, Cuong, "The Impact of Training and Development, Job Satisfaction and Job Performance on Young Employee Retention." *International Journal of Future Generation Communication and Networking*, vol. 13, no. 3, 1 May 1, 2020, https://doi.org/10.2139/ssrn.3930645.; Murtiningsih, Retno Sari. "The Impact of Compensation, Training, and Development and Organizational Culture on Job Satisfaction and Retention." *Indonesian Management and Accounting Research*, vol. 19, no. 1, Jan. 2020, https://doi.org/10.25105/imar.v19i1.6969.; Elsafty, Ashraf, and Mahmoud Oraby. "The Impact of Training on Employee Retention: An Empirical Research on the Private Sector in Egypt." *International Journal of Business and Management*, vol. 17, no. 5, 2022, https://doi.org/10.5539/ijbm.v17n5p58.; Papa, Armando, et al. "Improving Innovation Performance Through Knowledge Acquisition: The Moderating Role of Employee Retention and Human Resource Management Practices." *Journal of Knowledge Management*, vol. 24, no. 3, pp. 589–605, https://www.emerald.com/insight/content/doi/10.1108/jkm-09-2017-0391/full/html.